First World War
and Army of Occupation
War Diary
France, Belgium and Germany

57 DIVISION
172 Infantry Brigade
Prince of Wales's Volunteers (South Lancashire Regiment)
2/5th Battalion
28 January 1917 - 26 February 1918

WO95/2985/10

The Naval & Military Press Ltd
www.nmarchive.com
Published in association with The National Archives

Published by

The Naval & Military Press Ltd

Unit 10 Ridgewood Industrial Park,

Uckfield, East Sussex,

TN22 5QE England

Tel: +44 (0) 1825 749494

www.naval-military-press.com

www.nmarchive.com

This diary has been reprinted in facsimile from the original. Any imperfections are inevitably reproduced and the quality may fall short of modern type and cartographic standards.

Contents

Document type	Place/Title	Date From	Date To
Heading	WO95/2985/10 57 Divn. 172 Inf Brig 2/5 Sth Lancs Regt 1917 Feb-1918 Feb		
Heading	War Diary 2/5th S. Lan. R. From 28/1/17 To 28/2/17 With Appendices I & II		
War Diary	Blackdown Hants	28/01/1917	16/02/1917
War Diary	Folkestone	17/02/1917	20/02/1917
War Diary	Boulogne	21/02/1917	21/02/1917
War Diary	Bailleul	21/02/1917	21/02/1917
War Diary	Oultersteene	22/02/1917	22/02/1917
War Diary	Sailly	23/02/1917	23/02/1917
War Diary	Erquinghem Lys	24/02/1917	28/02/1917
Miscellaneous	2/5th Battalion South Lancashire Regiment	20/02/1917	20/02/1917
Miscellaneous	2/5th Battalion South Lancashire Regiment	28/02/1917	28/02/1917
Heading	War Diary 2/5th S. Lan. R. From 1/3/17 To 31/3/17 With Appendices III To VI		
War Diary	Erquinghem Lys	01/03/1917	03/03/1917
War Diary	Trenches	04/03/1917	13/03/1917
War Diary	Ruemarle	14/03/1917	20/03/1917
War Diary	Trenches	21/03/1917	31/03/1917
Miscellaneous	Defence Scheme For Left Battalion Holding The Rue Du Bois Sector		
Miscellaneous	Lewis Gun Positions		
Miscellaneous	Trench Mortars Co-Operation With Lewis Gun In BN Sector		
War Diary	Rue Du Bois Sub Sector		
Miscellaneous	Schedule Of Supplies Rue Du Bois Section		
Miscellaneous	O.C's "A", "B", "C", & "D" Coys.	13/04/1917	13/04/1917
Miscellaneous	Defence Scheme For Left Reserve Battalion. Rue Du Bois Sector.	21/03/1917	21/03/1917
Miscellaneous	O.'s C, "A", "B", "C" & "D" Coys.	14/04/1917	14/04/1917
Miscellaneous	2/5th Battalion South Lancashire Regiment	31/03/1917	31/03/1917
Miscellaneous	Appendix VI	06/04/1917	06/04/1917
Miscellaneous	Subsidiary line		
Miscellaneous	Strong Point Of Fleurbaix		
Miscellaneous	B A O St. Maur Bridgehead		
Heading	War Diary Of 2/5th S. Lan. R. From 1/4/17 To 30/4/17 With Appendices VII & VIII		
War Diary	Rue Dormoire Near Erquinghem-Lys	01/04/1917	13/04/1917
War Diary	Rue Marle	13/04/1917	19/04/1917
War Diary	Trenches	21/04/1917	29/04/1917
War Diary	Rue Marle	30/04/1917	30/04/1917
Miscellaneous	2/5th Battalion South Lancashire Regiment	30/04/1917	30/04/1917
Miscellaneous	2/5th. S. Lan. R.	07/05/1917	07/05/1917
Heading	War Diary Of 2/5th S. Lan. R. From 1/5/17 To 31/5/17 With Appendices IX To XI		
War Diary	Rue Marle	01/05/1917	07/05/1917
War Diary	Trenches Bois-Grenier Sector	08/05/1917	16/05/1917
War Diary	Rue Marle	17/05/1917	24/05/1917
War Diary	Trenches Bois Grenier Sector	25/05/1917	31/05/1917
Miscellaneous	Subject:- Musketry. Appendix IX	25/05/1917	25/05/1917

Miscellaneous	2/5th Battalion South Lancashire Regiment	31/05/1917	31/05/1917
Miscellaneous	2/5th. Bn. Sth. Lancs. Regt.	31/05/1917	31/05/1917
Heading	War Diary Of 2/5th S. Lan. R. From 1/6/17 To 30/6/17 With Appendices XII-XVI.		
War Diary	Trenches Bois Grenier Sector	01/06/1917	01/06/1917
War Diary	Rue Marle	02/06/1917	09/06/1917
War Diary	Trenches Bois Grenier Sector	10/06/1917	15/06/1917
War Diary	Rue Marle	16/06/1917	25/06/1917
War Diary	Trenches Bois Grenier Sector	26/06/1917	30/06/1917
Operation(al) Order(s)	2/5th. Bn. S. Lan. R., Operation Orders No. 20	12/06/1917	12/06/1917
Miscellaneous	Arrangements to be made at once pending information being received that the enemy has commenced to withdraw from his Front Line. Appendix I.		
Miscellaneous	Administration Appendix II		
Operation(al) Order(s)	2/5th S. Lan. R. Left Reserve Battalion Operation Orders No. 21	21/06/1917	21/06/1917
Miscellaneous	2/5th. Bn. South Lancs. Regt.	21/06/1917	21/06/1917
Miscellaneous	2/5th Battalion South Lancashire Regiment.	30/06/1917	30/06/1917
Heading	War Diary Of 2/5th S. Lan. R. From 1/7/17 To 31/7/17		
War Diary	Trenches Bois Grenier Sector	01/07/1917	09/07/1917
War Diary	Rue Marle	10/07/1917	17/07/1917
War Diary	Trenches Bois-Grenier Sector	18/07/1917	31/07/1917
Operation(al) Order(s)	2/5th. Bn. S. Lan. R., Operation Order No. 23	07/07/1917	07/07/1917
Miscellaneous	Action Of Parties. Appendix I		
Diagram etc	Phase 1		
Miscellaneous	Phase 2		
Diagram etc	Phase 3		
Diagram etc	Phase 4		
Miscellaneous	Appendix III		
Miscellaneous	2/5th. Sth. Lancs. Regt.		
Miscellaneous	Medical Arrangements		
Diagram etc	Phase I.		
Diagram etc	Phase 2.		
Diagram etc	Phase III		
Diagram etc	Phase 4		
Map	172nd Machine Gun Company		
Map	Map		
Miscellaneous	Report On Hostile Barrage And Expected Raid On Rue Du Bois Subsector Night 6/7th	06/07/1917	06/07/1917
Miscellaneous	Report On Entry Of Boche Raiding Party In Rue Du Bois Salient, Night July	06/07/1917	06/07/1917
Operation(al) Order(s)	2/5th. S. Lan. R., Operation Order No. 24		
Miscellaneous	Report On Dummy Raid Night 8/9th July	08/07/1917	08/07/1917
Miscellaneous	Military Medal	20/07/1917	20/07/1917
Miscellaneous	2/5th. Battalion South Lancashire Regiment		
Miscellaneous	2/5th Battalion South Lancashire Regiment	31/07/1917	31/07/1917
Heading	War Diary 2/5th S. Lan. R. From 1/8/17 To 31/8/17 With Appendices XXIV To XXXI Vol 7		
War Diary	La Rolanderie	01/08/1917	03/08/1917
War Diary	Trenches Bois Grenier Sector	04/08/1917	11/08/1917
War Diary	La Rolanderie	12/08/1917	19/08/1917
War Diary	Trenches Bois Grenier Sector	20/08/1917	27/08/1917
War Diary	Erquinghem La Rolanderie	27/08/1917	31/08/1917
Miscellaneous	Intelligence Report. From 6 a.m. to 6. p.m., 9th. August, 1917. Flamengrie Subsector.	09/08/1917	09/08/1917
Miscellaneous	Orders For Minor Operations	10/08/1917	10/08/1917

Miscellaneous	Report On Minor Operations Carried Out By "N" Battalion On Night	10/08/1917	10/08/1917
Miscellaneous	Intelligence Report. From 6 p.m. 10th. Aug. 1917 to 6 a.m., 11th Aug., 1917. Flamengrie Subsector.	11/08/1917	11/08/1917
Miscellaneous	Copy Of D.R.O. 1278	16/08/1917	16/08/1917
Operation(al) Order(s)	2/5th S. Lan. R. Orders For Minor Operation No. 2	22/08/1917	22/08/1917
Miscellaneous	2/5th Battalion South Lancashire Regiment.	31/08/1917	31/08/1917
Heading	War Diary 2/5th S Lan R. From 1/9/17 To 30/9/17 With Appendices XXII To XXVII		
War Diary	La Rolanderie	01/09/1917	04/09/1917
War Diary	Flamengrie Sub Sector	05/09/1917	10/09/1917
War Diary	Flamengrie Sub Sector Bois Grenier	11/09/1917	12/09/1917
War Diary	La Rolanderie	13/09/1917	17/09/1917
War Diary	Estaires	18/09/1917	18/09/1917
War Diary	Busnettes	19/09/1917	19/09/1917
War Diary	Laires	20/09/1917	30/09/1917
Operation(al) Order(s)	2/5th. S. Lan. R., Operation Order No. 40		
Operation(al) Order(s)	2/5th. S. Lan. R., Operation Orders No. 41	18/09/1917	18/09/1917
Miscellaneous	2/5th. S. Lan. R., Operation Order No. 42	19/09/1917	19/09/1917
Miscellaneous	Appendix XXV		
Miscellaneous	Programme Of Work	29/09/1917	29/09/1917
Miscellaneous	Programme Of Work.	28/09/1917	28/09/1917
Miscellaneous	Programme Of Work	27/09/1917	27/09/1917
Miscellaneous	Programme Of Work	26/09/1917	26/09/1917
Miscellaneous	Programme Of Work	25/09/1917	25/09/1917
Miscellaneous	Programme Of Work	24/09/1917	24/09/1917
Miscellaneous	2/5th Battalion South Lancashire Regiment.	30/09/1917	30/09/1917
War Diary	Laires	01/10/1917	18/10/1917
War Diary	Renescure	19/10/1917	19/10/1917
War Diary	Proven	20/10/1917	26/10/1917
War Diary	Elverdinghe	27/10/1917	31/10/1917
Miscellaneous	Brigade Trench To Trench Attack 2/5th. S. Lan, R., Preliminary Orders.	04/10/1917	04/10/1917
Miscellaneous	Brigade Trench To Trench Attack.	09/10/1917	09/10/1917
Miscellaneous	Administrative Arrangements. In Connection With Brigade "Trench To Trench Attack"	09/10/1917	09/10/1917
Operation(al) Order(s)	2/5th. S. Lan. R. Operation Order No. 1	03/10/1917	03/10/1917
Miscellaneous	Programme Of Training.	05/10/1917	05/10/1917
Miscellaneous	Programme Of Work	04/10/1917	04/10/1917
Miscellaneous	Programme Of Training	03/10/1917	03/10/1917
Miscellaneous	Programme Of Training	02/10/1917	02/10/1917
Miscellaneous	Programme Of Training	18/10/1917	18/10/1917
Miscellaneous	2/5th. 5th. Lancs. Regt.	08/10/1917	08/10/1917
Miscellaneous	2/5th. Sth. Lancs. Regt. Training Programme 3rd Week	10/10/1917	10/10/1917
Miscellaneous	Training Programme	11/10/1917	11/10/1917
Operation(al) Order(s)	2/5th. S. Lan. R., Operation Order No. 43	16/10/1917	16/10/1917
Miscellaneous	With Reference To Operation Order No. 43	16/10/1917	16/10/1917
Miscellaneous	2/5th Battalion South Lancashire Regiment	31/10/1917	31/10/1917
Miscellaneous	2/5th Battalion South Lancashire Regiment.	31/10/1917	31/10/1917
War Diary	Elverdinghe	01/11/1917	02/11/1917
War Diary	Elverdinghe And Pilkem	02/11/1917	05/11/1917
War Diary	Langemarck And Elverdinghe	06/11/1917	06/11/1917
War Diary	Langemarck Besinghe And Elverdinghe	07/11/1917	07/11/1917
War Diary	Boesinghe	08/11/1917	09/11/1917
War Diary	Audruicq	09/11/1917	09/11/1917
War Diary	Landrethun And Yeuse	09/11/1917	30/11/1917

Miscellaneous	Appendix XXXIV	03/11/1917	03/11/1917
Miscellaneous	Appendix XXXV	05/11/1917	05/11/1917
Operation(al) Order(s)	2/5th. S. Lan. R., Operation Orders No. 46		
Miscellaneous	Programme Of Work	30/11/1917	30/11/1917
Miscellaneous	Programme Of Work	29/11/1917	29/11/1917
Miscellaneous	Programme Of Work	28/11/1917	28/11/1917
Miscellaneous	Programme Of Work	27/11/1917	27/11/1917
Miscellaneous	Programme Of Work	26/11/1917	26/11/1917
Miscellaneous	Programme Of Work	24/11/1917	24/11/1917
Miscellaneous	Programme Of Work	23/11/1917	23/11/1917
Miscellaneous	Programme Of Work	22/11/1917	22/11/1917
Miscellaneous	Programme Of Work	21/11/1917	21/11/1917
Miscellaneous	Programme Of Work	20/11/1917	20/11/1917
Miscellaneous	Programme Of Work	19/11/1917	19/11/1917
Miscellaneous	Programme Of Work	17/11/1917	17/11/1917
Miscellaneous	Programme Of Work	16/11/1917	16/11/1917
Miscellaneous	Programme Of Work	15/11/1917	15/11/1917
Miscellaneous	Programme Of Work	14/11/1917	14/11/1917
Operation(al) Order(s)	2/5th. S. Lan. R., Operation Order No.	27/11/1917	27/11/1917
Miscellaneous	2/5th. Battn. Sth. Lancs. Regiment.	30/11/1917	30/11/1917
War Diary	Landrethun & Yeuse	01/12/1917	07/12/1917
War Diary	Herzeele	08/12/1917	18/12/1917
War Diary	Boesinghe	19/12/1917	25/12/1917
War Diary	Houthulst Forest Right. Sub Sector	26/12/1917	31/12/1917
Operation(al) Order(s)	2/5th. Bn. S. Lan. R., Operation Order No. 59	30/11/1917	30/11/1917
Operation(al) Order(s)	2/5th. Bn. S. Lan. R., Operation Order No. 52	06/12/1917	06/12/1917
Miscellaneous	Train Moves	07/12/1917	07/12/1917
Miscellaneous	Train Moves	17/12/1917	17/12/1917
Operation(al) Order(s)	2/5th Bn. S. Lan. R., Operation Orders No. 53		
Operation(al) Order(s)	2/5th Bn. S. Lan. R., Operation Orders No. 54	24/12/1917	24/12/1917
Miscellaneous	2/5th. S. Lan. R.	25/12/1917	25/12/1917
Miscellaneous	2/5th. Bn. S. Lan. R. Administrative Instructions	24/12/1917	24/12/1917
Miscellaneous	Administrative Instructions, No. 2.		
Miscellaneous	2/5 S. Lan. R. Operation Orders 55	27/12/1917	27/12/1917
Operation(al) Order(s)	2/5th South Lancashire Regiment Order No. 15	29/12/1917	29/12/1917
Miscellaneous	2/5th Battalion South Lancashire Regt.	31/12/1917	31/12/1917
Miscellaneous	2/5th Bn South Lancashire Regiment	31/12/1917	31/12/1917
War Diary	Boesinghe	01/01/1918	06/01/1918
War Diary	Pont-De Nieppe	06/01/1918	12/01/1918
War Diary	Houplines Left Sub Sector	13/01/1918	14/01/1918
War Diary	Houplines	14/01/1918	21/01/1918
War Diary	Pont De Nieppe	21/01/1918	27/01/1918
War Diary	Houplines	27/01/1918	30/01/1918
War Diary	Armentieres	31/01/1918	31/01/1918
Operation(al) Order(s)	2/5th. S. Lan. R., Operation Order No. 1	02/01/1918	02/01/1918
Operation(al) Order(s)	2/5th. S. Lan. R., Operation Order No. 2	04/01/1918	04/01/1918
Miscellaneous	Table "A"		
Operation(al) Order(s)	2/5th. S. Lan. R., Operation Orders No. 3	03/01/1917	03/01/1917
Miscellaneous	Time Table		
Operation(al) Order(s)	Preliminary Operation Order No. 4.	10/01/1918	10/01/1918
Operation(al) Order(s)	2/5th. S. Lan. R., Operation Orders No. 5	11/01/1918	11/01/1918
Miscellaneous	Table Attached 2/5th. S. Lan. R. O.O.5		
Operation(al) Order(s)	2/5th Bn. Sth. Lancs. Regt. Operation Order No. 6	17/01/1918	17/01/1918
Operation(al) Order(s)	2/5th Bn. Sth. Lancs. Regt. Operation Order No. 7	20/01/1918	20/01/1918
Operation(al) Order(s)	2/5th Bn. Sth. Lancs. Regt. Operation Order No. 8	28/01/1918	28/01/1918
Miscellaneous	Time-Table.		

Operation(al) Order(s)	2/5th. S. Lan. R., Operation Order No. 9	29/01/1918	29/01/1918
Miscellaneous	2/5 Battalion South Lancashire Regt.	31/01/1918	31/01/1918
Miscellaneous	2/5 Battalion South Lancs. Regt.	31/01/1918	31/01/1918
War Diary	Armentieres	01/02/1918	02/02/1918
War Diary	Steenwerck	03/02/1918	26/02/1918
Operation(al) Order(s)	2/5th. S. Lan. R., Operation Orders No. 11	01/02/1918	01/02/1918
Miscellaneous	2/5th. S. Lan. R.		

WO 95 2985/10

57 Divn; 172 Inf Brig
2/5 Sth Lancs Regt
1917 Feb – 1918 Feb

57

172
57

10

CONFIDENTIAL

Vol 1

Y. 1

WAR DIARY.

2/5th. S. LAN. R.

FROM. 28/1/17 TO. 28/2/17

WITH APPENDICES
I & II

Instructions regarding War Diaries and Intelligence Summaries are contained in F. S. Regs., Part II. and the Staff Manual respectively. Title Pages will be prepared in manuscript.

WAR DIARY
~~or~~
~~INTELLIGENCE SUMMARY~~
(Erase heading not required.)

Army Form C. 2118

106

Place	Date 1917	Hour	Summary of Events and Information	Remarks and references to Appendices
BLACKDOWN HANTS	Jan 28th		LT. S. J. FINK entrained at FARNBOROUGH to act as Divisional Entraining Officer at HAVRE.	RHB
— do —	Feb 1st		LT. T. McDONALD, LT. W. F. BRAZENER, LT A. W. MESSUM, LT J. E. GOODWIN, 2/LT. W. S. HALL and 14 other ranks entrained at FARNBOROUGH with 57th. Division's Advance Party. This party were sent out to obtain a knowledge of Sector Battn. would occupy.	RHB
— do —	14th	7 a.m.	First and Second line transport complete and 83 other ranks under Major A. BREWIS entrained at FRIMLEY for SOUTHAMPTON en route for HAVRE. Other officers with party were LT H. WEST and 2/LT L. E. TANTON.	RHB
— do —	16th	11.15 pm	Battalion less Transport left DETTINGEN BARRACKS and entrained at FARNBOROUGH STREET in two trains. "A" "B" + "C" Coys less one platoon of "C" Coy in first train. "D" Coy and one platoon "C" Coy in second train with half 2/9th K. L. R.	RHB For Officers with Battn. see Appendix I
FOLKESTONE	17th to 19th		Arrived FOLKESTONE about 5 a.m. Battalion went into Rest Camp – Officers to PAVILION HOTEL. Battalion was marched to the boat four times during the three days it spent in FOLKESTONE and on two of these occasions actually embarked. Weather very foggy all three days.	RHB
— do —	20th	9 a.m.	Battalion embarked on PRINCESS HENRIETTE. Sailed at 10 x 30 am & reached BOULOGNE about 12 x 30 pm. Proceeded to Rest Camp all ranks accommodated in tents except C. O. Battalion left England at full establishment strength of O. R but one officer short.	RHB.

1875 Wt. W593/826 1,000,000 4/15 J.B.C. & A. A.D.S.S./Forms/C. 2118.

Instructions regarding War Diaries and Intelligence Summaries are contained in F. S. Regs., Part II. and the Staff Manual respectively. Title Pages will be prepared in manuscript.

WAR DIARY

~~or~~

~~INTELLIGENCE SUMMARY~~

(Erase heading not required.)

Army Form C. 2118

Place	Date 1917	Hour	Summary of Events and Information	Remarks and references to Appendices
BOULOGNE	Feb 21st		Left Rest Camp at 6x30am. Entrained at 10am – two hours late. Very slow train journey	RHH
BAILLEUL			Reached BAILLEUL 6pm. and proceeded to billets at OULTERSTEENE.	
OULTERSTEENE	22nd		Day in billeting area. Got into touch with Transport which was at PRADELLES about 4 miles away. Box Respirators issued. Instruction for Officers and NCO'S by Divisional Gas Officer.	RHH
SAILLY	23rd		Moved to billets about half way between SAILLY and ESTAIRES.	RHH
ERQUINGHEM-LYS	24th		Relieved 1st OTAGO Battn. N.Z. as left Battalion of Brigade Reserve. Billeting area rather scattered – partly hutments, partly barns and houses. Battn H.Q. at LA ROLANDERIE. Quartermasters Stores in ERQUINGHEM-LYS village.	RHH
—do—	25th to 28th		Battalion in billets. Working parties daily in BOIS-GRENIER Sector. Emergency routes reconnoitred also Subsidiary Line of Trench System. In case of emergency Battalion would have moved up to Subsidiary Line by Emergency Routes. Situation quiet during this period except for occasional Artillery activity	RHH Officers with Unit at end of month. See Appendix II

R.H. Haywood Capt
Adjt. 2/5th. S. Lan. R.

1875 Wt. W593/826 1,000,000 4/15 J.B.C. & A. A.D.S.S./Forms/C. 2118.

APPENDIX I

2/5th BATTALION SOUTH LANCASHIRE REGIMENT

NOMINAL ROLL OF OFFICERS WHO EMBARKED WITH THE BATTALION AT FOLKESTONE ON 20th February 1917.

108

Lieut-Colonel	Bates	D,	
Major	Schultz	A.H.	
Captain	Gould	M.L.B.	
Captain	Wallis	A.C.	
Captain	Stephenson	C.W.	
Captain	Crowe	J.A.	
Captain	Hayward	R.C.	
Captain	Wood	R.H.	
Captain	Guest	E.L.	
Lieutenant	Hadfield	J.L.	
Lieutenant	Timson	H.H.	
Lieutenant	Dickinson	W,	
2nd Lieutenant	Dean	L.M.	
2nd Lieutenant	Holland	W.H.E.	
2nd Lieutenant	Nimmo	A.A.	
2nd Lieutenant	Paul	R.B.	
2nd Lieutenant	Cocking	J.C.O.	
Captain	Wood	R.L.	(R.A.M.C.)
Lieutenant	Gregory	H,	(Quartermaster)
Captain The Rev	Thomas	W.D.	(Chaplain attached).

APPENDIX II

109
SB

2/5th BATTALION SOUTH LANCASHIRE REGIMENT

NOMINAL ROLL OF OFFICERS AS ON 28th FEBRUARY 1917

HEADQUARTERS

Lieut-Colonel	D. Bates	Commanding Officer
Major	A.H. Schultz	Second in Command
Captain	R.C. Hayward	Adjutant.
Captain	R.L. Wood	Medical Officer
Lieutenant	H. Gregory	Quartermaster
Lieutenant	J.L. Hadfield	Bombing Officer.
Lieutenant	H.H. Timson	Signalling Officer
Lieutenant	W.F. Brazener	IntelligenceOfficer
Lieutenant	H. West	Lewis Gun Officer
2/Lieutenant	R.B. Paul	Assistant Adjutant
2/Lieutenant	L.E. Tanton	Transport Officer.

"A" COMPANY

Captain	A.C. Wallis	O/C Company
Lieutenant	A.W. Messum	Platoon Commander
2/Lieutenant	J.C.O. Cocking	Platoon Commander
Captain	E.L. Guest	Second in Command

"B" COMPANY

Captain	M.L.B. Gould,	O/C Company
Lieutenant	T.M. Donald	Second in Command
Lieutenant	S.J. Fink	Platoon Commander
2/Lieutenant	L.M. Dean	Platoon Commander

"C" COMPANY

Major	A. Brewis	O/C Company
Captain	J.A. Crowe	Second in Command
Lieutenant	J.E. Goodwin	Platoon Commander
2/Lieutenant	A.A. Nimmo	Platoon Commander

"D" COMPANY

Captain	C.W. Stephenson	O/C Company
Captain	R.H. Wood	Second in Command
Lieutenant	W. Dickinson	Platoon Commander
2/Lieutenant	W.H.E. Holland	Platoon Commander
2/Lieutenant	W.S. Hall	Platoon Commander

DETACHED

2/Lieutenant	R. Young	172nd Bde. L.T.M.B.
Captain	F.J. Frodsham	H.Q. 172nd Infantry Brigade
~~Captain~~	~~E.L. Guest~~	~~172nd Infantry Brigade~~

J 2

Vol 2

CONFIDENTIAL

WAR DIARY

2/5th S. LAN. R.

FROM 1/3/17 TO 31/3/17

WITH APPENDICES

III to VI.

Instructions regarding War Diaries and Intelligence Summaries are contained in F. S. Regs., Part II. and the Staff Manual respectively. Title Pages will be prepared in manuscript.

WAR DIARY
or
~~INTELLIGENCE SUMMARY~~
(Erase heading not required.)

Army Form C. 2118

Place	Date 1917	Hour	Summary of Events and Information	Remarks and references to Appendices
ERQUINGHEM-LYS	March 1st to 3rd		Battalion in billets at LA ROLANDERIE. Officers visited BOIS-GRENIER Sector. Nothing of note to record.	RLB
TRENCHES	4th		Relieved 2/4th S.L.R. in BOIS-GRENIER Sector by day. Relief quite Satisfactory. 2/10th K.L.R on our right, 37th Aust. Battn on our left. Line held – 'A' & 'C' Coys in Front Line, 'B' Coy in Support, 'D' Coy in Subsidiary. Trenches in fair condition – front line very bad in places.	RLB
	5th to 7th		Situation generally quiet. Orders received on 7th. to take over from 50% of 37th Aust. Battn. Advance parties sent same day to RUE DU BOIS Sector. Capt. E. L. GUEST to Brigade H.Q. on March 6th. for special duty.	RLB
	8th.		Took over from two Coys of 37th Aust. Battn. leaving 'A' Coy in left Company Sector of BOIS-GRENIER Sector. 'D' Coy moved along Subsidiary Line to left. Battalion H.Q. took over from 37th Aust. Bn. 2/4th. S.L.R. on left, 2/9th K.L.R. on right. Relief satisfactory. Divisional raiding School started. 2/Lt COCKING J.C.D and 2/Lt DICKINSON W with 20 other ranks sent to join school.	RLB
	9th to 12th		Situation normal. Only trouble experienced being in RUE DU BOIS Salient from enemy Snipers and fixed rifles which kept on firing all night. Enemy only 35/40 yards away in above salient. S.O.S. lines & Signal communication troublesome.	RLB

1875 Wt. W593/826 1,000,000 4/15 J.B.C. & A. A.D.S.S./Forms/C. 2118.

Instructions regarding War Diaries and Intelligence Summaries are contained in F. S. Regs., Part II. and the Staff Manual respectively. Title Pages will be prepared in manuscript.

WAR DIARY
~~or~~
~~INTELLIGENCE SUMMARY~~
(Erase heading not required.)

Army Form C. 2118

Place	Date 1917	Hour	Summary of Events and Information	Remarks and references to Appendices
TRENCHES	March 13th.		B & C relieved by 2/4th S L R in RUE DU BOIS Sector. A Coy relieved by 2/10th K.L.R. in BOIS-GRENIER Sector. Battn H.Q. relieved by 2/4th S.L.R. A B & C Coys go into Brigade Reserve at RUE MARLE taking over billets from two Coys 2/10th K.L.R. Battn H.Q. at CROWN PRINCE HOUSE which overlooks ARMENTIERES Station which is about 400 yards away. "D" Coy remained in Subsidiary Line. Relief carried out quite satisfactorily by day. No casualties during this tour of duty in trenches	RLtt Defence Scheme Appendix IV
RUEMARLE	14th to 19th		Three Companies in billets. Training during morning. One of these Coys supplying Picquet daily. "C" Coy relieved "D" Coy in Subsidiary Line on 17th.	
	20th.		Relieved 2/4th S.L.R. in RUE DU BOIS Sector. Relief carried out by day – Lewis Guns previous night. Found that it is impossible to get L.G.'s into position satisfactorily at night and decided in future to send them in by night and take up positions following morning. Dispositions three Coys in front line and Support line, one Coy in Subsidiary Line with one company from 2/4th S.L.R. (Bde Reserve) also in Subsidiary Line.	RLtt

1875 Wt. W593/826 1,000,000 4/15 J.B.C. & A. A.D.S.S./Forms/C. 2118.

Instructions regarding War Diaries and Intelligence Summaries are contained in F. S. Regs., Part II. and the Staff Manual respectively. Title Pages will be prepared in manuscript.

WAR DIARY
or
INTELLIGENCE SUMMARY
(Erase heading not required.)

Army Form C. 2118

Place	Date	Hour	Summary of Events and Information	Remarks and references to Appendices
TRENCHES	1917 March 21st to 28th		Capt. F J FRODSHAM and Capt E L GUEST returned to duty with Battn from 172nd Brigade H.Q. A C and D Coys in Front Line B Coy in Subsidiary Line. B Coy relieved A Coy on 24th inst. Situation during this period generally quiet. Front Line held by means of LOCALITIES and GAPS. Bombing and Lewis Gun Posts in LOCALITIES. 12 L.G's in Front Line and 4 in Support. On 27th inst. Right Coy Sector shelled by enemy during afternoon – H.E and Shrapnel but mostly H.E. Artillery reported suspected registering on our Sector. Special precautions taken night 27/28th Listening Posts put out in front of our wire. One Platoon and two Lewis Guns of 2/4th S.L.R pushed up to Support Line on left. Same precautions taken night 28/29th when in addition to above one company from 2/4th S.L.R. (Brigade Reserve) in Subsidiary Line during night. Summer Time taken into use on 24th. March 27th 2/Lt AA NIMMO and 33 O.R sent to 172nd Brigade Pioneer Coy.	Defence Scheme Appendix III [initials]

1875 Wt. W593/826 1,000,000 4/15 J.B.C. & A. A.D.S.S./Forms/C. 2118.

Instructions regarding War Diaries and Intelligence Summaries are contained in F. S. Regs., Part II. and the Staff Manual respectively. Title Pages will be prepared in manuscript.

WAR DIARY
~~or~~
~~INTELLIGENCE SUMMARY~~

(Erase heading not required.)

Army Form C. 2118

Place	Date 1917	Hour	Summary of Events and Information	Remarks and references to Appendices
TRENCHES	March 29th		Relieved by 2/6th K.L.R. by night. Lewis Guns came in previous night and took up positions morning of 29th. Relief satisfactory. Battalion goes into Divisional Reserve at RUE DORMOIRE about half way between ERQUINGHEM-LYS and BAC ST MAUR. Four casualties – two killed two wounded during this tour of duty.	RHH
	30th to 31st		In Divisional Reserve. One day's rest and then practically whole Battalion on working parties under R.E.	Scheme for Occupying defensive position in emergency Appendix VI RHH
			March 31st. Conference of C.O's at Brigade H.Q. re training of platoon instructors in Bombing, Sniping, Physical Training and Bayonet Training, Lewis Gun, Platoon Commander's duties.	
			Nothing of note to record on these days.	
			Following officers joined for duty during the month on dates stated –	List of officers with unit at end of month Appendix V.
			2/Lt. A.R. ST GEORGE 3rd S. Lan R. 25/3/17.	
			2/Lt. V. HARTLEY —do— 25/3/17.	
			2/Lt. S.P. SMITH —do— 25/3/17	
			2/Lt. A.R. STONE —do— 26/3/17	
			2/Lt. R.V. HOPE —do— 30/3/17.	
			R H Hayward Capt. Adjt. 2/5th. S. Lan R.	

1875 Wt. W593/826 1,000,000 4/15 J.B.C. & A. A.D.S.S./Forms/C. 2118.

APPENDIX III

DEFENCE SCHEME FOR LEFT BATTALION HOLDING THE RUE DU BOIS SECTOR.

- o -

Ref. Map Sheet 36 N.W.4 1/10,000

Description of Front.

(1)

The Sector consists of Front Line Breastworks from PARK ROW AVENUE exclusive, I.20.d.25.50. to PEAR TREE FARM exclusive at I.16.b.28.67., and is divided for artillery purposes into sub-sectors I.20.1, I.21.1,2,3,4 & 5, I.15.1 & 2, I.16.1,2,& 3. Many of these sub-sector boards are at present non-existent but their areas have been plotted on Company C.O.'s maps.

1st. SUPPORT LINE practically unheld.

2nd. SUPPORT LINE - BURNT FARM, STURT ROAD, QUEEN STREET, PARADISE ALLEY, and terminates at LILLE POST

SUBSIDIARY LINE from PARK ROW AVENUE exclusive to LEITH WALK inclusive, and also connected to 2nd. Support Line by good C.T., WELLINGTON, HAYSTACK, WINE, COWGATE.

Distribution for Defence.

(2)

The front breastworks are held by 3 Companies as lightly as possible by day; and by 2 platoons from each Company, i.e. 6 Platoons, and also 2½ platoons called Fighting Patrols by night, -- 2 Platoons per company in the 2nd. Support Line, and 2 full Companies in Subsidiary Line as a local reserve, one of these Companies being provided by the Battalion in Brigade Reserve.

In addition to the Infantry Garrison 12 Lewis Guns are suitably placed in the Front Line to dominate N.M.L. and cover gaps unheld, and 4 Lewis Guns in the 2nd. Support Line. A Machine Gun Company under Brigade arrangements also cover N.M.L. on front and flanks in addition to the overland approaches from Subsidiary Line to Front Line.

Lewis Gun positions see Appendix 1.

4 Light Trench Mortars assist in the defence from sunken emplacements, and for agressive purposes from separate emplacements. For positions see Appendix.

Action for Defence.

(3)

The front line breastworks will be held, and will not be abandoned if line is pierced by attack.

In the event of a breach a local counter attack will immediately be made. Troops from Support Line will move to localise the breach by forming defensive flanks on both sides.

To assist the one Company local Reserve in Subsid. Line will move up by overland routes, their place being filled by a Company from Brigade Reserve.

It must be understood that the troops holding the Defensive Flanks must hold their ground at all costs and localise the breach even if the breach penetrates some distance, and make every endeavour by concentrated fire to prevent the breach being widened at the Front Line. In the event of a raid in force, the 2nd. Support Line will form the main line of defence.

In the event of the breach occurring by the Battns. on our Right or Left being driven in, defensive flanks as above will be immediately formed from the garrison holding our flanks, companies assisted by reinforcements from Subsid. Line who will endeavour to use their Lewis Guns to the best advantage, and have their men well spaced to minimise casualties as the communication trenches are certain to be shelled.
For water supply see Appendix 4.

Patrols. (4)

At least one patrol will go out nightly from each Company, the arrangements being supervized by the Scout Officer. Internal duck-board Patrols will maintain contact between companies in our Sector as well as with Companies on our Right and Left-hand flanks. Two Fighting Patrols will be provided from dusk to midnight every night, one for each half sector, and to be relieved at mid-night by two fresh patrols who carry on till daylight: Officers to command these patrols if available. These patrols are authorised to have a "roving commission", can move to any position in their sector, and to act in the first place as a mobile force strengthening the front line in case of an attack. They are however to understand that their job is essentially an agressive one, and they must rush in to any threatened point, and either drive a raiding party off their line of communication, or bottle him up against our wire, so that he cannot get back to his own lines undamaged. The Officer or N.C.O. in charge must use his own initiative as to where and when to attack, bearing in mind that the quicker he acts, the better he will cause disorganization, and confusion in the raider's ranks, which will put them to a great disadvantage. These Fighting Patrols may go out into N.M.L. and seek a hostile force, but in such a case they should previously advise the Scout Officer and their Company Commanders of the Section from which they go out and come in.

Gas. (5)

A local gas attack, i.e. one issuing from gas-shells, must immediately be warned to all troops locally by means of gongs or mouth-horns, but not by the compressed air power horns. These local gongs etc. will be taken up by gas-guards etc. in the vicinity only if the gas-shells are within their radius or the gas emanating is drifting their way.
A gas-cloud attack emanating from the enemy's lines is to be signalled by the blowing of mouth-horns - gongs, and by the compressed air horns, and by all the noises available, and is to be taken up and carried on along the flanks. In each case gas-masks must be put on at once and kept on until ordered to remove, given by an Officer or a gas N.C.O. During a gas attack men will man the defences, but otherwise stand still, working and carrying parties stopping work.

(Sheet 3.)

Liaison. (6)	An Officer from each Company occupying a flank position will visit the Company H.Q. of the Flank Company of next Battalion daily, this includes the Subsidiary Companies.
Water. (7)	The available water supply is scheduled in Appendix 8
S.O.S. (8)	Trench Officers are in communication with Artillery direct of his sector, and the signal in case of alarm is S.O.S. Trench No. giving the artillery reference, in accordance with the position of line attacked. The artillery being responsible for passing message on. In addition coloured signal rockets will be discharged as near as possible on the flanks of the attacking force, the signal and rockets being repeated until it is clear that the artillery is providing the necessary support. The S.O.S. message is never to be used when only a Test Round is to be fired.
Gas Attack. (9)	The Telephone Signal for gas attack when enemy do not advance is GAS ATTACK, followed by Trench No., which is to be treated in the same manner as the S.O.S. message. If infantry attack follows a gas discharge the ordinary S.O.S. message will be sent.
Bombers. (10)	In the event of a successful assault bombers will be responsible for the C.T.'s, the position of Bombing Posts being as per Appendix 3. The junction of 2nd. Support Line and C.T.:s must be held at all costs. Bombers working towards the threatened points and proceeding with the necessary barricades. Bombers will not withdraw from the Support Line until orders are received from Bn. H.Q. The Battalion Bombing Officer will remain in the Subsidiary Line, and superintend the distribution of bombs, and endeavour to get into touch with the Bombing Officer of the Battalion in reserve.
Transport. (11)	On an alarm of attack being given the regimental transport and Q.M. Stores will prepare to move at short notice.
Battn. H.Q. (12)	Battalion Headquarters will remain at I.14.d.4.8.

D Bates

Lieut.Col.
Commanding.
2/5 L. N. Lancs Regt

To:-- G.O.C. Brigade.
C.O.
2nd. in Command.
Adjutant.
C.O. opposite number.
C.O. do do 171 Bde.

APPENDIX I

LEWIS GUN POSITIONS.

Position of Lewis Guns in Batt. Sector.

12 Lewis Guns in Front Line.
4 Lewis Guns in Support Line.

FRONT LINE.

No.of Gun	Map Ref.	S.O.S. Line. Mag.	True.	Position.
1.	I.20.D.55.32.	181	168	Right Sector.
2.	I.21.C.05.78.	83	70	Right Sector.
3.	I.21.A.80.26.	88	75	Right Sector.
		Alt.137	124	
4.	I.15.D.34.06.	109	96	Centre Sectr.
5.	I.15.D.56.21.	196	183	Centre Sector.
6.	I.15.D.99.49	103	90	Centre Sector.
7.	I.16.C.15.62.	200	187	Centre Sectr.
8.	I.16.C.49.69.	193	180	Left Sector.
9.	I.16.C.83.93.	232	219	Left Sector.
10.	I.16.B.10.21.	159	146	Left Sector
11	I.16.B.19.48.	193	180	Left Sector.
12.	I.16.B.7.3.	-	70	Left Sector.

SUPPORT LINE.

No.of Gun	Map Ref.	S.O.S. Line. Mag.	True.	Position.
13.	I.21.A.55.49.	121	108	Right Sector.
14.	I.21.A.80.92	178	165	Centre Sector.
15.	I.15.D.00.54.	175	162	Centre Sectr.
16.	I.9.D.92.15.	101	148	Left Sector.

SUBSIDIARY LINE.

4 Lewis Guns in reserve belonging to the Reserve Coy. of 2/4th. S.L.R., 2 of them with the two right Platoons between PARK ROAD & WELLINGTON AVENUE, 2 with the two left platoons between WINE AVENUE & LEITH WALK.

These are in readiness in case of counter-attack, and to replace guns in Front that are put out of action.

---o---

SUPPORT FROM FLANK BATTALION.

Our right Sector RUE DU BOIS, is supported by 2 Lewis Guns of the 2/10th. or 2/9th. K.L.R.'s.

No.of Gun.	Map Ref.	S.O.S. Line. Mag.	True.
7.	I.26.C.81.99.	60	47
9	I.20.D.34.02.	102	89

Our Left Sector, CHARDS FARM, is supported by 1 Lewis Gun and 1 Vickers Gun of the Australian Battn.

200 yd. to the left of PEAR TREE FARM Australian Bn. have one Lewis Gun covering our Left Sector Front. S.O.S. Line about 180 true.

In addition our extreme left Support Line is covered by an Australian Vickers Gun in position at I.10.C.75.50.

On our left of the Subsid. Line LEITH AVENUE there are two Aust. Vickers at I.9.C.99.99. 200 yds. apart, S O S line 5 & 95 true.

APPENDIX II.

TRENCH MORTARS CO-OPERATION WITH LEWIS GUN IN BN SECTOR.

The L.T.M.B. co-operate with the Lewis Gun as follows:--

1. L.T.M. at 20.D.72.94 covers with Left Traverse WILLOW GAP. With Centre Traverse PARK GAP. Right Traverse PARK LOCALITY.

1. L.T.M. at 21.A.42.41. covers with left traverse RUE DU BOIS GAP. Centre Traverse RUE DU BOIS LOCALITY. Right Traverse WILLOW GAP.

1. L.T.M. at 15.A.91.39 has a traverse of 300 yards covering both SALOP GAP and WINE DALE LOCALITY.

1. L.T.M. at 16.A.79.62 has traverse of 450 yards straight towards front, and covers CHARDS FARM LOCALITY.

Appendix 3.

RUE DU BOIS SUB-SECTOR

No. 15 Squad.	At bottom of WELLINGTON AVENUE to reinforce No. 20
No. 16 "	At bottom of HAYSTACK AVENUE to reinforce No. 22 or 21 or both.
No. 17 "	At bottom of WINE AVENUE to reinforce Nos 23 or 24 or both.
No. 18 "	At bottom of Cowgate Avenue to reinforce No. 25.
No. 19 "	At bottom of LEITH WALK to reinforce No. 26.
No. 20. "	About DEAD COW FARM to hold WILLOW AVENUE.
No. 21. "	At bottom of RUE DU BOIS to hold same and co-operate with No. 27.
No. 22 "	At bottom of SALOP AVENUE to hold same.
No. 23 "	At bottom of WINE STREET to hold same.
No. 24 "	At bottom of AVONDALE ROAD to hold same.
No. 25 "	About COWGATE LOOP with PARADISE ALLEY to hold COWGATE AVENUE.
No. 26 "	About junction of LEITH WALK with LILLE POST to hold LEITH WALK.
No. 27 "	In and about RUE DU BOIS SALIENT - normally to harass the enemy with rifle grenades. In case of hostile attack to act as directed for No. 14 Squad and to fall back if necessary and co-operate with 21.
DISTRIBUTION.	Companies in FRONT & SUPPORT LINES to provide squads 21 - 27 inclusive, plus one of the squads in SUBSIDIARY LINE. The remaining four squads to be found by Company in Subsidiary Line. The three remaining squads of the battalion to report if possible as reinforcements to Battalion Bombing Officer.
Battn. BOMBING OFFICER.	At No. 10 (Brigade Reserve) Grenade Store at bottom of COWGATE AVENUE to act similarly to the Bombing Officer of BOIS GRENIER sub-sector in conjunction with Bombing Officer of left Reserve Battalion, and will act as defined in Defence Orders.

Appendix 4.

SCHEDULE OF SUPPLIES

RUE DU BOIS SECTION.

W A T E R.

Right Company.

Pump - BURNT FARM (broken)
Pump - SALOP GAP.

Centre Company.

Pump - WINE AVENUE (near Orchard)
2 Tanks - 400 Gal - WINE AVENUE (near Orchard)
Pump - COWGATE AVENUE (middle)
Petrol Tins - 120 Gal - ORCHARD
2 Tanks - 400 Gal - COWGATE AVENUE (need repair)

Left Company.

Pump - LILLE POST
Wooden Tub 220 Gal - LILLE POST.

Subsidiary Line.

2 Tanks - 400 Gal - Battalion Headquarters.
Pumps - Near Signal Box.
2 Tanks - 350 Gal - COWGATE AVENUE (bottom)
1 Tank - 200 Gal - LEITH WALK (bottom)

I R O N   R A T I O N S.

Right Company - WELLINGTON AVENUE (top) - 760.
Centre Company- ORCHARD - 50.
Left Company - LILLE POST - 250.
Subsidiary Line -
Battalion Headquarters. - 1000.
COWGATE AVENUE (bottom) - 700.

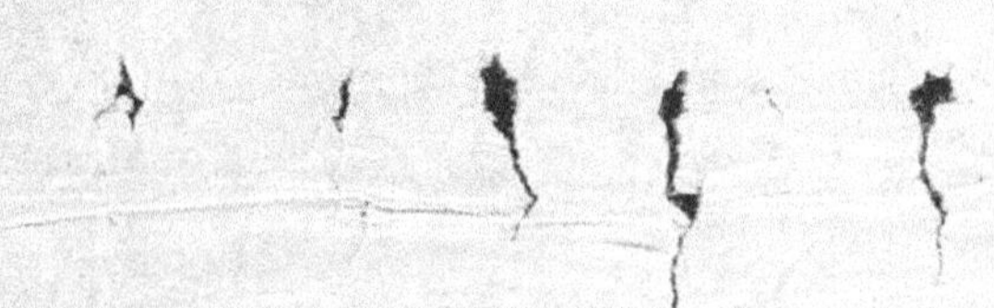

To - O.C.'s "A", "B", "C" & "D" Coys. APPENDIX IV Ref. No. D. 14.

1. Herewith copy of Defence Scheme for Left Reserve Battalion This will be handed over in relief.

2. Reference para. 4 Companies will fall in on heir own alarm posts and await orders.

3. Reference para. 5, Lewis Gun ammunition will be carried in buckets--Nos. 3,4,5,&6 carry two buckets each slung round the neck. Guns will be slung.

4. Reference para. 9, Each company in billets will detail one picked bomber per platoon. This will give 4 per company or a total of 12. Six of these bombers must be always available to report at once to the Bombing Officer at Battalion H.Q. on the alarm being given. O.C.'s Companies will ensure in granting passes that two of these bombers always remainin Billetting Area.
Names of men select d will be sent in to Battalion H.Q. forthwith and in future as soon as billets are taken over.

Captain,
Adjutant,
"N" Battalion.

13th. April, 1917.

Ref:- Maps,
Trench Maps,
Sheet 36 N.W.4
Scale $\frac{1}{10,000}$.

Copy No......

DEFENCE SCHEME

for

Left Reserve Battalion.
RUE DU BOIS SECTOR.

To be attached to Defence Scheme for Left Front Battalion in above Sector.

---

1. The Left Reserve Battalion will furnish one Company as ~~Reserve~~ Garrison for the Subsidiary Line and this Company is under the orders of the O.C. Left Front Battalion, (the Battalion in occupation of the trenches.)

2. Three Companies are in billets, one of which will always be ready to move at a moments notice by day or night.
   This Company will be detailed daily in Routine Orders, under the name of Inlying Picquet.

3. The remaining 2 Companies will be in readiness to move at one hours notice by day and night.
   50% of passes may be granted to these Companies, and this percentage applies to Officers as well.

4. On the alarm being given the Inlying Picquet and the other 2 Companies will fall in on the Battalion Alarm Post, and the Senior Major's horse will be saddled and brought to the Alarm Posts with the greatest speed.
   The 2nd. in Command or a substitute will report mounted to Brigade Headquarters, as soon as possible.
   No move will be made until orders are received. On the receipt of order: "Move", the Inlying Picquet will proceed immediately to the Subsidiary Line, and will occupy it between WELLINGTON AVENUE and COWGATE AVENUE: and on arrival this Company will come under the Orders of the O.C. Battalion in occupation of the trenches; reporting to him on its arrival in the Sunsidiary Line at I.14.d.5.9.
   The remaining two companies will await further orders on the Battalion Alarm Post.

5. Lewis Guns will be carried and accompany their platoons.

6. Dress:-- Battle Order; unexpended rations to be carried.

7. Each Company may leave behind cooks and servants up to a maximum of TEN under the C.Q.M.S.; one of this number will be permanently told off to remain incharge of all stores left behind, but in the event of theBattalion not returning to Billets within six hours the remainder will be marched up under the C.Q.M.S. and rejoin their Companies.

8. In the event of a rupture of our line, on the left of our Brigade Front, a defensive flank will be formed on receipt of orders from the Brigade composed of 2 Platoons with 2 Lewis Guns.
   The party willproceed to LEITH WALK, and face the left flank from that line.

9. The Battalion Bombing Officer and 6 Battalion Bombers will accompany the Inlying Picquet when it moves forward from the Alarm Post to the Sunsidiary Line.
   One Bomber will take post at each Genade Dump in the Subsidiary Line to superintend the distribution of Grenades.
   The Battalion Bombing Officer will try to gain touch with the Bombing Officer of the Battalion in occupation of the trenches and to co-operate with him in the defence of main C.T.'s and flanks.

(Continued.)

(Continued.)

10: Overland routes to the Sunsidiary Line will be reconnoitred by all Officers, and known to 1 N.C.O. in each platoon.

(Signed) T. H. MARCHANT, Lieut.Col.
Commdg.

21/3/17. 2/4th. Battn Sth. Lancashire Regiment.

ISSUED TO:-

Copy No. 1 - Headquarters, 172nd. Infantry Brigade.
" No. 2 - O.C. A Coy.
" No. 3 - O.C. B Coy.
" No. 4 - O.C. C. Coy.
" No. 5 - O.C. "D" Coy.
" No. 6 - Battalion Bombing Officer.
" No. 7 - Commanding Officer.
" No. 8 - Office Copy.

S E C R E T.   Ref.No. O.36.

To - O.'s C, "A", "B", "C" & "D" Coys.

1. With referenee to Defence Scheme for Left Reserve Battalion and H.Q. No. O,35 dated 13/4/17. The question of action of Lewis Guns of Company on work at night has been raised.

2. The Company referred to will leave behind in billets three Lewis Gunners per gun. The Guns, spare parts, and S.A.A. will be left in one easily accessible billet and the 12 men detailed will remain with them.

3. In the event of an alarm the guns and three men per gun as detailed will come under the orders of the Lewis Gun Officer who will supplement the teams from H.Q. personnel.
Guns will become a mobile reserve under the hand of the Commanding Officer.

4. It must be clearly understood that the Company detailed as Inlying Picquet will not move until direct orders to do so are received from Battalion H.Q.

5. The Inlying Picquet must sleep with clothes and boots on, and with skeleton equipment ready to put on at once in case of alarm.

6. Immediately on receipt of the alarm O.'s C, Companys will report in person at Battalion H.Q. for instructions --- this of course does not apply to the Company in the Subsidiary Line.

7. This instruction will be added to Defence Scheme for Left Reserve Battalion as an appendix.

Captain.
Adjutant,
"N" Battalion.

14/4/17.

APPENDIX. V.

2/5th BATTALION SOUTH LANCASHIRE REGIMENT

NOMINAL ROLL OF OFFICERS AS ON 31st MARCH 1917.

HEADQUARTERS

Lieut-Colonel	D. Bates	Commanding Officer
Major	A.H. Schultz	Second in Command
Captain	R.C. Hayward	Adjutant
Captain	F.J. Frodsham	Assistant Adjutant
Captain	R.L. Wood	Medical Officer.
Lieutenant	H. Gregory	Quartermaster.
Lieutenant	J.L. Hadfield	Bombing Officer
Lieutenant	W.F. Brazener	Intelligence Officer
Lieutenant	H.H. Timson	Signalling Officer
Lieutenant	H. West	Lewis Gun Officer.
2/Lieutenant	L.E. Tanton	Transport Officer

"A" COMPANY

Captain	A.C. Wallis	O/C Company.
Captain	R.H. Wood	Second in Command
Lieutenant	A.W. Messum	Platoon Commander
2/Lieutenant	J.C.O. Cocking	Platoon Commander
2/Lieutenant	A.R. Stone	Platoon Commander
2/Leiutenant	H.P.W. Davis	Platoon Commander

"B" COMPANY

Captain	M.L.B. Gould	O/C Company
XXXXXXX		
Lieutenant	T.M. Donald	Second in Command
Lieutenant	S.J. Fink	Platoon Commander
2/Lieutenant	L.M. Dean	Platoon Commander
2/Lieutenant	A.R. St. George	Platoon Commander

"C" COMPANY

Major	A. Brewis	O/C Company
Captain	E.L. Guest	Second in Command
Lieutenant	J.E. Goodwin	Platoon Commander
2/Lieutenant	R.B. Paul	Platoon Commander
2/Lieutenant	V. Hartley	Platoon Commander
2/Lieutenant	R.V. Hope	Platoon Commander

"D" COMPANY

Captain	C.W. Stephenson	O/C Company
Captain	J.A. Crowe	Second in Command
Lieutenant	W. Dickinson	Platoon Commander
2/Lieutenant	W.H.E. Holland	Platoon Commander
2/Lieutenant	W.S. Hall	Platoon Commander
2/Lieutenant	S.P. Smith	Platoon Commander

DETACHED

2/Lieutenant	R. Young	172nd Brigade L.T.M.B.
2/Lieutenant	A.A. Nimmo	172nd Brigade Pioneer Company.

Ref. Maps.
Sheet 36 N.W. 1/20,000.
Sheet 36 N.W.3 1/10,000.
Sheet 36 N.W.4 1/10,000.

To- O.'s C. "A", "B", "C", & "D" Coys.

APPENDIX VI

SECRET.

--o--

1. Whilst in Divisional Reserve for the purpose of the Divisional Defence Scheme this Unit is known as "B" Battalion.

2. There are four different dispositions which the Battalion might be called up on to make, viz:--
   1. To reinforce the Subsidiary Line.
   2. To garrison the STRONG POINT of FLEURBAIX.
   3. To garrison the works of BAC ST MAUR BRIDGEHEAD.
   4. To reinforce Divisions on our right and left.

   The dispositions to be made in case of 1, 2, or 3, being ordered are laid down in Appendices I, II, & III attached. With regard to 4, orders would be received from Brigade.

3. Certain emergency routes have been selected and marked out which lead from the ESTAIRES - SAILLY - ARMENTIERES road up to the Front Line system.
   These routes are more likely to escape the artillery and indirect Machine Gun fire which the enemy is certain to put down on the main roads.
   The roads can only be reconnoitred at present between the Front Line System and RUE DU QUESNES - RUE DELETREE line on account of cultivation but would of course be used in an emergency.
   The routes allotted to "B" Battalion are:--
   "F" Commencing at G.13.c.2.8.
   "G" Commencing at G.13.b.2.3.
   "H" ~~Commencing at~~ Branching off from "G" Route at H.20.a.7.0.

4. The first order to be issued to the Battalion when operations become iminent will be for all personnel to get dressed ready to move but to remain in Billets. Horses will be harnessed but kept in stables.

5. On the alarm being given Companies and Hedaquarters personnel will at once fall in on their own alarm posts and await orders. The Second in Command of each Company will proceed to Battalion H.Q. and remain there until definite instructions are issued. The Second in Command of the Battalion will proceed at once to Brigade H.Q.

6. The guides mentioned in Appendices I, II, & III will be assembled by the Sniping Officer and held in readiness to proceed to Companies as soon as required.

7. In the event of dispositions 1, 2, or 3 par. 2 being ordered packs will be neatly packed by Platoons in one billet, and left behind with one man per Company as guard. Battalion will proceed to allotted positions in "Battle Order."

(Continued.)

7 - Contd. Lewis Guns will be conveyed as under:--
No. 1 of each team to carry Gun slung also spare parts Wallet.
Nos 2, 3, 4, 5, & 6 will each carry two "Buckets" of Magazines slung round the neck.
Gun Boxes and Tin Box Carriers will be left in billets.

8. In the event od disposition 4, para. 2 being ordered instructions as to dress will be issued.
Lewis Guns in boxes, spare parts, Tin Boxes, etc. will be brought to the large barn at Battalion H.Q. and left there with Nos. 1 & 2 of each team.

9. All ranks will proceed in case of a move with full water bottles and full complement of ammunition.

10. Guides have reconnoitred all posts which may have to be occupied, and it is necessary unlesss special orders are issued for O.'s C. Coys. to personally reconnoitre their areas, though Officers and N.C.O.'s proceeding on working parties should take every opportunity of familiarizing themselves with the place would be at night.

R.H. Hayward Captain.
Adjutant.

6th. April, 1917.

PAINT.

APPENDIX I.

SUBSIDIARY LINE.

Name of Post.	Map Reference.	Garrison.	By whom found.	Guide.	Remarks.
COMMAND POST.	H.29.b.5.0.	1 Coy.	"A" Coy.	241374, Rfn. Tilley.	If not sufficient room in post itself trenches extend to left.
SMITH'S VILLA.	H.29.c.80.75.	2 Platoons.	"B" Coy.	240787, Rfn. Entwistle.	
CHAPEL FARM.	H.29.c.20.65.	2 Platoons.	"B" Coy.	240333, Rfn. Burrows S.	
ELBOW FARM.	H.29.c.1.1.	1 Coy.	"C" Coy.	240796, Rfn. Curran.	
CROIX MARECHAL.	H.34.a.90.65.	1 Coy.	"D" Coy.	240790, L/C. Forsyth.	

Battalion H.Q. will move forward to ELBOW FARM.

APPENDIX II.

S T R O N G   P O I N T   O F   F L E U R B A I X.

Name of Post.	Map.Ref.	Garrison.	By whom found.	Guide.	Remarks.
CAIN POST.	H.27.a.1.1.	2 Sections with 1 L.G.	"B" Coy.	241142, Rfn. Hughes.	
ABEL POST.	H.27.a.3.5.	2 Sections.	"B" Coy.	241978, Rfn. Richards.	
FERRETS POST.	H.27.b.0.0.	1 Platoon.	"B" Coy.	240361, L/C. Ellenthorpe.	
CONTINUOUS LINE.	H.27.b.4.0. to H.22.c.7.8.	2 Platoons & 2 Sections.	"A" Coy.	242236, Rfn. Bagley.	1 Platoon & 2 Sections south of & 1 Platoon North of GRANDE RUE.
LIMIT POST.	H.22.a.5.0.	1 Platoon.	"A" Coy.	242206, Rfn. Traverse.	
BOMB SCHOOL.	H.21.d.4.9.	2 Platoons.	"C" Coy.	240872, Rfn. Urquhart.	
RUE DE BIACHES.	H.21.a.4.3.	1 Platoon.	"C" Coy.	242171, Rfn. Rhodes.	
DURHAM POST.	H.21.c.6.1.	2 Platoons.	"B" Coy.	241934, Rfn. Norris.	
NORTH KEEP.	H.21.d.8.4.	2 Sections with 1 L.G.	"A" Coy.	242236, Rfn. Bagley.	
SCHOOL KEEP.	H.21.c.9.5.	1 Platoon.	"C" Coy.	241158, Rfn. Hornby.	
CENTRE KEEP.	H.21.d.2.0.	1 Coy.	"D" Coy.	240882, Cpl. McCormack.	

Battalion Headquarters will move forward to CENTRE KEEP.

11

APPENDIX III

B A C S T. M A U R B R I D G E H E A D.

Name of Post.	Map Ref.	Garrison.	by whom Found.	Guide.	Remarks.
RUE DE BRUGES POST.	G.23.b.9.7.	1 Platoon.	"D" Coy.	240790, L/C. Forsyth.	
CROSSING POST.	G.24.c.6.9.	2 Platoons.	"D" Coy.	240796, Rfn. Curran.	1 Platoon on each side of Road.
DU QUESNOY.	G.24.d.7.3.	1 Platoon.	"D" Coy.	241893, Rfn. Wiseman.	
FOURTEEN TREES.	H.19.c.5.8.	2 Platoons.	"C" Coy.	241262, Rfn. Topping.	
YORK POST.	H.19.b.0.7.	2 Platoons.	"C" Coy.	241181, Rfn. Byrom.	
SCREEN POST.	H.19.b.4.9.	---	---	240333, Rfn. Burrows.	
RUE BATTAILLE.	H.13.d.9.6.	1 Company.	"B" Coy.	241944, Rfn. Gandy.	
TWENTIETH POST.	H.14.a.& c.	1 Company.	"A" Coy.	240758, Rfn. Brophy.	

Battalion Headquarters will move forward to H.13.c.6.6.

---77

CONFIDENTIAL

Army Form A 2007.

CENTRAL REGISTRY.

Central Registry No. and Date.	Attached Files.
Vol 3 WAR	DIARY

SUBJECT, AND OFFICE OF ORIGIN.

of

2/5th S. LAN. R.

Referred to	Date	Referred to	Date	Referred to	Date
From	1/4/17	to	30/	4/17	

P.A.	Date

Schedule of Correspondence

With Appendices VII & VIII

Wt. W3019—1684 750m. 5/15. M. & H. Ltd. (M 50242)

Forms A 2007. 6

Instructions regarding War Diaries and Intelligence Summaries are contained in F. S. Regs., Part II. and the Staff Manual respectively. Title Pages will be prepared in manuscript.

WAR DIARY

~~or~~

~~INTELLIGENCE SUMMARY~~

(Erase heading not required.)

Army Form C. 2118

Place	Date April	Hour	Summary of Events and Information	Remarks and references to Appendices
RUE DORMOIRE Near ERQUINGHEM-LYS.	1917 1st to 13th.		Battalion in Divisional Reserve. Employed on working parties in trenches mostly by night The Scheme for training Platoon Instructors started on April 2nd but had to be abandoned on April 4th owing to Officers and NCO's being required for working parties. Found essential that if satisfactory work is to be done Platoons must have their officers and senior N.C.O's as otherwise the amount and quality of work suffers. Three of the classes referred to viz. Bombing - Lewis Gun and Sniperscout were carried on and results were entirely satisfactory	RHB
	10th.		The raid by "PAYNTER'S PARTY" (trained at Divisional School) took place not successful as enemy seemed to expect it. Our casualties in raid were :- 2/Lt. J. C. O. COCKING Missing 3 Other Ranks Missing. 7 Other Ranks Wounded.	RHB
	12th.		LT. COL. D. BATES left the Battalion for England and Major A. H. SCHULTZ assumed temporary command.	
	13th.		Relieved 2/6th Bn. KINGS L'POOL REGT. in Left Brigade Reserve of BOIS GRENIER - RUE DU BOIS Sector. B C and D Coys went into billets at RUE MARLE	RHB

1875 Wt. W593/826 1,000,000 4/15 J.B.C. & A. A.D.S.S./Forms/C. 2118.

Instructions regarding War Diaries and Intelligence Summaries are contained in F. S. Regs., Part II. and the Staff Manual respectively. Title Pages will be prepared in manuscript.

WAR DIARY

~~or INTELLIGENCE SUMMARY~~

(Erase heading not required.)

Army Form C. 2118

Place	Date April 1917	Hour	Summary of Events and Information	Remarks and references to Appendices
RUE MARLE	13th		'A' Coy went into Subsidiary line as 5th Coy. In addition to having one company in Subsidiary line one other company now sent each night for work in front line trenches.	RHB
RUE MARLE	14th to 21st		In Left Brigade Reserve. Two companies training during mornings also classes for Lewis Gunners and Bombers under Specialist officers. Nothing of note to record during this period.	RHB
	19th		Lieut. S. J. FINK seriously wounded by shrapnel whilst in charge of a carrying party taking Medium Trench Mortar Bombs up to the front line. Lt. FINK died of wounds on 20th.	RHB
Trenches.	21st.		Relieved 2/4th S. LAN. R. in RUE DU BOIS Subsector. Lewis Guns sent up previous night and relieved by day on 21st. Battalion relieved by night. Relief quite satisfactory.	RHB
	22nd	1.40 a.m.	2/Lieut S. P. SMITH and batman caught by small raiding party of Boches in RUE DU BOIS Salient. Enemy were hiding in our trench and fired on 2/Lt SMITH and his batman with automatic pistols. The batman was wounded but remembered seeing 2/Lt SMITH	RHB

1875 Wt. W593/826 1,000,000 4/15 J.B.C. & A. A.D.S.S./Forms/C. 2118.

Instructions regarding War Diaries and Intelligence Summaries are contained in F. S. Regs., Part II. and the Staff Manual respectively. Title Pages will be prepared in manuscript.

WAR DIARY

~~or~~

~~INTELLIGENCE SUMMARY~~

(Erase heading not required.)

Army Form C. 2118

Place	Date	Hour	Summary of Events and Information	Remarks and references to Appendices
TRENCHES	April 1917. 22nd		dragged away by enemy. The whole affair was evidently over in a few seconds and what had happened was not known till 2 a.m. when 2/Lt. N.H.E HOLLAND came up to relieve 2/Lt SMITH and found the wounded batman. The steel helmet and cane of the missing officer were found in the salient also three soft infantry pattern caps, three stick grenades and an automatic pistol left behind by the raiding party who had evidently decamped in a great hurry. The nearest post was about 60 yards away and this put up very lights and opened fire on hearing shouting in NO MAN'S LAND. This had apparently no effect. This occurrence was reported to Brigade in Situation report at 6 a.m. when details could be ascertained. This was much too late and in future any contact with enemy is to be reported at once and must reach Brigade H.Q within ~~three~~ 20 min. ~~hours~~ of occurrence. Owing to capture of 2/Lt SMITH it was made a standing order that no patrol in front line must be less than four strong. One man with fixed bayonet well in front and two others behind.	RJW

1875 Wt. W593/826 1,000,000 4/15 J.B.C. & A. A.D.S.S./Forms/C. 2118.

Instructions regarding War Diaries and Intelligence Summaries are contained in F. S. Regs., Part II. and the Staff Manual respectively. Title Pages will be prepared in manuscript.

WAR DIARY

~~or~~

~~INTELLIGENCE SUMMARY~~

(Erase heading not required.)

Army Form C. 2118

Place	Date	Hour	Summary of Events and Information	Remarks and references to Appendices
TRENCHES.	April 1917. 23rd		Generally quiet. Good deal of movement heard behind enemy lines. Transport trams and trains reported.	[illegible]
	24th		Weather turned fine at last. Much aerial activity. Enemy aeroplane brought down in our lines in flames after fight with one of our planes, fell in NO MAN'S LAND in front of BOIS-GRENIER sector.	[illegible]
	25th & 26th		Very quiet, nothing special to report.	
	27th		Left Front Company ("A" Coy) heavily shelled during morning and Right Front Company ("C" Coy) shelled during afternoon. Latter retaliation for Trench Mortar "shoot". Left front company had been firing a fair number of NEWTON Rifle Grenades and this probably drew fire on to them. Seems that if Infantry are to keep up the aggressive spirit they must have backing of artillery if enemy retaliate.	[illegible]
	28th 29th		Gas attack from sector on our left at 12.30am 29th. Enemy put up red and green clusters and his artillery opened fire. Relieved by 2/4th S. LAN. R. on night of 29/30th. Relief commenced at 9.30pm completed at 11.50pm. Relief satisfactory. Casualties during this tour: 1 Officer Missing 2 O.R. Killed 19 O.R. Wounded	[illegible]

1875 Wt. W593/826 1.000,000 4/15 J.B.C. & A. A.D.S.S./Forms/C. 2118.

Army Form C. 2118

Instructions regarding War Diaries and Intelligence Summaries are contained in F. S. Regs., Part II. and the Staff Manual respectively. Title Pages will be prepared in manuscript.

WAR DIARY
~~or~~
~~INTELLIGENCE SUMMARY~~

(Erase heading not required.)

Place	Date April (1917)	Hour	Summary of Events and Information	Remarks and references to Appendices
TRENCHES	29th		Battalion went into Left Brigade Reserve at RUE MARLE.	
RUE MARLE	30th		Three companies (A B + C) in billets and D Coy in Subsidiary line as 5th Company.	RKH
			Battalion Strength at end of April 32 Officers 922 Other Ranks.	See Appendix vii for nominal Roll of Officers. See Appendix viii for statement of strength.
			R.K. Hayward Capt. Adjt 2/5th S. Lan. R	

1875 Wt. W593/826 1,000,000 4/15 J.B.C. & A. A.D.S.S./Forms/C. 2118.

APPENDIX VII.

2/5th BATTALION SOUTH LANCASHIRE REGIMENT

***** ********* ***** ********** ********

NOMINAL ROLL OF OFFICERS AS ON 30th APRIL 1917.

HEADQUARTERS

Major	Schultz A.H.	Acting Commanding Officer.
Major	Brewis. A.	Acting Second in Command.
Captain	Hayward R.C.	Adjutant.
Captain	Frodsham F.J.	Assistant Adjutant.
Captain	Wood R.L.	Medical Officer.
Lieutenant	Gregory H,	Quartermaster.
Lieutenant	Hadfield J.L.	Bombing Officer.
Lieutenant	Brazener W.F.	Intelligence Officer.
Lieutenant	Timson H.H.	Signalling Officer.
Lieutenant	West H.	Lewis Gun Officer.
2/Lieutenant	Tanton L.E.	Transport Officer.

"A" Company

Captain	Wallis A.C.	O/C Company.
Captain	Wood R.H.	Second in Command.
Lieutenant	Messum A.W.	Platoon Commander.
2/Lieutenant	Stone A.R.	Platoon Commander.
2/Lieutenant	Davis H.P.W.	Platoon Commander.

"B" Company

Captain	Gould M.L.B.	O/C Company.
Lieutenant	Donald T.M.	Second in Command.
2/Lieutenant	Dean L.M.	Platoon Commander.
2/Lieutenant	St. George. A.R.	Platoon Commander.

"C" Company

Captain	Guest E.L.	Acting O/C Company.
Lieutenant	Goodwin J.E.	Platoon Commander.
2/Lieutenant	Paul R.B.	Platoon Commander.
2/Lieutenant	Hartley V,	Platoon Commander.
2/Lieutenant	Hope R.V.	Platoon Commander.

"D" Company

Captain	Stephenson C.W.	O/C Company.
Captain	Crowe J.A.	Second in Command
Lieutenant	Dickinson W.	Platoon Commander.
2/Lieutenant	Holland W.H.E.	Platoon Commander.
2/Lieutenant	Hall W.S.	Platoon Commander.

DETACHED.

2/Lieutenant	Young R.	172nd Bde L.T.M.B.
2/Lieutenant	Nimmo A.A.	172nd Bde Pioneer Company.

APPENDIX VIII

2/5th. S. Lan. R.

STATEMENT SHOWING FLUCTUATIONS OF STRENGTH.

Date.		Strength.	
		Officers.	O.R.
Feb. 16th.	(Battalion left BLACKDOWN, HANTS.)	29.	985.
" 20th.	(Battalion landed in FRANCE.)	29	983.
" 28th.		29	975.
March, 31st.		34	964.
April, 30th.		31	922※

※ Trench Strength of other ranks on April 30th. ... 724.

198 Other Ranks not on Strength Strength made up as under:--

Transport & Grooms.	49.
Q.M. Stores (includes C.Q.M.S.)	37.
R.A.M.C. Water Duties.	5.
Courses of Instruction.	15.
Hospital.	9.
Detention.	1.
O.R. Sergeant at Base.	1.
Detached:--	
Employed at Brigade & Division.	26.
Town Guard. ARMENTIERES.	12.
Light T.M.B. (not supernumerary.)	9.
Signallers with M.G. Coy.	2.
Brigade Pioneer Coy.	32.
TOTAL.	198.

7th. May, 1917.

1/2/5/1

9.8.

CONFIDENTIAL

WAR DIARY

OF

2/5th. S. LAN. R.

FROM 1/5/17 TO 31/5/17

WITH APPENDICES IX to XI

Instructions regarding War Diaries and Intelligence Summaries are contained in F. S. Regs., Part II. and the Staff Manual respectively. Title Pages will be prepared in manuscript.

WAR DIARY ~~or INTELLIGENCE SUMMARY~~

(Erase heading not required.)

Army Form C. 2118

Place	Date	Hour	Summary of Events and Information	Remarks and references to Appendices
RUE MARLE	May 1917 1st to 4th		Battalion in Brigade Reserve. Usual working parties found and training carried out. RUE ALLÉE – RUE FLEURIE – LA VESÉE line and L'ARMÉE line reconnoitred. Former is an almost continuous line about a mile behind Subsidiary Line of Front system of trenches. Latter consists of posts at fair intervals. 2/Lieut J.S. WOOLLETT, 3rd S. LAN. R. joined for duty on 1st inst. This period generally quiet though some shelling of back areas, notably ERQUINGHEM, with heavies took place.	RLB
—do—	5th to 6th		Quiet with no special feature. 2/Lieut A. L. GACE, 3rd S. LAN. R. joined for duty on 6th inst. Lewis Guns went into line on night of 6th – ready for Battalion Relief on night 7th/8th.	RLB
—do—	7th	4.30 pm.	Notification received that all guns of 2nd Army would put up a hurricane bombardment twice between 8x30pm and midnight	RLB
		7.45 pm.	Gas Alarm heard north of ARMENTIERES. Taken up. Box Respirators worn for an hour. No gas came into our area and	

1875 Wt. W593/826 1,000,000 4/15 J.B.C. & A. A.D.S.S./Forms/C. 2118.

Instructions regarding War Diaries and Intelligence Summaries are contained in F. S. Regs., Part II. and the Staff Manual respectively. Title Pages will be prepared in manuscript.

WAR DIARY
or
INTELLIGENCE SUMMARY
(Erase heading not required.)

Army Form C. 2118

Place	Date	Hour	Summary of Events and Information	Remarks and references to Appendices
RUE MARLE	7th.		respirators were taken off. This gas attack was part of a raid which took place on ARMENTIÈRES Sector. Owing to possibility of retaliation for 2nd Army Shoot, relief postponed for 24 hours.	RCH
TRENCHES BOIS-GRENIER SECTOR.	8th to 9th		Relieved 2/4th S. LAN. R. in RUE DU BOIS Subsector on night 8th/9th. Situation very quiet. Relief satisfactory. Complete by 11x45 p.m. CAPT. R.H. WOOD and Lieut T.M. DONALD undertook organization of two small raiding parties to obtain identification. (Referred to later as WOOD'S party and DONALD'S party.) 241031 R/m MADDEN J. A. awarded Military Medal for bravery on April 26th in digging out a comrade under heavy fire in CHARD'S FARM salient.	RCH
	10th		Major W. L. OWEN, M.C. 1/5th Battn. Kings L'pool Regt arrived and took over command of the Battalion.	
	11th.		Situation quiet. Patrols out nightly from WOOD'S and DONALD'S parties.	
	12th to 13th	12 midt to 2.30 a.m.	Patrol of 7. O.R. from DONALD'S party went out to reconnoitre gaps in wire. 3 went into wire - 4 lay outside about 30 yards in rear. Boche patrol came across covering party - scrap ensued. 5 of patrol (1 wounded) got back to our lines. 2 missing. 3 Boche hit	RCH

1875 Wt. W593/826 1,000,000 4/15 J.B.C. & A. A.D.S.S./Forms/C. 2118.

Instructions regarding War Diaries and Intelligence Summaries are contained in F. S. Regs., Part II. and the Staff Manual respectively. Title Pages will be prepared in manuscript.

WAR DIARY
or
INTELLIGENCE SUMMARY
(Erase heading not required.)

Army Form C. 2118

Place	Date	Hour	Summary of Events and Information	Remarks and references to Appendices
TRENCHES BOIS GRENIER SECTOR.	13th.		believed killed.	
			Raid by DONALD's party had to be abandoned as enemy watched this part of his line too closely after events of night 12th/13th.	RCA
			Enemy showing signs of nervousness at night	
	14th	12 midt	WOOD's party went out, made up as under:–	
			Party to enter Boche trench 5.	
			Parapet Party 2.	
			Guides in enemy wire 2	
			Covering Party 12 with 1 officer	
			2 Lewis Guns on Flanks 4	RCA
			25.	
			Fighting patrol standing by in our front line trench.	
			Nothing happened till 2x30 a.m. when our men discovered in his wire. Enemy manned his parapet and bombed his wire. Party withdrew	
			No casualties.	
	15th	1	Quiet day.	
		10.30 pm	Patrol of 1 N.C.O. 6 men of "C" Company went out. Made an attempt	RCA

1875 Wt. W593/826 1,000,000 4/15 J.B.C. & A. A.D.S.S./Forms/C. 2118.

Instructions regarding War Diaries and Intelligence Summaries are contained in F. S. Regs., Part II. and the Staff Manual respectively. Title Pages will be prepared in manuscript.

WAR DIARY

~~or~~

~~INTELLIGENCE SUMMARY~~

(Erase heading not required.)

Army Form C. 2118.

Place	Date	Hour	Summary of Events and Information	Remarks and references to Appendices
TRENCHES BOIS GRENIER SECTOR	15th		to get a prisoner. They were however discovered	
	16th	2.30am	Patrol leader and three men returned but left three men out. Nothing was seen of these men until 3x30pm. when they doubled across N.M.L. and reached our lines safely only one shot being fired at them.	
			Relieved by 2/4th S. Lan. R. at night commencing 9x30pm. Relief complete at 11x40pm.	
			Battalion less "A" Coy went into billets at RUE MARLE.	RLD
			Casualties during 8 days in trenches 1 killed 12 wounded 2 missing – no officer casualties	
RUE MARLE	17th to 19th		Companies in billets training.	
			241031 Rfn MADDEN J. received Military Medal from Army Commander II Army.	
			Went into XI CORPS I ARMY from 2nd ANZAC CORPS 2nd ARMY.	
	20th	noon	2/Lieut A. L. GACE. left to go to Chinese Labour Battn	
	21st		Nothing unusual. Relieved 2/4th S. Lan. R. in RUE DU BOIS Subsection	RLD
	22nd to 24th		Relief commenced at 8pm. being put forward two hours owing to expected discharge of gas projectors on FLAMENGRIE Subsection. Relief complete 10x30pm.	

1875 Wt. W593/826 1,000,000 4/15 J.B.C. & A. A.D.S.S./Forms/C. 2118.

Instructions regarding War Diaries and Intelligence Summaries are contained in F. S. Regs., Part II. and the Staff Manual respectively. Title Pages will be prepared in manuscript.

WAR DIARY
or
~~INTELLIGENCE SUMMARY~~
(Erase heading not required.)

Army Form C. 2118

Place	Date	Hour	Summary of Events and Information	Remarks and references to Appendices
TRENCHES BOIS GRENIER Sector	25th to 27th		Enemy exceptionally quiet. Musketry Practices started in front line. Found that men were forgetting how to use their rifles.	APPENDIX IX.
	28th		Enemy slightly more active – mostly M.G's and Artillery. Received notification that enemy might be expected to withdraw on this front, being extension of retirement further south.	
	29th		Conference with Trench Mortar Officers to secure cooperation and retaliation.	
	31st	10.30 pm	Opened fire for 5 minutes with all rifles, Lewis Guns, Rifle Grenade Batteries and 3" Stokes Mortars. Some retaliation but not serious. Enemy seemed to think we were going to attack and put up red & green lights. Had good effect on our men – keeps up offensive spirit. Strength of Battalion May 31st. 34 Officers 905 Other Ranks	APPENDICES X & XI

R. Haygarth Capt.
Adjt. 2/5th Bn. South Lancs. Regt.

1875 Wt. W593/826 1,000,000 4/15 J.B.C. & A. A.D.S.S./Forms/C. 2118.

APPENDIX. IX.

SUBJECT:- Musketry Ref. No. M.33.

To O.'s C. "A", "B", "C", & "D" Coys.

O.'s C. Companies will ensure that the following practices are carried out daily:-

1. RAPID LOADING.
To be practiced using 6 clips of live rounds during each practice, a record of the time taken being kept.
A cork or a wedge made of wood must be put in behind the trigger when this practice is being done

2. Each Section Commander in the Front Line will put out during the hours of darkness one of the targets issued.
These will be fixed up 50 yards in front of his Section's position with the white side of the target towards our own trenches.
The Section Commander will then order 10 rounds rapid fire at this target, and afterwards send in a return to Company Headquarters showing:-
(a) Number of men firing at the target.
(b) The number of hits made.

O.'s C. Companies must impress upon Platoon and Section Commanders that they are all responsible for seeing that these practices are carefully and thoroughly carried out. Men not in the Front Line will be practiced in rapid loading, and also in rapid firing as opportunity offers.

The Commanding Officer wishes Company Commanders to bring the result of the previous night's practice for rapid firing and times taken for rapid loading to the daily Conference.

Everything should be done to stimulate a spirit of competition in the men, and between sections and platoons in carrying out these practices.

R Hayshaw
Captain
25th May. 1917. Adjutant
2/5th Battalion South Lancashire Regt.

APPENDIX. X.

2/5th BATTALION SOUTH LANCASHIRE REGIMENT

****

NOMINAL ROLL OF OFFICERS AS ON 31st MAY. 1917

****

HEADQUARTERS

Lieut-Colonel.	Owen W.L. M.C.	Commanding Officer.
Major	Schultz. A.H.	Second in Command.
Captain	Hayward R.C.	Adjutant
Captain	Frodsham F.J.	Assistant Adjutant
Captain	Wood R.L.	Medical Officer
Lieutenant	Gregory H.	Quartermaster.
Lieutenant	Hadfield J.L.	Bombing Officer.
Lieutenant	Brazener W.F.	Intelligence Officer.
Lieutenant	Timson H.H.	Signalling Officer.
Lieutenant	West H.	Lewis Gun Officer.
2/Lieutenant	Tanton L.E.	Transport Officer.

"A" Company

Captain	Wallis A.C.	O/C Company
Captain	Wood R.H.	Second in Command
Lieutenant	Messum A.W.	Platoon Commander
2/Lieutenant	Stone A.R.	Platoon Commander.
2/Lieutenant	Davis H.P.W.	Platoon Commander.

"B" Company

Captain	M.L.B. Gould	O/C Company.
Lieutenant	Donald T.M.	Second in Command.
2/Lieutenant	Dean L.M.	Platoon Commander.
2/Lieutenant	St. George A.R.	Platoon Commander.
2/Lieutenant	Bullen H.G.	Platoon Commander.

"C" Company

Major	Brewis A.	O/C Company
Captain	Guest E.L.	Second in Command
Lieutenant	Goodwin J.E.	Platoon Commander.
2/Lieutenant	Nimmo A.A.	Platoon Commander.
2/Lieutenant	Hope R.V.	Platoon Commander.
2/Lieutenant	Woollett J.S.	Platoon Commander.

"D" Company

Captain	Stephenson C.W.	O/C Company
Captain	Crowe J.A.	Second in Command
Lieutenant	Dickinson W.	Platoon Commander.
2/Lieutenant	Holland W.H.E.	Platoon Commander.
2/Lieutenant	Handley W.C.	Platoon Commander.

Detached

2/Lieutenant	Young R.	172nd Bde L.T.M.B.
2/Lieutenant	Hall W.S.	172nd Bde Pioneer Coy.
2/Lieutenant	Paul R.B.	172nd Brigade School of Instruction.

,........................

APPENDIX. XI.

2/5th. Bn. Sth. Lancs. Regt.

...

STATEMENT

- SHOWING FLUCTUATIONS OF STRENGTH. -

34 Officers. --- 905 Other Ranks.

Trench Strength, 31/5/17 --- 701 Other Ranks.

204 Other Ranks not on Trench Strength made up as under:-

Transport & Grooms.	46.
Q.M. Stores.	34.
R.A.M.C. (Water Duties.)	5.
Courses of Instruction.	23.
Hospital.	8.
Detention.	1.
O.R. Sergeant at Base.	1.

Detached:-

Employed at Bde. and Divn.	26.
Town Guard, ARMENTIERES.	12.
A.P.M.	5.
Light T.M.B. (not superny.)	8.
Signallers with M.G. Coy.	2.
Brigade Pioneer Company.	33.
Total.	204.

172/57 Original #13R

Vol 5

CONFIDENTIAL

WAR DIARY

OF

2/5th S. LAN. R.

FROM 1/6/17 to 30/6/17

WITH APPENDICES XII - XVI.

Instructions regarding War Diaries and Intelligence Summaries are contained in F. S. Regs., Part II. and the Staff Manual respectively. Title Pages will be prepared in manuscript.

WAR DIARY

~~or~~

~~INTELLIGENCE SUMMARY~~

(Erase heading not required.)

Army Form C. 2118

Place	Date	Hour	Summary of Events and Information	Remarks and references to Appendices
TRENCHES BOIS GRENIER SECTOR	1st.		Relieved by 2/4th S. Lan. R. in RUE DU BOIS Subsector. Relief complete 10x30 pm. Battalion less A Coy went into billets at RUEMARLE. Casualties during tour 1 OR killed 6 OR wounded.	RCH
RUEMARLE	2nd.		Copy of London Gazette 31/5/17 received. All officers go back to original seniority. Battn left with Lt. Col and 3 Captains remainder subalterns.	
	3rd & 4th		Companies training. Enemy shelling back areas, apparently counter battery work. B Coy billets received ten 5.9's on 4th but whole company away training so no casualties. B Coy sent into new billets.	
	5th & 6th		Situation quiet. B Coy relieved A Coy in Subsidiary Line on evening 6th.	
	7th.	3.10 am.	II Army Push at MESSINES commenced. Zero 3.10 a.m. Distinctly heard mines blown from here.	
		4 pm.	Enemy shelled billeting area. Continued for an hour. Casualties 1 Killed 11 wounded	
		9 pm.	Shelling recommenced and continued intermittently throughout the night.	
		1.30 am	Battalion H.Q. at CROWN PRINCE HOUSE received attention. R.S.M. wounded. All men spent night out in cover trenches and open ground.	
	8th.	7.30 am.	18 pdr Battery at HALFWAY HOUSE knocked out. After this billets not shelled.	RCH
		2 pm.	Orders received to be prepared to move to left to assist 171st Brigade in defence of ARMENTIERES. Two Battalions of Brigade on our right (170th) to be	

1875 Wt. W593/826 1,000,000 4/15 J.B.C. & A. A.D.S.S./Forms/C. 2118.

Instructions regarding War Diaries and Intelligence Summaries are contained in F. S. Regs., Part II. and the Staff Manual respectively. Title Pages will be prepared in manuscript.

WAR DIARY

~~or~~

~~INTELLIGENCE SUMMARY~~

(Erase heading not required.)

Army Form C. 2118

Place	Date	Hour	Summary of Events and Information	Remarks and references to Appendices
RUE MARLE.	8th		ready to support this Brigade (172nd) These preparations on account of reported massing of enemy troops North of ARMENTIERES at WARNETON.	
			Parties from Companies and Battn. H.Q. reconnoitred positions to be taken up in case of move to our left.	R.C.O.
			2/Lieut R. HARGREAVES joined for duty. Lt J E GOODWIN to England - damaged knee	
	9th		Conference of O/C Coys to consider Brigade Operation Orders No 4 with reference to voluntary BOCHE withdrawal.	
			Relieved 2/4th S Lan. R in RUE DU BOIS Subsector. Relief satisfactory. Arrangements made that 2/4th S. Lan R. would do all patrolling during this tour in preparation for their raid.	
			Battalion Operation Orders No. 20. (BOCHE voluntary withdrawal issued)	APPENDIX. XII
TRENCHES BOIS GRENIER Sectn.	10th		Lt. Col OWEN to C.O's conference at BOULOGNE representing 57th Division.	
			Daylight patrol of 2 NCO's and 1 man (240508 L/Sgt BICKERSTAFFE, 240790 L/Cpl FORSYTH and 240796 Rfn CURRAN) reconnoitred ground where patrol of 2/4th S Lan. R. had been bombed just outside our own wire previous night. Patrol very successful. Discovered place where enemy patrol had laid up & track back to his own lines.	R.C.O.
	11th		Scheme for rewiring of whole front started. Permission received from Brigade to put out French Wire entanglement with apron instead of ordinary Fence Wire. This means great saving of time.	

1875 Wt. W593/826 1,000,000 4/15 J.B.C. & A. A.D.S.S./Forms/C. 2118.

Instructions regarding War Diaries and Intelligence Summaries are contained in F. S. Regs., Part II. and the Staff Manual respectively. Title Pages will be prepared in manuscript.

WAR DIARY

~~or~~

~~INTELLIGENCE SUMMARY~~

(Erase heading not required.)

Army Form C. 2118

Place	Date	Hour	Summary of Events and Information	Remarks and references to Appendices
TRENCHES	12th	6 pm	Daylight patrol consisting of 2/Lieut L.M. DEAN and 2 NCO's reconnoitred N.M.L. in front of CONRATE GAP (Left Sub Sector)	
BOIS GRENIER Sector				RWC
	13th		Subsidiary line shelled with 5.9's and 4.2's No casualties.	
			2/Lieut E. B. LE MARE joined for duty	
	14th		12th PORTUGESE Battn. came into FLAMENGRIE Subsector (on our right)	
	15th	11.15pm	~~[illegible]~~ Silent Raid by 2/4th. S. Lan. R. from RUE DU BOIS Subsector.	
			No identification obtained.	
	16th		Relieved by 2/4th. S. Lan. R. on night of 17th inst. Relief complete 11pm	
RUE MARLE	to 17th		Battn less 'A' Coy went into billets at RUE MARLE (Casualties during tour 1 OR killed 6 wounded).	
			Lt. Col. OWEN returned from C.O.'s conference.	
	18th		Divisional Horse Show. We won three prizes. First, Transport Group, First, Mules, Second, Single Horse Vehicle.	
	19th to 20th		Less shelling of back areas. A great many heavy guns in ARMENTIERES	
			Orders for Battn. when in Reserve in case of Enemy withdrawal issued, also Instruction No. I for O.O 20	APPENDICES XIII & XIV
	21st		Lieut Gen. R. G. BROADWOOD C.B. wounded at PONT NIEPPE by Shrapnel. Died of wounds received, later in the day.	
			'C' Coy relieved 'A' Coy in Subsidiary line.	
	22nd to 23rd		No Special feature.	RWC
			2/Lieut J. CLARKE joined for duty 23/6/17.	
	24th	2pm	Billeting area shelled. No casualties	

1875 Wt. W593/826 1,000,000 4/15 J.B.C. & A. A.D.S.S./Forms/C. 2118.

Instructions regarding War Diaries and Intelligence Summaries are contained in F. S. Regs., Part II. and the Staff Manual respectively. Title Pages will be prepared in manuscript.

WAR DIARY

~~or~~

~~INTELLIGENCE SUMMARY~~

(Erase heading not required.)

Army Form C. 2118

Place	Date	Hour	Summary of Events and Information	Remarks and references to Appendices
RUE MARLE	25th		Relieved 2/4th S Lan. R in RUE DU BOIS Subsector. Relief satisfactory. Complete at 11 pm	
TRENCHES BOIS GRENIER Sector	26th to 28th		No special feature except that enemy much more active with "Minnies". Received notification from Division on 28th that Artillery observers considered that, increased "Minnie" activity and also the fact that enemy aeroplanes had been flying low over our lines, indicated enemy intention to raid probably on Centre company sector. Special precautions taken accordingly. 2/Lieut B. C. ADAMS joined for duty 26/6/17.	RHK
	29th	3.5 pm	2/10th K.L.R did daylight raid from FLAMENGRIE Subsector on our right. Some retaliation from Minnies on this subsector also about 40 7.7 cm's and heavier shells round about Battalion H.Q. Very little damage and 1 slight casualty.	
			BOCHE very restless at night sending up many very lights	
		10.30 to 11 pm	LA CHAPELLE D'ARMENTIÈRES heavily shelled	
		11.35 pm	Very bright Star shell sent up. Fell between Support and Subsidiary lines in Centre Company Sector. Followed later by another which failed to burst. These were apparently fired from a field gun and gave tremendous light on bursting	
	30th.		Weather very wet and much colder. "B" Coy training and reconnoitring for "OWEN'S 'OP'". Final orders not yet completed.	RHK

Army Form C. 2118

Instructions regarding War Diaries and Intelligence Summaries are contained in F. S. Regs., Part II. and the Staff Manual respectively. Title Pages will be prepared in manuscript.

WAR DIARY

~~or~~

~~INTELLIGENCE SUMMARY~~

(Erase heading not required.)

Place	Date	Hour	Summary of Events and Information	Remarks and references to Appendices
TRENCHES BOIS GRENIER Sector	30th		Enemy continued active with Minnies otherwise situation quiet Strength of Battalion June 30th 1917. 37 Officers 851 Other Ranks. R.L. Hayward Lieut & Adjt 2/5th S. Lan Regt.	[illegible] APPENDICES XV & XVI

1875 Wt. W593/826 1,000,000 4/15 J.B.C. & A. A.D.S.S./Forms/C. 2118.

APPENDIX - XII

SECRET.

Copy No ..9....

2/5th. BN. S. LAN. R., OPERATION ORDERS NO. 20.

Ref. Map,
Sheet 36 N.W.4
1/10,000.

12th. June, 1917.

1. INFORMATION.

There are various indications of a voluntary withdrawal by the enemy owing to the crumbling process which is taking place further South.

This may be expected to extend to this Sector, and in the event of this happening prompt action is essential.

The present enemy defences consist of two main lines:-

(a) Front Line and Supports.
(b) Second Line shown on map as:- INDENT INDEED, INCUMBENT, and INADEQUATE Trenches.

In between those two lines there are two intermediary lines of resistance:-

(i) DISTILLERY - WEZ MACQUART - RUELLE DE LA NOIX Road.
(ii) Line LE QUESNE - GRAND MARAIS - CHAU. D'HANCARDRY - FME DE L'EPERONNERIE - LA BLEUE.

The withdrawal is not expected to go beyond the enemy's second line as shown in (b)

NOTE.-- GRAND MARAIS is the Battalion's main objective, and any resistance from this quarter will be overcome with the least possible delay.

2. INTENTION.

In the event of the enemy withdrawing voluntarily it is the intention that the Battalions in occupation of our Front System will follow him up with vigour.

3. PRELIMINARY ACTION.

Details for the action to be taken prior to the enemy's withdrawal are stated in Appendix I

4. NOTIFICATION OF ENEMY'S INTENTION TO WITHDRAW.

In the event of information being received that the enemy intends to withdraw, a message in the following code will be sent to all Companies.

"ENEMY IS WITHDRAWING FROM RUE DU BOIS SUB-SECTOR .... RUE DU BOIS CUTTING"

"ENEMY HAS WITHDRAWN FROM RUE DU BOIS SUB-SECTOR .... RUE DU BOIS CUT."

Information of the enemy's withdrawal on the flanks of the Battalion will be communicated in the above manner substituting the name of the Sub-sector concerned.

(Continued.)

5. ACTION ON RECEIVING NOTICE OF ENEMYS IN TENTION TO WITHDRAW.

The Operations will be divided into 5 phases as under:-

FIRST PHASE. General Stand-to and Preparations for a move. Reconnaissance and Establishment of Patrols in Enemy's Front System.
(a) On receipt of the first code message referring to this Frontage, a general stand-to for all Coys. will be ordered at once and preparations made for a move.
(b) Each Front Line Company will immediately send forward a small patrol to reconnoitre the enmy's Front Line. If found unoccupied the patrols will establish themselves at the point of entry and send back information to their Company Commanders who will at once send forward the remainder of the Platoon from which the Patrol was detailed, to establish posts in the enemy's Front System in the following localities.--

RUE DU BOIS SUB-SECTOR.

Right Coy.	I.21.d.00.70 & I.21.c.30.03.
Centre Coy.	I.21.b.80.20.
Left Coy.	I.16.d.57.70 & I.22.a.82.87.

The enemy's Support Line in the immediate vicinity will be reconnoitred, and Bombing Squads will be established at the junction of the Support Line and Communication Trenches.
On Code-word signifying enemy's withdrawal being received from Battalion Headquarters (for code-words see para. 4) patrols will take immediate action and proceed by previously arranged routes to enemy Front Line, and reconnoitre their respective frontages to ascertain.

(i) Whether the enemy has withdrawn from Front Line system.
(ii) Whether enemy has withdrawn from first first intermediary line.
(iii) Whether enemy has withdrawn from second intermediary line.
(iv) Whether enemy has withdrawn from Second Main Line of Defence.

(c) The remaining platoons of the front line companies will move up to our front line and get ready to move forward as soon as the second phase takes place.

(d) Battalion Headquarters will be moved to:-

ORCHARD POST.

Continued.)

2nd. PHASE. Occupation and Consolidation of Enemy's Front Line System, and General Move Forward of Battalions in Reserve, Machine Gun Coy., Light T.M.B. etc.

(a) At the discretion of Officers Commanding Coys. the remaining Platoons of each Front Line Company will cross NO MAN'S LAND to support the leading platoons, and the enemy's entire Front and Support Lines will be occupied by mutually supporting posts. One Platoon for each Company being detailed for carrying up material and ammunition etc. 2 Sections of this Platoon will be allotted to each of the two consolidating platoons.

(b) It may be wise not to dig strong points in the German Front Line system, but to go 30 to 50 yards beyond so as to avoid hostile shelling by being away from his old line which will have been most accurately registered.

(c) The enemy's trenches will be consolidated at once, and covering patrols sent forward as far as the general line FARM HOUSSAIN - LA MOTTE HOUSSAIN - LE QUESNE - thence along the DISTILLERY ROAD through VEZ MACQUART.
Bombing Squads will push forward along the Main Communication Trenches and establish "blocks" South-east of this Line.

(d) If a voluntary withdrawal takes place it is very improbable that he will have any isolated posts in his Front Line, and it is anticipated that he will vacate the whole Front Line system.
It is however more than probable that he will leave M.G.'s in isolated positions such as the DISTILLERY, PETIT MARAIS, GRAND MARAIS, LARGE FARM BREWERY, EST. DE LA BARRIERE, VEZ MACQUART --- in fact at any point where he could cause us loss and delay, and these isolated posts will have to be summarily dealt with by Stokes Guns, M.G.'s, Rifle Grenades and if necessary by small "ousting" attacks by sections and platoons with the help of artillery.

(e) Company Headquarters will be established in the enemy's trenches and marked with large white notice boards placed out of view from the enemy marked in black as under:-

RUE DU BOIS SUB-SECTOR.

Companies from Right to Left, I, II, III (Roman Figs.)

These boards are to assist Artillery Observation Officers in locating the position of Companies from our O.P.'s in rear.

(Continued.)

(f) The Fourth Company of each Battalion in the trenches will occupy a central position in our Front Line and establish Headquarters in the vicinity of I.15.1., RUE DU BOIS SUB-SECTOR.

(g) The "Fifth Company" will remain in its position in the Subsidiary Line and rejoin its own Unit when the Battalions in Brigade Reserve move up.

(h) The Battalion in Brigade Reserve will move up to the Subsidiary Line. Battalion Headquarters will be established in the present Sub-sector Battalion Headquarters.

(i) Left Reserve Battalion will detail one company to dig a Communication Trench across NO MAN'S LAND at approximately Point I.21.c.8.9. to INCLINE TRENCH. The Company detailed for this work will work under R.E. supervision, who will issue instructions as to rendezvous, tools, etc. It will be prepared to occupy our Front Line in an emergency.

(j) One Section of the 172nd. Machine Gun Coy. will occupy our original Front Line trench taking up previously selected positions.

(k) Brigade Headquarters will move to advanced Brigade Headquarters at I.13.c.9.8.

3rd. PHASE. Establishment of Outposts along the General Line from FME. HOUSSAIN - LA MOTTE HOUSSAIN LE QUESNE - HOTEL (I.27.c.8.9.) - PETIT MARAIS - DISTILLERY ROAD - EST. de la BARRIERE - CROSS ROADS WEZ MACQUART as far as Point I.17.c.35.10.

(a) As soon as the patrols report that the enemy have retired from the General Line named above, the leading Companies will immediately establish outposts along this line and push out patrols to maintain touch with the enemy.

(b) Special patrols will be sent to reconnoitre selected points as under:-
Junction of INCUBATOR TRENCH and INCOMPLETE DRIVE GRAND MARAIS, locality I.28.b.8.5. CHAU D'HANCARDRY FME de L'EPERONNERIE.

4th. PHASE. Occupation of selected points mentioned in (b) 3rd. PHASE, and the construction of Strong Points.

(a) As soon as patrols report that the enemy has withdrawn from any of the above mentioned localities the leading Company Commanders will receive orders from Battalion Headquarters to occupy them and consolidate them. (See 3rd. PHASE (b)).

(Continued.)

(b) As soon as localities mentioned in 3rd. PHASE (b) have been occupied, and supposing GRAND MARAIS to be still holding out the 4th. Company (Subsidiary Coy.) will take steps to attack and occupy same.

5th. PHASE. Continuation of the Advanced.
Should the enemy continue to withdraw behind his main second line of defence, orders will be issued by the Brigade for advance guards to move forward and keep in touch with him.

6. BOUNDARIES. Battalion Boundaries.

(y) RIGHT. Junction of PARK ROW and Front Line (I.20.d.45.80) - junction of INCOME LANE and INCOME TRENCH - HOTEL (I.21.c.8.9.) thence along the line of INCOME DRIVE - INCOMPLETE DRIVE - MONTE PINDO - the road from MONTE PINDO - LA VALEE.
This line inclusive.

(z) LEFT. Line joining points I.16.b.3.7. - I.16.d.50.90 - along the ditch to I.17.c.35.10 - I.17.c.2.0. - along the ditch to I.23.b.05.25.

COMPANY BOUNDARIES.

Right Boundary of each Company as under:-

Right Coy. as (y)

Centre. I.21.a.8.4. - I.21.b.2.1. (GERMAN HOUSE) - I.28.a.35.85 - I.35.a.6.8.

Left. I.16.c.5.7. - I.22.a.75.80 EST. DE LA BARRIERE exclusive - CHAU. D'HANCARDRY exclusive - I.29.b.6.3.

Left Bounday of Left Coy. as (z)

7. MACHINE GUNS. As soon as Companies are established in German Front Line system two Vickers M.G.'s will go forward and one will report to O.C. Left Coy. and one to O.C. Right Coy. who will place these guns forward of their flanking strong points to allow of good flanking or cross fire. Two other guns will take up positions in our present front line at I.26.a.55.75 and I.21.b.10.90 to co-operate on any points of resistance with direct and indirect fire. The remaining four guns will occupy with four L.G.'s (from the 5th. Coy.) our present defence line running along the Support Line.

(Continued.)

- 4 -

8. LIGHT T.M. BATTERY. 1 Section, L.T.M.B. will be attached to the Battalion, distribution being one gun to each Coy. in Front Line, 1 Gun in reserve, Battn. H.Q. In the event of GRAND MARAIS or any other point holding out the O.C. 172nd. L.T.M.B. will use the guns as required. The O.C. 172nd. L.T.M.B. will remain at Battalion Headquarters at ORCHARD POST.

9. ARTILLERY. (a) One Artillery Liaison Officer will report to Battalion Headquarters and one to the Centre Company.

(b) The same batteries that cover Companies in the Front Line, as shown in the Defence Scheme will continue to cover Companies when they move forward to the enemy's Front Line system. Zones for S.O.S. will conform to the phases of the infantry action as under:-

(i) During first and second phases artillery will cover the front opposite the enemy's Support Line.

(ii) When the third phase is completed the zone for S.O.S. will cover the front opposite the general line of outposts.

(c) Company Commanders requiring a concentration of fire on any locality will inform the artillery by reference to the 1/10,000 Map, Sheet 36 N.W.4.

(d) The O.C. Centre Group Artillery will make arrangements for the movement and action of Medium Trench Mortar Batteries.

10. LIAISON. One Officer or Sergeant with a runner will be sent to the Battalion Headquarters on either flank. One Officer from Battalion Headquarters and a runner will report to advanced Brigade Headquarters I.13.c9.8. The above arrangements for liaison will be instituted as soon as the 2nd. Phase has commenced.

11. COMMUNICATIONS. (a) Officers Commanding Front line Companies will establish telephone communication from their new Company Headquarters in the enemy's lines to the Company Posts in our present front line.

(b) The Battalion Signalling Officer will arrange for communication from these Company posts to the new Battalion Headquarters at ORCHARD POST.

(c) As soon as the second phase commences two runners will be sent from Battalion Headquarters to report to Brigade Signalling Officer at Advanced Brigade Headquarters (I.13.c.9.8.)

11. Continued. (d) Special instructions for visual signalling and other arrangements for communication will be issued to the Battalion S.O. by Brigade Signalling Officer.

12. ADMINISTRATIVE ARRANGEMENTS. Arrangements for supply of rations, water ammunition and material etc., are set forth in Appendix II.

13. MEDICAL. Advanced R.A.P. will be at junction of WINE STREET and WINE AVENUE
The two present R.A.P.'s at Battalion Headquarters and bottom of LEITH WALK will be available and occupied by M.O. and S.B.'s of Reserve Battalion.

14. REPORTS. Patrol-leaders will keep Company Headquarters informed of progress made, and as each objective is reached and found vacated or otherwise a comprehensive report will be sent by runner to Advance Company's Headquarters at I.16.b.10.30, I.15.d.85.50 and I.21.c.85.90 respectively, and forwarded to Battalion H.Q.

R.H. Hayward
Lieutenant,
Adjutant,
2/5th. S. Lan. R.

Issued at 11am by runner to

Copy No. 1 ... O.C.
" " 2 ... "A" Coy.
" " 3 ... "B" "
" " 4 ... "C" "
" " 5 ... "D" "
" " 6 ... T.O.
" " 7 ... Q.M.
" " 8 ... Office.
" " 9 ... War Diary. X
" " 10 ... Bde H.Q.
" " 11 ... L.T.M.B.
" " 12 ... M.T.M.B.
" " 13 ... M.G.Coy.
" " 14 ... O.C. Battn. in Bde. Res.
" " 15 ... Spare.

APPENDIX I.

Arrangements to be made at once pending information being received that the enemy has commenced to withdraw from his Front Line.

1. OBSERVATION OF THE ENEMY. The closest observation will be maintained constantly of the enemy's trenches, and any signs of evacuation will be reported at once. This will be carried out by Infantry and Artillery Observers. At night, NO MAN'S LAND, will be carefully patrolled throughout the hours of darkness, and patrols will lie up close to the enemy's parapet and ascertin whether he is still in occupation. Besides the policy of small raiding parties as laid down in Letter B.M. 97/5 dated 3/3/17 patrols will enter the unoccupied portions of the enemy'sFront Line and establish listening posts throuhout the night.

2. DETAILS. Officers, N.C.O.'s and men detailed to remain behind in the event of the withdrawal developing into an attack will report to Transport Lines, the Senior Officer taking command of the party.

3. MATERIAL. Sites will be selected for a Dump of R.E. material tools, etc. by each Company in the front line. These dumps will contain:-

60 Shovels.
30 Picks.
2,000 Sand-bags.
5 Coils of French Wire.
50 Coils of Barbed wire.
20 Long Screw Posts. (4' 6")
2 Wire-cutters.
2 Mauls.
Pickets, angle, iron, 3' 6" ... 160.
" " " 5' ... 60.

In addition to the above there will be two reserve dumps of material established at:-

(i) QUEEN STREET adjoining Railway. I.21 a.05.65.
(ii) Off LEITH WALK between LILLE POST and CHARDS FARM.

Material for all these dumps has been indented for by the Brigade, and will be sent up to the trenches. Companies will be informed whenthis material is to arrive and will commence stocking their front line dumps first. The exact amount of material for the reserve dumps is given in para. 6 of this appendix. Separate R.E. Dumps are being arranged by the 505th. Company R.E. These are quite independent of the Infantry Dumps mentioned above.

P.T.O.

4. AMMUNITION.

(a) Ammunition dumps will be formed for each Front Line Company. These dumps will be commenced forthwith and if not complete when Companies are relieved will be handed over to the incoming Companies for completion.

Dumps to contain:-

20 Boxes S.A.A.
20 Boxes, Mills Grenades No. 23, with blanks.
20 Boxes, Mills Grenades, No. 5
2 Boxes Rifle Grenades No. 20. with blanks.
1 Box 1" Very Lights.

Ammunition Dumps will be situated at:-

Right Coy.	I.21.c.85.97.
Centre Coy.	I.15.d.50.12.
Left Coy.	I.16.c.70.80.

(b) O.C. Light Trench Mortar Battery will form small dumps of Stokes Gun Ammunition on each Company Front.

5. GENERAL.

(a) All the above mentioned dumps will be marked with a notice-board "EMERGENCY DUMP." The material will not be used for any other purpose than that required in these operations unless orders are issued to the contrary from Battalion Headquarters.

(b) All Lewis Gun Magazines will be kept filled.

6. MATERIAL IN RESERVE DUMPS.

Boxes, Water Lined 10 galls.	1.
Bridges, trench. 9' - 12'	6.
Corr. Iron Sheets.	24.
Duckwalks.	50.
"A" Frames, 3' 0"	25.
Frames folding breastwork.	50.
Hurdles, revetting, wood.	25.
Panels, revetting, light.	25.
Pickets, wood, 3'	25.
Pickets, wood, 3'	170.
Pickets, angle iron 5'	35.
Windlass.	50.
Wire, barbed, coils.	50.

ADMINISTRATION. APPENDIX II.

1. TRANSPORT. When ordered by the Brigade, Transport will move to field at H.4.d.5.8. near ERQUINGHEM CHURCH where they will be brigaded under the B.C.O. All vehicles will be loaded, watercarts and coal-bunkers filled.
Two mounted orderlies from each Unit will report at H.E.2 and await instructions.

2. SURPLUS STORES. Surplus Stores will be deposited at School Buildings, H.4.d.40.35.
The 2/8th. K.L.R. and 2/10th. K.L.R. will also use this place as a dump.
The personnel already detailed will remain with surplus stores at the place mentioned above and await orders from the Brigade Salvage Officer.

3. BRIGADE SCHOOL. The Officers and N.C.O.'s at the Brigade School will remain in their present billets and send an Officer to report to H.E.2 for Orders.

4. RATIONS. The O.C. No. 4 Company Divisional Train will deliver the rations for all units of the Brigade at H.4.d.40.35.
Companies will notify Battalion Headquarters who will probably notify Brigade Headquarters the most suitable time and place for delivery of rations, and arrange for guides for the distribution to companies.

5. DRESS AND EQUIPMENT. On receipt of enemy's intention to withdraw all ranks will immediately be made up to:-

Inaddition to BATTLE ORDER:-

(a) 1 Spade or Pick. (70% Spades 30% Picks.)
(b) 2 No. 5 Bombs.
(c) 2 Sand-bags.
(d) 1 Extra Bandolier S.A.A.
(e) In addition each Bombing Section will carry three boxes of bombs, and each Rifle Bombing Section 3 Boxes of No. 20 Rifle Grenades.
(f) One 1" Very Light.

Water Bottles will be filled and the iron ration carried.
Companies will move forward in Battle Order less greatcoats. Packs will be dumped near Company Headquarters under a guard of one man.
All packs must be carefully marked with the regimental number, rank and name of the owner.

S E C R E T APPENDIX XIII Copy No...9...

2/5th S. LAN.R. LEFT RESERVE BATTALION OPERATION ORDERS NO. 21.

Ref. Map
Sheet 36 N.W.4.
1/10,000
Operation Orders
No. 20.

LEFT RESERVE BATTALION.

1. On receipt of code message "RUE DU BOIS CUTTING" there will be a general Stand-to and preparations made for a move.
In addition to the Iron Ration, one day's ration will be carried by each man. These rations will be drawn from Battalion Headquarters at CROWN PRINCE HOUSE.

ACTION BY COMPANIES IN BRIGADE RESERVE.

2. On receipt of orders to move to the SUBSIDIARY LINE Companies in Brigade Reserve will move by half platoons at 200 yards distance to the following positions in ~~XXXXXXXXX~~SUBSIDIARY LINE:-

"A" COMPANY will occupy from LEITH WALK to COWGATE AVENUE exclusive.
"B" COMPANY will occupy from COWGATE AVENUE inclusive to HAYSTACK AVENUE exclusive.
"C" COMPANY will occupy from HAYSTACK AVENUE to the point where the SUBSIDIARY LINE cuts the road at I.20.a.80.99.
"D" COMPANY will occupy from I.20.a.80.99 to PARK ROW.

RECONNAISSANCE

3. Each Company and Platoon Commander will at once reconnoitre an emergency route from Billets to its Company position in the SUBSIDIARY LINE, and also from this latter position to the FRONT LINE.

ROUTES.

4. In the event of there being no enemy shelling:-

"A" Company will proceed via, CROWN PRINCE HOUSE-SAND-BAG-CORNER-BRICKFIELDS.
"B" Company via the Emergency Route running from CROWN PRINCE HOUSE into RAILWAY ROAD.
"C" Company Via the Emergency Route running from near their present billets through RUE FLEURIE to the SUBSIDIARY LINE.
"D" Company via L'ARMEE-GUNNER FARM and the Emergency Route to the SUBSIDIARY LINE.

COMPANY HEADQUARTERS.

5. Company Headquarters in SUBSIDIARY LINE will be as follows:-

"A" Company at I.9.c.75.64.
"B" Company at I.14.b.8.5.
"C" Company at I.14.b.76.08.
"D" Company at I.20.a.74.90.

COMMUNICATION TRENCH DIGGING PARTY.

6. Upon arriving in the SUBSIDIARY LINE "D" Company will upon receipt of further orders report to Lieut. Lloyd, R.E., WINE AVENUE, I.14.b.8.6. for the purpose of digging the Communication Trench across NO MAN'S LAND.
The Company will approach the Rendezvous under cover by the SUBSIDIARY LINE by platoons at intervals of not less than 100 yards and will draw tools at the rate of one shovel per man and in addition each second man will take a pick

OPERATION ORDERS NO.21. (Sheet 2).

Lieutenant,

21st. June 1917. Adjutant 2/5th Batt: South Lancashire Regt.

Issued at.........by runner.

Copy No 1 to Commanding Officer.
" " 2 to O/C "A" Company.
" " 3 to O/C "B" Company.
" " 4 to O/C "C" Company.
" " 5 to O/C "D" Company.
" " 6 to Transport Officer.
" " 7 to Quartermaster.
" " 8 to FILE.
" " 9 to War Diary.
" " 10 to Brigade Headquarters.
" " 11 to L.T.M.B.
" " 12 to M.T.M.B.
" " 13 to M.G. Company.
" " 14 to O/C Battalion in Line.
" " 15 to Captain Brewis.
" " 16 Spare.

APPENDIX XIV

S E C R E T.

Copy No. 9....

2/5th. BN. SOUTH LANCS. REGT.

Ref.Map,
Sheet 36 N.W.4,
1/10,000

- INSTRUCTIONS. No - 1

To be attached to Operation Orders No. 20.

21st. June, 1917.

BATTALION IN THE LINE.

1. Upon moving into the Line for the next tour of duty each Company will take into the trenches two Hurricane Lamps in complete working order with wick and oil.
These lamps will be used to show the place of entry into the enemy line in case the move forward takes place at night.

COMPANY RATIONS.

2. Upon information being received from Patrols that the enemy's front line system is clear of the enemy, orders will be issued to O/C Coys. to draw from the BRIGADE RESERVE RATION DUMPS one extra day's ration.
These will be carried forward on the men and will be in addition to the unexpired portion of the day's rations and also the Iron Emergency Ration.

POINTS OF EXIT AND ENTRY.

3. The Right Company will leave our Front Line at:-
I.20.d.90.53, and at
I.21.c.90.90.
and will enter the Enemy Front Line at
I.21.d.00.70, and
I.21.c.30.03.
The CENTRE COMPANY will leave our Front Line at
I.21.a.95.76 and
I.16.c.53.71.
and will enter the enemy Line at
I.21.b.13.04., and
I.22.a.73.80.
The LEFT COMPANY will leave our Front Line at
I.16.c.70.70., and
I.16.b.18.20
and will enter the Enemy Front Line at
I.22.a.80.80., and
I.16.d.80.70.

COMPANY EMERGENCY DUMPS.

4. Emergency Dumps should be made near points of exit. They should be placed well under the parapet and camouflaged. Suitable Boards showing places of exit and entry will be obtained by O/C Coys. from Battalion Headquarters and placed in Emergency Dumps ready for use.
The Machine Gun Company will deposit their ammunition for the operation in these Front Line Emergency Dumps. This will be carried forward to the Company Headquarters Dumps in the enemy line by the platoons of each Company detailed for carrying parties.
The dumps to be formed in the enemy's lines must be near roads, tracks, or trenches.

P.T.O.

In addition to the Company Emergency Dumps there will also be advanced ~~EMMH~~ Emergency R.E. Dumps at the following points:-

RIGHT COMPANY. I.21.a.95.05.
Centre COMPANY I.15.d.3.1.
LEFT COMPANY. I.16.c.5.7.

SIGNALLERS. 5. At least one Signaller will go forward with our patrols They will take with them suitable Visual Signalling apparatus.

LIAISON. 6. O.'s C. Right and Left Companies will upon receiving information that the enemy are withdrawing, send one Lance Corporal and one Runner to the Companies of the Battalions on their Right and Left who will send a report to their respective Company Headquarters upon completion of each phase.

MAPS. 7. "A" and "B" Maps will be issued to each Platoon Commander These will be marked by him showing after each phase:-

(a) His Position.
(b) Position of Enemy.
(c) Position of troops on his flanks.

These maps will be forwarded to Battalion Headquarters after each phase.

ACTION OF L.T.M.B. 8. On receipt of warning that the enemy is withdrawing, one L.T.M. will immediately proceed to each Company Sector in Front Line and get into position for firing against hostile Machine Guns, which may attempt to impede our advance.

The position of the detachments in our Front Line will be as follows:-

RIGHT COMPANY. I.21.1.
CENTRE COMPANY. I.21.5.
LEFT COMPANY. I.16.2.
Reserve Mortar in the ORCHARD.

O/C Coys. will get into touch with these Mortars and will notify the Detachment when they desire them to proceed across NO MAN'S LAND.

The detachment will them move over and take up such positions as will enable them to fire in support of the Company in front, in the event of it being attacked while consolidating.

Afterwards detachments will be in readiness to advance with Companies with a view to the destruction of enemy strong points.

RATIONS. 9. Companies will ration their L.T.M. Detachments and C.Q.M.S. will obtain these rations from the L.T.M.B. Q.M.

CARRYING PARTIES. 10. The Platoon of each Company finding the carrying parties will send one section of 1 N.C.O. and 7 men to report to the O/C L.T.M. Detachment in his Company's Sector for the purpose of carrying ammunition.

MACHINE GUNS. 11. Para. 7 of Operation Orders No. 20 is deleted and the following instructions substituted:-

O/C No. 3 Section, 2/Lieut. GREENWOOD with two M.G.'s Nos. 12 and 13 will report to C/O 2/5th. S. Lan. R. at ORCHARD POST and will come under his orders for the operations

Two M.G.'s Nos. 14 and 15 under Section Sergeants will move as follows:-

One to about I.15.d.6.3. firing right and left.
One to about I.16.b.3.7. firing right and left.

No. 4 Section will supply two teams from No. 3 and No. 11 positions which will move as follows:-

No. 3 to about I.21.b.1.8. firing right and left
No. 11 to about I.20.d.4.2. firing left and right.

O.'s C Nos. 3 and 4 Sections will get into touch with O/C Coys in Front Line, and will arrange to send a man by

by night with the Infantry Patrols into NO MAN'S LAND so that some ~~man~~ member of each team will be familiar with the ground to be crossed.
2/Lieut.'s GREENWOOD and JONES will get into touch with the C/O 2/5th Bn. S. Lan. R. and with the O.'s C. Coys and discuss the methods they are to use, and the tactical features the M.G.'s are to be responsible for.
A Dump will be established near I.21.c.8.9. by O/C No. 3 M.G. Section for M.G., S.A.A. etc. Spare Belts for M.G.'s will also be put into Company Emergency S.A.A. Dumps together with two petrol tins of water per gun. These will be carried forward by the carrying parties when the 2nd. phase takes place.

AMENDMENT. 12. 2nd. Line in para (a) 2nd Phase in Operation Orders No. 20 will be amended as follows:-
For "Coys" read "Battalions."

VERY LIGHTS AND BOMBS. 13. Boxes of Very Lights and Bombs to be carried by the men will be placed ready in the Emergency Dumps.

DUMPS IN ENEMY LINES. 14. Upon arriving in the enemy lines all additional S.A.A. Bomb Stores etc. carried on the men as provided in para 3 of Operation Orders No. 20 will be deposited in the Company Dump in the Enemy's lines.

RIFLE GRENADES. 15. Each Rifle Bomber will carry 20 No. 20 Rifle Grenades.

R Ellery Ward
Lieutenant
Adjutant
"N" Battalion

Issued at by runner to:-

Copy No 1 to O/C
" 2 to O/C "A" Coy.
" 3 to O/C "B" Coy.
" 4 to O/C "C" Coy.
" 5 to O/C "D" Coy.
" 6 to T.O.
" 7 to Q.M.
" 8 to Office
" 9 to War Diary.
" 10 to Bde. H.Q.
" 11 to L.T.M.B.
" 12 to M.T.M.B.
" 13 to M.G. Coy.
" 14 to O/C Battn. in Bde Reserve.
" 15 to Captain Brewis.
" 16 to Spare.

APPENDIX. XV.

2/5th Battalion South Lancashire Regiment.

NOMINAL ROLL
of Officers, as on 30th June, 1917.

HEADQUARTERS.

Lieut-Colonel	Owen, W.L. M.C.	Commanding Officer.
Captain	Schultz, A.H.	Second in Command.
Captain	Wood, R.L.	Medical Officer.
Lieut.	Hayward, R.G.	Adjutant.
Lieut.	Gregory, H.	Quartersmaster.
Lieut.	Hadfield, J.L.	Bombing Officer.
Lieut.	Brazener, W.F.	Intelligence, Officer.
Lieut.	Timson, H.H.	Signalling Officer.
Lieut.	West, H.	Lewis Gun Officer.
2/Lieut.	Tanton, L.E.	Transport Officer.

"A" COMPANY.

Lieut.	Wallis, A.C.	O.C. Company.
2/Lieut.	Hargreaves, R.	Platoon Commander.
2/Lieut.	Davies, H.P.W.	Platoon Commander.
2/Lieut.	Wood, R.H.	Second in Command.
2/Lieut.	Messum, A.W.	Platoon Commander.
2/Lieut.	Stone, A.R.	Platoon Commander.

"B" COMPANY.

Lieut.	Donald, T.M.	O.C. Company.
2/Lieut.	Bullen, H.G.	Platoon Commander.
2/Lieut.	Dean, L.M.	Second in Command.
2/Lieut.	St George, A.R.	Platoon Commander.
2/Lieut.	Clarke, J.	Platoon Commander.

"C" COMPANY.

Captain	Brewis, A.	O.C. Company.
2/Lieut.	Le Mare, E.B.	Platoon Commander.
2/Lieut.	Nimmo, A.A.	Platoon Commander.
2/Lieut.	Guest, E.L.	Second in Command.
2/Lieut.	Hope, R.V.	Platoon Commander.
2/Lieut.	Adams, B.C.	Platoon Commander.
2/Lieut.	Woollett, J.S.	Platoon Commander.

"D" COMPANY.

Lieut.	Stephenson, C.W.	O.C. Company.
Lieut.	Crowe, J.A.	Second in Command.
Lieut.	Frodsham F.J.	Platoon Commander.
2/Lieut.	Dickinson, W.	Platoon Commander.
2/Lieut.	Holland, W.H.E.	Platoon Commander.
2/Lieut.	Handley, W.C.	Platoon Commander.

DETACHED.

Captain	Gould, M.L.B.	Divisional Salvage Coy.
2/Lieut.	Hall, W.S.	172nd Infantry Bde Pioneer Coy.
2/Lieut.	Paul, R.B.	172nd Infantry Bde Instructor.

-------------oOo-------------

APPENDIX XVI

2/5th Battalion South Lancashire Regiment.

STATEMENT
SHOWING FLUCTUATIONS OF STRENGTH.

37 Officers.   851 Other Ranks.

Trench Strength 30th June, 1917 634 Other Ranks.

217 Other Ranks not on Trench Strength made up as under:-

Transport and Grooms	45
Q.M.Stores.	29
R.A.M.C. (Water duties)	5
Courses of instruction.	46
Hospital.	5
O.R.Sergeant at Base.	1
Rest Camp (1st Army).	3

Detached :-

Employed at Bde and Div.	15
Town Guard, ARMENTIERES.	9
A.P.M.	5
L.T.M.B.	9
Signallers with M.G.Coy.	2
Brigade Pioneer Coy.	33
Total.	217.

ORIGINAL

35807. W16879/M1879 500,000 3/17 R.T. (1074) Forms W3091/3

Army Form W.3091.

CONFIDENTIAL

Cover for Documents.

Vol 6

172/57

Nature of Enclosures.

WAR DIARY

OF

2/5th. S. Lan. R.

From 1/7/17 to 31/7/17

Notes, or Letters written.

With APPENDICES

XVII to

Instructions regarding War Diaries and Intelligence Summaries are contained in F. S. Regs., Part II. and the Staff Manual respectively. Title Pages will be prepared in manuscript.

WAR DIARY

~~or~~

~~INTELLIGENCE SUMMARY~~

(Erase heading not required.)

Army Form C. 2118

Place	Date 1917 July	Hour	Summary of Events and Information	Remarks and references to Appendices
TRENCHES BOIS GRENIER Sectr	1st.	2.10 am.	Enemy raided Brigade on our left. Heavy barrage put on which lasted about half an hour. Our subsector not affected. Division cut down scheme for "OWEN'S 'OP".	
	2nd		Enemy aeroplanes flying low over our lines. C.T.'s registered. Special precautions taken by front line coys at night. B Coy training for "OWENS 'OP". Trenches taped out in rear of Subsidiary Line behind existing screens. Daylight patrolling carried out each day. Grass in NML very long and gave good cover.	RCCO
	3rd.	4pm.	Three NCO's of C Coy went out on daylight patrol & did not return. No sign of any fighting or bombing heard.	
	4th.		Preparations for OWEN'S 'OP complete. C.O. summoned to Brigade during afternoon.	OWEN'S 'OP APPENDIX XVII
		4pm.	Message received postponing raid. C.O. brought back information that one of our aeroplanes had taken a photo on July 2nd near LOMME (about 3 miles behind BOCHE lines) shewing clearly a section of our trenches dug on a training ground. Section shewn by photo lies between COWGATE AVENUE and WINE AVENUE both inclusive, going as far back as 2nd Support line	RCCO

1875 Wt. W593/826 1,000,000 4/15 J.B.C. & A. A.D.S.S./Forms/C. 2118.

Instructions regarding War Diaries and Intelligence Summaries are contained in F. S. Regs., Part II. and the Staff Manual respectively. Title Pages will be prepared in manuscript.

WAR DIARY

~~or~~

~~INTELLIGENCE SUMMARY~~

(Erase heading not required.)

Army Form C. 2118

Place	Date	Hour	Summary of Events and Information	Remarks and references to Appendices
TRENCHES BOIS GRENIER Sector	4th		This was found out by Corps Intelligence Dept. A photograph taken ten days previously of same area did not shew these trenches. The following precautions taken at night:– (i) Front line cleared from PEAR TREE FARM to RUE DU BOIS Salient inclusive (ii) Strong patrol of B Coy lay up in ditch on right of CHARDS FARM salient with two Lewis Guns. (iii) All artillery to open on enemy Front and Support lines 5 minutes after enemy barrage opens. (iv) All our M.G's and T.M.'S laid on threatened area in our own trenches to catch BOCHE if he gets in. Night passed quietly. BOCHE patrol seen in NML by B Coys patrol. They were moving towards CORDATE. Very few very lights were fired from BOCHE trenches during the night and his conduct rather pointed to the fact that enemy was waiting for our raid.	RCH
	5th		Quiet day. Some registration specially "minnies". Line held by day by L.Gs. Posts strengthened by addition of bombers. All usual periscopes left up. Same precautions taken at night as on 4th inst.	RCH
	6th		Quiet day. Heavy barrage put on to us at night. BOCHE raiding party entered RUE DU BOIS salient during barrage.	See APPENDIX XVIII

1875 Wt. W593/826 1,000,000 4/15 J.B.C. & A. A.D.S.S./Forms/C. 2118.

Instructions regarding War Diaries and Intelligence Summaries are contained in F. S. Regs., Part II. and the Staff Manual respectively. Title Pages will be prepared in manuscript.

WAR DIARY

~~or~~

~~INTELLIGENCE SUMMARY~~

(Erase heading not required.)

Army Form C. 2118

Place	Date	Hour	Summary of Events and Information	Remarks and references to Appendices
TRENCHES BOIS GRENIER Sector	7th		Quiet day except for MINNIES. Same precautions taken by day as previously. Whole of Front and Support lines cleared at night. Raid on area between CONFATE and WINE Stile anticipated. Quiet night	R.E.O.
	8th		"OWEN'S 'OP'" definitely cancelled. Quiet day.	
	9th	1.35 am	Dummy raid Zero Hour 1.35 am. Took place in accordance with orders. No identification. Minnies active during day. Specially with "air bursts" Relieved at night by 2/4th. S. Lan. R. Relief satisfactory - complete 10.50pm Casualties during tour 6 OR. Killed. 3 OR. Missing. 2 OR. died of wounds. 34 O.R. wounded	APPENDIX XIX APPENDIX XX
RUE MARLE	10th to 13th		Battalion in billets. Generally quiet except for shelling of battery positions in vicinity of billets.	
	14th		Orders received that Battalion is to take over FLAMENGRIE Subsector from 2/9th. K. L. R. on night 17th/18th July. Reason for this that we may have to do a show from FLAMENGRIE Subsector. 2/10th K. L. R. to take our place in RUE DU BOIS Subsector.	R.E.O.
	15th		B Coy's billets shelled. 2 O.R. wounded. 1 civilian killed & 2 wounded. B Coy had to take over new billets. Owing to shelling billets getting scarce in RUE MARLE	

1875 Wt. W593/826 1,000,000 4/15 J.B.C. & A. A.D.S.S./Forms/C. 2118.

Army Form C. 2118

Instructions regarding War Diaries and Intelligence Summaries are contained in F. S. Regs., Part II. and the Staff Manual respectively. Title Pages will be prepared in manuscript.

WAR DIARY

~~or~~

~~INTELLIGENCE SUMMARY~~

(Erase heading not required.)

Place	Date	Hour	Summary of Events and Information	Remarks and references to Appendices
RUE MARLE	16th & 17th.		Generally quiet. Relieved 2/9th R. L. R. in FLAMENGRIE Subsector on night of 17th. Relief satisfactory but late owing to our company in Subsidiary line RUE DU BOIS Subsector being relieved late by 2/10th R. L. R. New method of holding line adopted viz:- Lewis Gun Posts of not more than 15 men in Front line with a Bombing Post in support of each. Remainder of Front line companies being in Support and Subsidiary lines All companies went into the trenches organized into three platoons instead of four. This necessary to keep up section organization of four complete sections of not less than 1 N.C.O. and 6 men.	HCH
TRENCHES BOIS-GRENIER Sector	18th to 20th.		Generally quiet. Enemy planes active flying low over our lines but apparently no registration. On 20th bombs were dropped on our lines but no damage done.	
	21st & 22nd	10.45 pm.	2/Lieut DICKINSON and 10 men left our lines and entered enemy trenches at 12.45 a.m. Observed enemy patrol of 6 men returning to their own lines & withdrew to get into favourable position but saw no further sign of enemy.	HCH
	23rd		Rough orders for "OWENLY WAY" started	

1875 Wt. W593/826 1,000,000 4/15 J.B.C. & A. A.D.S.S./Forms/C. 2118.

Instructions regarding War Diaries and Intelligence Summaries are contained in F. S. Regs., Part II. and the Staff Manual respectively. Title Pages will be prepared in manuscript.

WAR DIARY

~~or~~

~~INTELLIGENCE SUMMARY~~

(Erase heading not required.)

Army Form C. 2118

Place	Date	Hour	Summary of Events and Information	Remarks and references to Appendices
TRENCHES	24th		2/Lieut DICKINSON accidentally wounded by bayonet when returning from patrol.	
BOIS GRENIER Sector	25th		Quiet day. Relieved by 2/9th R.L.R. at night. Relief complete by 11.30pm. Battalion went into billets at LA ROLANDERIE and ERQUINGHEM. Battn. H.Q. at ARTILLERY FARM, about 1½ miles nearer the line than ERQUINGHEM. We found FLAMENGRIE Subsector generally quieter than RUE DU BOIS. Casualties during tour 1 Officer and 7 O.R. wounded.	RCH
	26th to 29th		Battalion in Billets. Usual working parties found and training carried out. ARMENTIERES heavily shelled with gas shells night 28th/29th. Gas drifted towards ERQUINGHEM. Alarm lasted about 3½ hours. Midnight to 3.30am.	
	30th	9pm	Orders received that owing to casualties suffered by 171st Brigade it may be necessary for 3 companies of this Battalion and one company of Left Reserve Battalion to go to ARMENTIERES to reinforce that sector. Companies in billets to stand-by. No action night 30th/31st.	
	31st		241394 L/Cpl BLACKHURST. S. and 241945 Rfn HAYES J. awarded Military Medal, date of award 20/7/17.	See APPENDIX XXI
			Offensive in north commenced. Barrage heard all night 30th/31st. News good. Generally quiet in this sector – rather less shelling of back areas. Strength of Battalion 31/7/17 35 Officers 808 Other Ranks.	APPENDICES XXII + XXIII

RCHaywood Lieut
Adjt 2/5th. S. Lan. R.

1875 Wt. W593/826 1,000,000 4/15 J.B.C. & A. A.D.S.S./Forms/C. 2118.

APPENDIX XVII

SECRET. Copy No. 8.

"OWEN's OP."

2/5th. BN. S. LAN. R., OPERATION ORDER NO. 23.

-------*------

Map Ref.
Sheet 36 N.W.4
BOIS GRENIER E.A.7.A
1/10,000

1. INTENTION. To raid enemy Front Line System known as INCLEMENT TRENCH and INCLEMENT SWITCH between I.21.b.78.20 and I.22.a.05.32,
the object being to:-
(a) Destroy enemy personnel.
(b) Bring back prisoners for identification.
(c) Destroy enemy's defences, dug-outs, M.G. Emplacements.
(d) Decrease the morale of the enemy.

2. RAIDING PARTY. "B" COMPANY. Commanded by Lieut. T.M. DONALD will carry out the raid assisted by Lieut. J.L. HADFIELD, the Battalion Bombing Officer.

3. SCHEME. On "X" night, 4 Bangalore Torpedoes will be placed under enemy's wire at I.21.b.94.35 by HADFIELD'S PARTY. They will be in position at ZERO - 30, and will be fired at ZERO + 6. Immediately after the explosion the raiding parties will enter through gap made (24 yards gap) and act as detailed in APPENDIX I. Under cover of Artillery, and M.G. fire withdrawal will commence at ZERO + 30.

4. DIVERSIONS. The following diversions to attract enemy fire will be made:-

(a) RIGHT FLANK. "D" COMPANY.
No. 16 Platoon commanded by 2/Lieut. W. DICKINSON under cover of M.G., L.T.M.B. and Projector fire on enemy Support Line between I.21.c.19.32 and I.21.d.15.52 will enter enemy Front Line at I.21.c.88.58, and will endeavour to bring out enemy sentry post.
Trench junctions at I.21.c.82.46 and I.21.c.99.68 will be engaged by this platoon with Rifle Grenades and L.G. fire from N.M.L.
A Bangalore Torpedo will be placed in enemy's wire at I.21.c.85.60 and will be fired at ZERO + 6. L.G.'s in N.M.L. will engage M.G.'s at point blank range.

(b) CENTRE. "C" COMPANY.
1 Section of "C" Company will enter enemy's front line at I.22.a.42.66 at ZERO + 6, and will endeavour to bring out enemy sentry post. A Bangalore Torpedo will be placed in enemy wire opposite this point and will be fired at ZERO + 6. 2 L.G.'s each supported by half a section of rifle grenades, will be placed in N.M.L. at I.22.d.40.95 and I.22.a.22.80, and will deal with enemy M.G.'s at point blank range.

(Continued.)

4. DIVERSIONS (Contd)

(c) LEFT FLANK. "A" COMPANY.

"A" COMPANY will enter enemy's trenches at I.16.d.28.58 and will endeavour to bring back enemy sentry post.

2 L.G.'s each supported by half a section rifle bombers will be placed in N.M.L. at I.16.b.50.31 and I.16.d.26.95 to cover raiding party, and to deal with enemy M.G.'s at point blank range.

12 Dummy Figures will be used from Zero + 6 to ZERO + 30, which will be worked by men in shell-holes in N.M.L. 100 yards from enemy front line.

A Bangalore Torpedo will be placed in wire opposite point of entry and will be fired at ZERO 6.

An Artillery Box Barrage to be combined with an Artillery Smoke Screen will be placed on enemy trenches from ZERO + 6 to ZERO + 81 opposite CHARDS FARM.
Projectors will fire on Enemy Front Line System in WEZ MACQUART.

5. PROJECTORS.

Projectors firing oil drums will be used to help to create the diversion on both left and right flanks. 210 will be fired on WEZ MACQUART and 40 on INCLUDE SUPPORT.

6. ACTION OF M.G.'s.

Machine Guns will enfilade INCLEMENT SUPPORT and junction of latter with SWITCH LINE, also Communication Trench running between I.22.a.15.44 and I.22.a.30.32.
Two M.G.'s will be in N.M.L. at I.21.b.50.75 and I.21.b.93.85 for protection of main raiding parties.
One Machine Gunner will accompany GREENALL'S Party and one with CLARKE'S PARTY to deal with hostile M.G.'s.

7. L.T.M.B.

Eight Mortars will take part in the raid; three to form a barrage as a diversion on INCLUDE SUPPORT, three on INCLEMENT SWITCH close to junction with Support Line, and two on M.G. Emplacement at I.21.b.55.22.

8. M.T.M.B.

Three guns will fire on INCIDENT SUPPORT.

9. RECONNAISSANCE.

Reconnaissance will be principally carried out by day. Reconnoitring patrols of 2 to 4 O.R. will lay up close to enemy wire and do their reconnaissance in daylight.
O/C Raid, each Platoon Commander concerned and the Bombing Officer will carry out the reconnaissance.

10. LEWIS GUN & RIFLE GRENADE PARTIES.

The object of these parties in N.M.L. is to deal with enemy M.G. fire, and so to assist the main raiding party by engaging enemy M.G.'s and silencing them.
The Rifle Grenade Parties in conjunction with the former will firstly, deal with enemy M.G.'s and secondly, will support and protect the Lewis Gunners.
These parties will play a very important part in the raid, and enemy M.G.'s must be engaged with the greatest persistency.

11. COMMUNICATION.

Communication will be maintained to Advanced Coy., H.Q., by Runner and Telephone. The Signalling Officer will arrange for Communications with

(Continued.)

11 - Continued. Artillery, M.G. Coy., and L.T.M.B. Runners and telephones will be in position at ZERO - 30. A wire will be run out with O/C Assault.

12. O/C RAID HEADQUARTERS. O/C Raid Headquarters will be at I.15.d.52.20. Position Call:- H.H.7.

13. ASSEMBLY. Parties will keep together and in their order. Raiding Parties will assemble in the Subsidiary Line (in their order of going out as shown in APPENDIX I.) between WINE AVENUE and HAYSTACK AVENUE at a time to be notified later.
They will proceed up WINE AVENUE at suitable intervals and will go out into N.M.L. immediately, and lie down there awaiting orders to advance from O/C Raid.

14. WITHDRAWAL. Withdrawal will commence at ZERO + 30. On regaining our Front Line the Raiders will return to their "bivvies" in the Subsidiary Line handing in their tallies to the Police Control Posts at the junctions of C.T.'s with Subsidiary Line. These Tallies will be forwarded to B.H.Q.

15. COLLECTING STATION. As soon as kit has been collected all parties will proceed to cross-roads at H.6.d.65.65 (RUE MARLE) where they will be taken by Motor Lorries to ERQUINGHEM.

16. TALLY OFFICER. 2nd. Lieut. A.R. ST.GEORGE will check all raiders at point mentioned in Para. 15.

17. EQUIPMENT. See APPENDIX III.

18. PRISONERS. Prisoners will be sent back as soon as captured and will not be kept until the withdrawal commences. On arriving in our Front Line they will be sent down to Battalion Headquarters when they will be despatched immediately to Brigade Headquarters.

19. BOOTY. All booty will be handed in at Battalion Headquarters and will be passed on to Brigade Headquarters.

20. PROTECTION. The two M.G.'s referred to in Para. (6) will protect the advance and withdrawal of the raiding parties.

21. SIGNALS. In the event of it being found necessary to postpone operations blue rockets will be sent up by O/C Raid and will be repeated at Battalion Headquarters at I.14.d.5.7. This will be confirmed by 'phone.
At ZERO + 30 Green Very Lights will be sent up from each post in Front Line which will be the signal for withdrawal.

22. CODE. The following Code Words will be used throughout the operations:-

OPERATIONS POSTPONED	SPARROW.
CEASE FIRE	BLACKBIRD
PARTY ENTERING FIRST LINE	CHAFFINCH
PARTY ENTERING SECOND LINE	BULLFINCH
ALL DOING WELL	ROBIN
WEAK RESISTANCE	THRUSH
MUCH RESISTANCE	HAWK
RESERVES REQUIRED	PARTRIDGE
PRISONERS RETURNING	OWL
CASUALTIES	PIGEON

(Continued.)

22 - Contd.	PARTY RETURNING ALL IN	DONE PHEASANT

23. SUPPORT. The Bangalore Carrying Party consisting of 24 men will remain in Front Line to act as Support.

24. SYNCHRONIZATION OF WATCHES. On the evening preceding "X" night the Signalling Officer will take 3 watches to Brigade Headquarters at 6 p.m.
He will synchronize watches at Battalion Headquarters at 9 p.m. when all with watches taking part in the Raid will attend.

Lieut.Col.,
Commanding,
2/5th. S. Lan. R.

Issued 7/7/17.

No. 1 Copy to O/C "B" Coy.
2 " to O/C 172nd. M.G.Coy.
3 " to O/C 172nd. L.T.M.B.
4 " to 2nd.Lt. A.R.ST.GEORGE.
5 " to 2nd.Lt. H.G. BULLEN.
6 " to Battn. Bombing Officer.
7 " to 2nd.Lt. L.M. DEAN.
8 " to H.Q., 57th. Division.
9 " Spare.
10 " to C/O.
11 " to 2nd.Lt. J. CLARKE.
12 " to H.Q., Centre Group, R.A.
13 " to H.Q., 172nd. Inf. Bde.
14 " to O/C "N" Coy., R.E.
15 " to H.Q., Div. R.A.
16 " WAR DIARY.

ACTION OF PARTIES.

APPENDIX I.

Parties in order of attack	Party Leader.	Party	Action
1.	LT. HADFIELD.	BANGALORE TORPEDO PARTY.	Leaves our trenches at about 10.15 p.m. on "X" night. Four Torpedoes will be placed under the enemy wire at approximately I.21.b 94 35. Torpedoes will be in position at ZERO - 30 when party will withdraw 30 yards. At ZERO + 6 the torpedoes will be fired simultaneously The party will immediately rush in and take up position on the enemy parapet, to cover advance of the raiding party. When raiders are in the enemy trenches this party will damage the wire as much as possible and make additional gaps to facilitate the withdrawal of the raiding party. These gaps will be clearly marked with chalk. Prisoners will be taken back by this party.
2.	PRICE.	PARAPET PARTY RIGHT	Party will be on the enemy front line parapet and will move along two or three yards in advance of the Front Line bombing parties. Their duties are to protect the bombing parties by bombing and Lewis Gun fire, to beat off a counter attack from the Boche Support Line and to engage Machine Guns at point blank range and silence them. These parties will remain on the parapet to protect the flanks of the raiding party and to cover their withdrawal.
[illegible]	DUTTON.	FRONT LINE BOMBING PARTY RIGHT	Follows HOMES' PARTY, and jumping into E.F.L. will move along trench to the right and block it at least 30 yards from the junction of the SWITCH with Front Line. Two men will be posted at the block, and remainder of the party will assist ROWLEY'S PARTY in mopping up front line.
3.	HOLMES.	PARAPET LEFT	Works as PRICE'S PARTY but left.
	HATTON.	FRONT LINE BOMBING LEFT.	Follows Left Parapet Party, and jumping into E.F.L. will move along trench a distance of 80 yards, to the left. They will block the trench at this point leaving two men at the block. Remainder of party will assist CLARKE'S PARTY in mopping up the Front Line.
4.	2/Lt. DEAN.	PARAPET PARTY CENTRE.	2/Lieut. DEAN, O/C Assault will be with this party which will be stationary on the centre of the enemy parapet. Their duties are similar to those of Nos. 2 and 4 parties. O/C Assault will be in telephonic communication with O/C Raid and O/C E.T.M.B. This party will be the last to withdraw and will cover the withdrawal of the Raiders with Lewis Gun and Rifle fire.

(Continued)

Parties in order of attack.	Party Leader	Party.	Action.
4 (Contd)	OAKES.	CENTRE C.T. BOMBING PARTY.	This party jumps into Front Line and works along to the Centre C.T. ON reaching this two men of the party will work on the parapet of the C.T. (one at each side) The remainder will work down the C.T. to the switch and block it at its junction with the S. Side of the Switch. When GREENALLS PARTY have reported right end of Switch clear, OAKES PARTY will withdraw and block C.T. at its junction with N. Side of Switch.
5.	GREENALL.	SWITCH BOMB- -ING PARTY.	Will follow DUTTON S PARTY along F.L. and work down the switch mopping up and demolishing dug-outs etc. as they move along. If casualties occur and party is weakened, reinforcements will be obtained from OAKES' PARTY. Party will withdraw up left C.T. covered by BRADY"S PARTY, leave the front line as soon as it is reached and return to our trenches.
	BRADY.	LEFT C.T. BOMBING PARTY.	Works along front line to the left. Bombs down left C.T. to the SWITCH. Will form a block of 30 yards left of the end of the C.T. When GREENALL S PARTY reaches C.T. BRADY S PARTY will form a rear guard to it and withdraw up C.T. to front line.
6.	QUINN.	SAP BOMBING PARTY	On B.T. s exploding, QUINN S PARTY will rush the Sap and clean it up with bombs and if necessary L.G. fire. They will work up to the Front Line and reinforce ROWLEY S PARTY, and assist in mopping it up. The Lewis Gun will be used for additional protection of the flanks and for dealing with possible counter-attack from N.M.L. It will also engage enemy M.G.
	ROWLEY.	OCCUPATION PARTY. FRONT LINE, RIGHT	Duties same as CLARKE S PARTY.
	2/Lt. CLARKE.	OCCUPATION PARTY. FRONT LINE, LEFT.	This party mops up front line and supervision trench (if any). Will demolish dug-outs, emplacements, etc Prisoners sent up from SWITCH LINE will be passed back to HADFIELD S PARTY.
	BICKERSTAFFE	IDENTIFIC- -ATION PARTY.	Has a roving Commission. Its principal duty is to search dug-outs for papers map, and all possible identifications.

NOTE. As soon as prisoners are taken they will be passed back to HADFIELD S PARTY and sent direct to our Front Line.

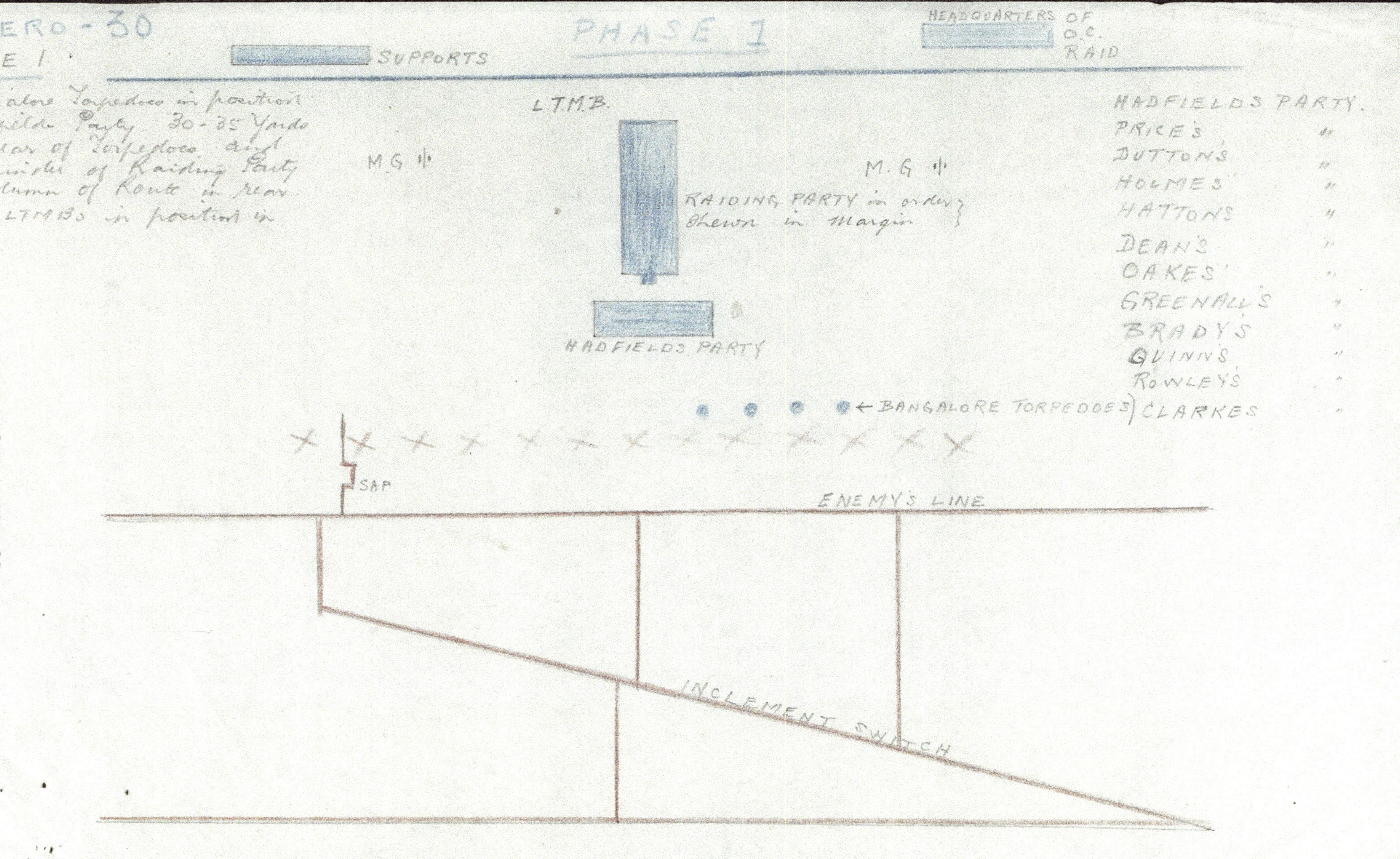
ZERO-30
PHASE I.
SUPPORTS
PHASE I
HEADQUARTERS OF O.C. RAID
Bangalore Torpedoes in position Hadfields Party 30-35 Yards in rear of Torpedoes and remainder of Raiding Party in column of Route in rear. MGs: LTMBs in position in NML
L.T.M.B.
M.G.
M.G.
RAIDING PARTY in order shewn in Margin
HADFIELDS PARTY
HADFIELDS PARTY.
PRICE'S "
DUTTON'S "
HOLMES' "
HATTONS "
DEAN'S "
OAKES' "
GREENALL'S "
BRADY'S "
QUINNS "
ROWLEYS "
CLARKES "
← BANGALORE TORPEDOES
SAP
ENEMY'S LINE
INCLEMENT SWITCH
APPENDIX II.

ZERO + 6 - ZERO + 7

PHASE 2.

PHASE 2

SUPPORTS

O.C. RAID H.Q

Immediately after explosion of Bangalore Torpedoes, Parties entering enemy trenches HADFIELD'S PARTY rush on to parapet to deal with any local resistance and remainder of raiding party follow

M.G. 1/1

LTMB

1/1 M.G

QUINNS PARTY

CLARKE'S PARTY
ROWLEY'S "
QUINNS "
BRADYS "
GREENALL'S "
OAKES' "
DEANS "
HATTONS "
HOLMES' "
DUTTON'S "
PRICES "
HADFIELD'S PARTY

ENEMY FRONT LINE

INCLEMENT SWITCH

ZERO + 7
ZERO + 30
PHASE 3 Parties having entered trenches established blocks, mopped up etc

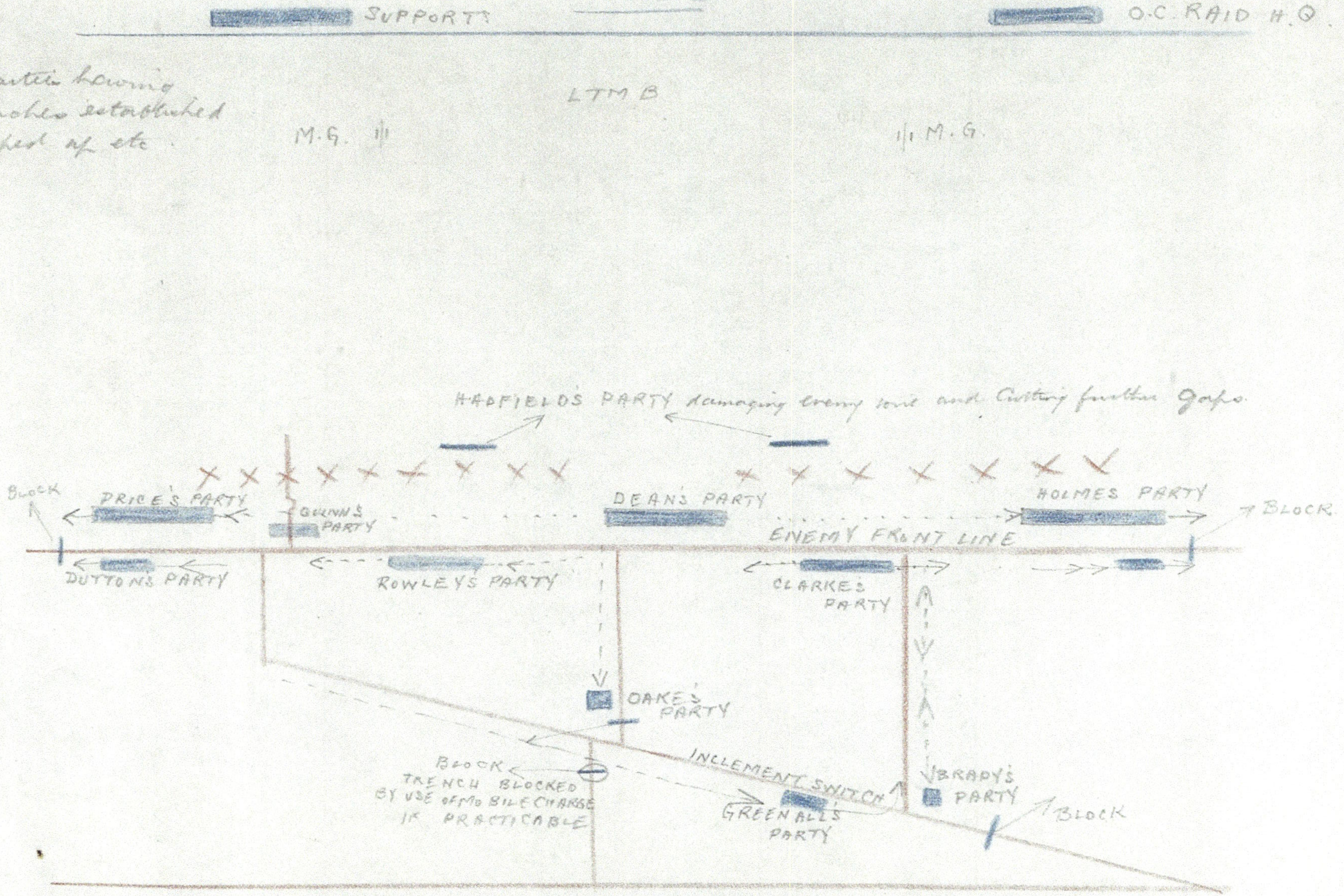

PHASE 3

ZERO + 35

PHASE 4

SUPPORTS.

O.C. RAID H.Q.

PHASE 4 Withdrawal across N.M.L. PARAPET PARTIES last to leave enemy trenches.

1/1 M.G.

L.T.M.B.

1/1 M.G

PRICES PARTY

DEAN'S PARTY

HOLME'S PARTY

E.F.L.

xx additional gaps made by HADFIELDS PARTY to facilitate withdrawal

INCLEMENT SWITCH

APPENDIX III.

PARTY NOMENCLATURE	Officers	N.C.O.'s	Men	Rifles & Bayonets	S.A.A.	Armour Pierc-ing S.A.A.	Revolvers	do Ammunition	Hand weapon	Bombs	Bangalore Torpedoes	Mobile Charges	Stokes Shells	Wire Cutters	Rope	P. Bombs.	Lewis Guns	Magazines filled.	Very Pistols	P. Cartridges	Flash Lamps.	Compass Luminous	Sandbags Empty	Distingu-ishg Marks	Mats.	Tape	Chalk	P.H. Helmets	Blocking Material	Trench Stretchers	Whistles.	REMARKS.
1. BANGALORE TORPEDO PARTY.	1	5	9	-	-	-	6	72	-	30	4	-	-	14	1	-	-	-	-	-	-	2	-	15	3	-	4	15	-	-	1	
2. PARAPET PARTY FRONT LINE LEFT	-	1	3	3	100	50	1	12	3	30	-	-	-	4	-	-	1	12	1	12	-	-	-	4	2	-	-	4	-	-	1	
3. PARAPET PARTY FRONT LINE CENTRE	1	3	5	9	450	-	2	24	7	30	-	-	-	4	1	-	1	12	1	12	1	2	-	9	-	1	-	9	-	-	1	
4. PARAPET PARTY FRONT LINE RIGHT	-	1	3	3	100	50	1	12	3	30	-	-	-	4	-	-	1	12	1	12	-	-	-	4	2	-	-	4	-	-	1	
5. FRONT LINE BOMB -ING PARTY LEFT	-	1	6	7	350	-	-	-	7	70	-	2	2	3	1	14	-	-	-	-	1	-	-	7	-	-	-	7	1	2	1	1 Coil French Concertina.
6. Front LINE BOMB -ING PARTY R.	-	1	6	7	350	-	-	-	7	70	-	2	2	3	1	14	-	-	-	-	1	-	-	7	-	-	-	7	1	2	1	do.
7. CENTRE C.T. BOMBING PARTY.	-	1	6	7	350	-	-	-	7	70	-	2	2	3	1	14	-	-	-	-	1	-	-	7	-	-	-	7	1	-	1	do.
8. FRONT LINE OCC -UPATION PARTY LEFT.	1	2	7	10	500	-	2	24	9	50	-	2	2	6	1	6	-	-	-	-	2	1	2	10	-	-	-	10	-	2	1	
9. FRONT LINE OCCUPATION PARTY RIGHT.	-	4	6	10	500	-	1	12	10	50	-	2	2	6	1	6	-	-	-	-	2	1	2	10	-	-	-	10	-	2	1	
10. LEFT C.T. BOMB -ING PARTY.	-	1	6	7	350	-	-	-	7	70	-	2	2	3	1	6	-	-	-	-	1	-	2	7	-	-	-	7	1	-	1	1 Coil French Concertina
11. SAP. BOMBING PARTY.	-	1	6	6	300	-	1	12	7	30	-	-	-	4	1	-	1	12	-	-	1	-	2	7	-	-	-	7	-	-	1	
12. SWITCH BOMBING PARTY.	-	2	7	9	450	-	-	-	9	70	-	2	2	-	1	14	-	-	1	12	2	-	4	9	-	-	-	9	-	-	1	
13. O/C RAID PARTY.	1	2	3	4	200	-	2	24	4	-	-	-	-	-	-	-	-	-	-	-	-	-	-	-	-	-	-	-	-	-	-	
14. IDENTIFICATION PARTY.	-	2	-	2	100	-	1	12	2	10	-	2	-	-	1	2	-	-	-	-	-	2	-	2	2	-	-	2	-	-	1	

APPENDIX IV.

2/5th. STH.LANDS.REGT.

"B" Company,

DETAILS OF PARTIES.

--o--

O/C RAID PARTY.

Lieutenant DONALD	T.M.	O/C Raid.
240557, C.S.M. DEAN	H.	
241993, Cpl. DARBYSHIRE	P.	
240743, Rfn. SMITH	E.	Runner
241508, " LYONS	F.	"
242008, " WIDDOWS	A.	"

Party No. 1.

BANGALORE TORPEDO PARTY.

Lieutenant HADFIELD	J.L.	Leader.
241677, Sgt. ROBINSON	F.	Deputy Leader.
241347, Cpl. LANE	P.	
241977, L/C. BOWDEN	P.J.	
241986, " HESKETH	F.	
242239, Rfn. JAMESON	T.	
241497, " FINNEY	J.	
240686, " FINNEY	W.	
241363, " SHAW	J.	
242651, " WILKINSON	W.E.	
241974, " MACKIN	N.	
241706, " BARRETT	E.	
241465, " WOODALL	A.	
242670, " EDWARDS	G.	
241044, L/C. HUGHES T.	T.	

Party No. 2.

PARAPET PARTY LEFT.

240696, Cpl. HOLMES	M.	Leader.
241001, Rfn. O'BRIEN	P.	Deputy Leader.
241314, " BLEVIN	J.	
240872, " URQUHART	C.	Sniper.

Party No. 3,

PARAPET PARTY CENTRE.

2nd. Lieut. DEAN	L.M.	O/C Assault.
241268, Sgt. BALL	T.H.	Leader.
241211, L/C. HENDERSON	J.	Deputy Leader.
241479, Rfn. SMITH	P.	
241120, " RIGBY	A.	
242236, " BAGLEY	W.	Sniper.
241378, " BRIODY	J.	Telephnoists.
241330, " LANGTHORNE	G.	Telephnoists.
240149, L/C. HORNBY	P.	Telephnoists.

(Continued.)

242625, Rfn. DUDDELL S. Runner.
242619, " ROBERTS T.C. do.

Party No. 9.

FRONT LINE OCCUPATION PARTY RIGHT.

241221, Sgt. ROWLEY A. Leader.
241573, Cpl. SMITH A.E. Deputy Leader.
241105, L/C. PICKAVANCE T.
242666, Rfn. LODER W.
242002, " TOMLINSON W.
242225, " RIGBY R.
242218, " RIGBY E.
241006, " SHARKEY T.
242010, " ECCLES R.
67532, Machine Gunner Cpl. TRICKETT R.S.

Party No. 10.

LEFT COMMUNICATION TRENCH BOMBING PARTY.

242216, Cpl. BRADY J. Leader.
241390, Rfn. PENNINGTON C. Deputy Leader.
241978, " RICHARDS A.
241383, " TAYLOR S.O.
240605, " THOMPSON P.
242220, " BAIRD J.
240255, " OWEN J.

Party No. 11.

BOMBING PARTY SAP.

241101, L/C. QUINN J. Leader.
240653, Rfn. O'CONNOR P. Deputy Leader.
242641, " EDWARDS E.T.
241454, " SYMONDS D.
242639, " JONES J.W.
242664, " HAMILTON A.J.
242646, " ELLIS H.M.

Party No. 12.

BOMBING PARTY SWITCH LINE.

241464, L/S. GREENALL Leader.
241994, L/C. DAVIES L.
241997, Rfn. DIXON J.J.
241335, " COLLINS J.
242003, " JACKSON A.
242657, " WARRINGTON T.
241340, " FENNEY W.
242660, " JONES H.
67568, M. Gunner BRAID J.

(Continued.)

Party No. 4.

PARAPET PARTY RIGHT.

241572,	L/C.	PRICE	W.	Leader.
241500,	Rfn.	DONOGHUE	J.	Deputy Leader.
241987,	"	BACON	A.	
241374,	"	TILLEY	F.	Sniper.

Party No. 5

BOMBING PARTY FRONT LINE LEFT.

241561,	L/C.	HATTON	J.	Leader.
241322,	Rfn.	PRICE	B.	Deputy Leader.
241710,	"	TAYLOR	T.	
242227,	"	BESWICK	E.	
241594,	"	HODGSON	A.	
242233,	"	ALMOND	A.	
241715,	"	HUGHES	J.	

Party No. 6.

BOMBING PARTY FRONT LINE RIGHT.

242009,	L/C.	DUTTON	H.M.	Leader.
242515,	Rfn.	WORTHINGTON	T.	Deputy Leader.
242228,	"	MOODY	R.	
241456,	"	CROMPTON	J.	
241995,	"	STEELE	W.	
242649,	"	JONES	H.	
240731,	"	TANNER	H.	

Party No. 7.

RIGHT COMMUNICATION TRENCH BOMBING PARTY.

241102,	Cpl.	OAKES	D.	Leader.
241310,	Rfn.	TRAVERSE	J.	Deputy Leader.
241334,	"	BANKS	J.	
241501,	"	BILLINGE	G.	
241476,	"	JENNIONS	C.	
242217,	"	FAIRCLOUGH	J.	
242000,	"	DEAN	E.	

Party No. 8.

FRONT LINE OCCUPATION PARTY LEFT.

2nd. Lieutenant		J. CLARKE.		Deputy O/C Assault.
240690,	Sgt.	OWEN	A.E.	Leader
241970,	L/C.	COOK	A.	Deputy Leader
242237,	Rfn.	TUNSTALL	G.	
241505,	"	MARKEY	F.	
242238,	"	OWENS	C.	
241598,	"	BREEM	M.	
242672,	"	WILLIAMS	J.	
241327,	"	BAXTER	J.	
241005,	"	CONQUEROR	O.	

(continued.)

IDENTIFICATION PARTY.

240508, L/Sgt. BICKERSTAFFE A. Leader.
240882, Cpl. McCORMACK B.

CARRYING PARTY BANGALORE TORPEDOES AND SUPPORTS.

241261, L/C. WALKER F.
241998, Rfn. BISHOP E.W.
242828. " BEDDOES G.H.
242870, " EDWARDS G.
240794, " BRISCOE W.
242234, " BAGNALL W.
241446, " MARSH J.
241266, " HUNT T.
242656, " WEBB H.
242007, " CLEWORTH P.
240727, " MAHER J.
242634, " ROBERTS D.
242224, " CULLEY J.
241656, " DISLEY T.
242667, " JONES W.T.
242621, " WATKINS A.G.
242663, " BROPHY G.
241493, " EDEN D.
241989, " TAYLOR F.H.
241556, " CRITCHLEY M.
242669, " OWEN D.L.
242005, L/C. RIMMER T.
241494, Rfn. LAMB D.
240185. " HEWITT R.

APPENDIX V.

MEDICAL ARRANGEMENTS.

Advanced R.A.P.'s will be established at the following points:-

RIGHT. Junction of STURT TRENCH & WELLINGTON AVENUE.

CENTRE. JUNCTION of AVONDALE and front Line I.15.d.46.13.

LEFT. Concrete dug-out at LILLE POST.

Parties of S.B.'s with equipment will be posted at each Advanced R.A.P.
S.B.'s will not attempt to remove casualties from front line during operations unless a favourable opportunity occurs.
Walking Cases will find their own way to R.A.P. at Battalion Headquarters.
Officers will be detailed for duty at R.A.P.'s in Subsidiary Line.
M.O. will be at R.A.P. at Battalion Headquarters.

ZERO - 30.

P H A S E   I.

Bangalore Torpedoes in position HADFIELD'S PARTY. 30 - 35 yards in rear of Torpedoes, and remainder of raiding party in column of Route in rear. M.G.'s, L.T.M.B."s in position in N.M.L.

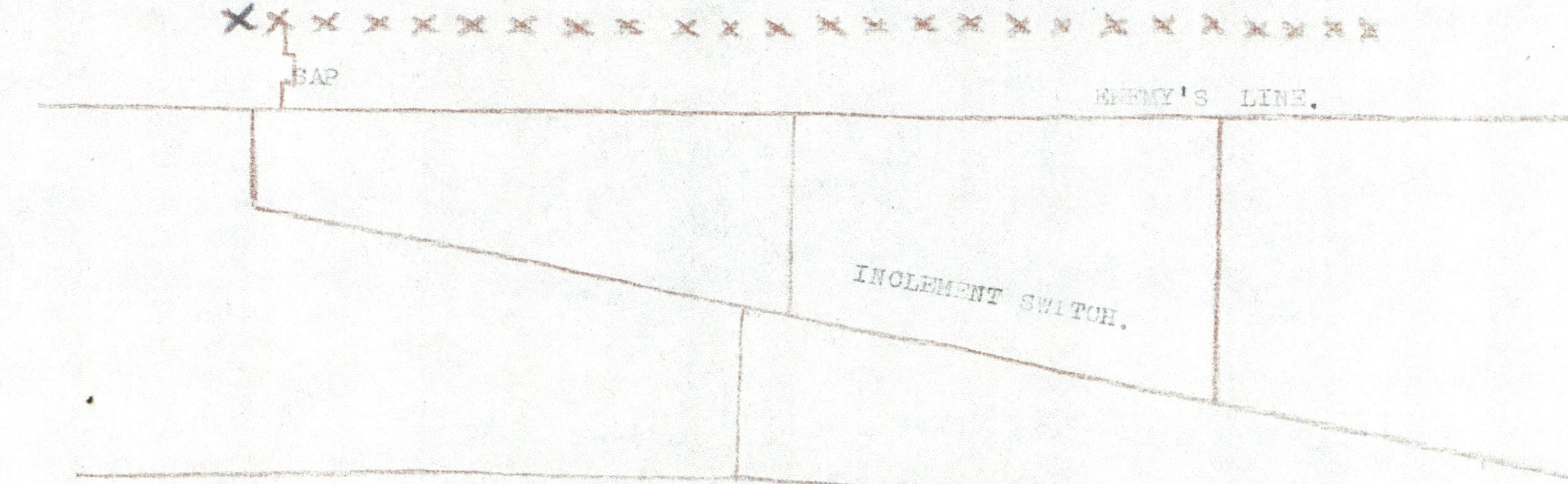

HADFIELDS PARTY.
PRICE'S "
DUTTON'S "
HOLMES "
HATTONS "
DEANS "
OAKES "
GREENALLS "
BRADY'S "
QUINN'S "
ROWLEY'S "
CLARKE"S "

ZERO - 6 to ZERO + 7

PHASE 2.

Immediately after explosion of Bangalore Torpedoes. Parties entering enemy trenches HADFIELD'S PARTY rush on to parapet to deal with any local resistance and remainder of raiding party follow.

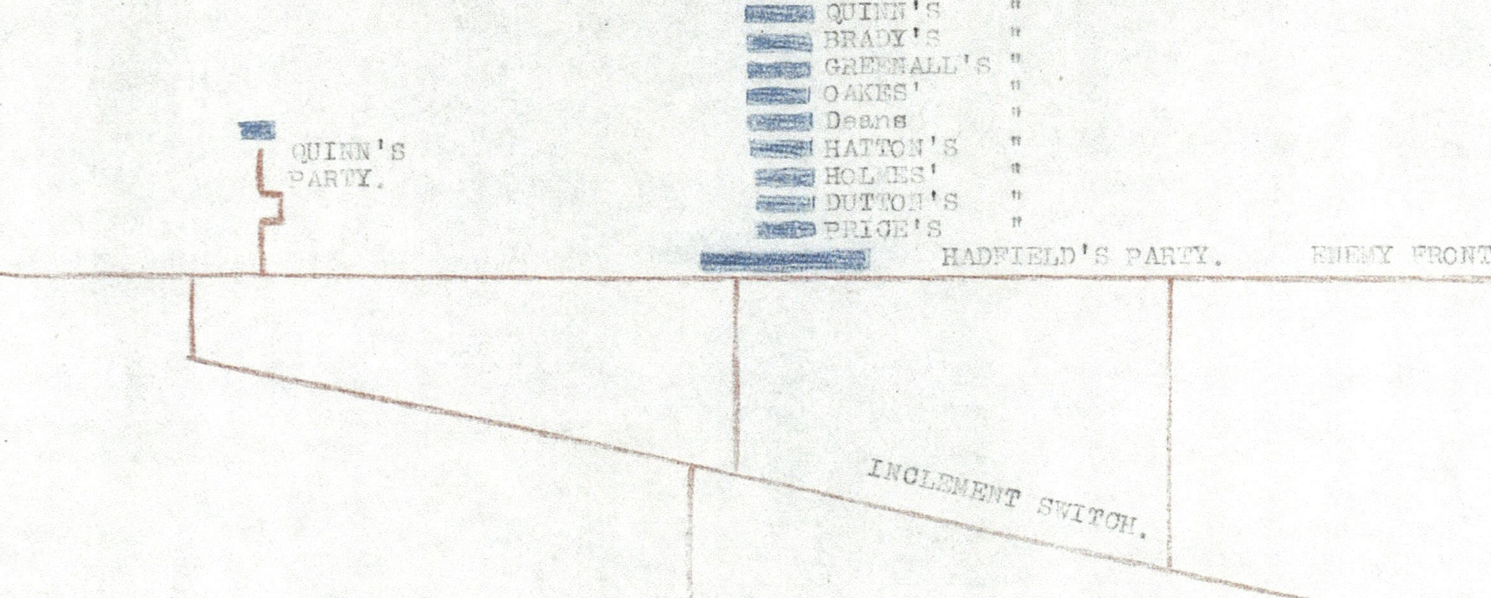

PHASE III.

ZERO + 7 to
ZERO + 30.

Parties having entered trenches established blocks, mopped up etc.

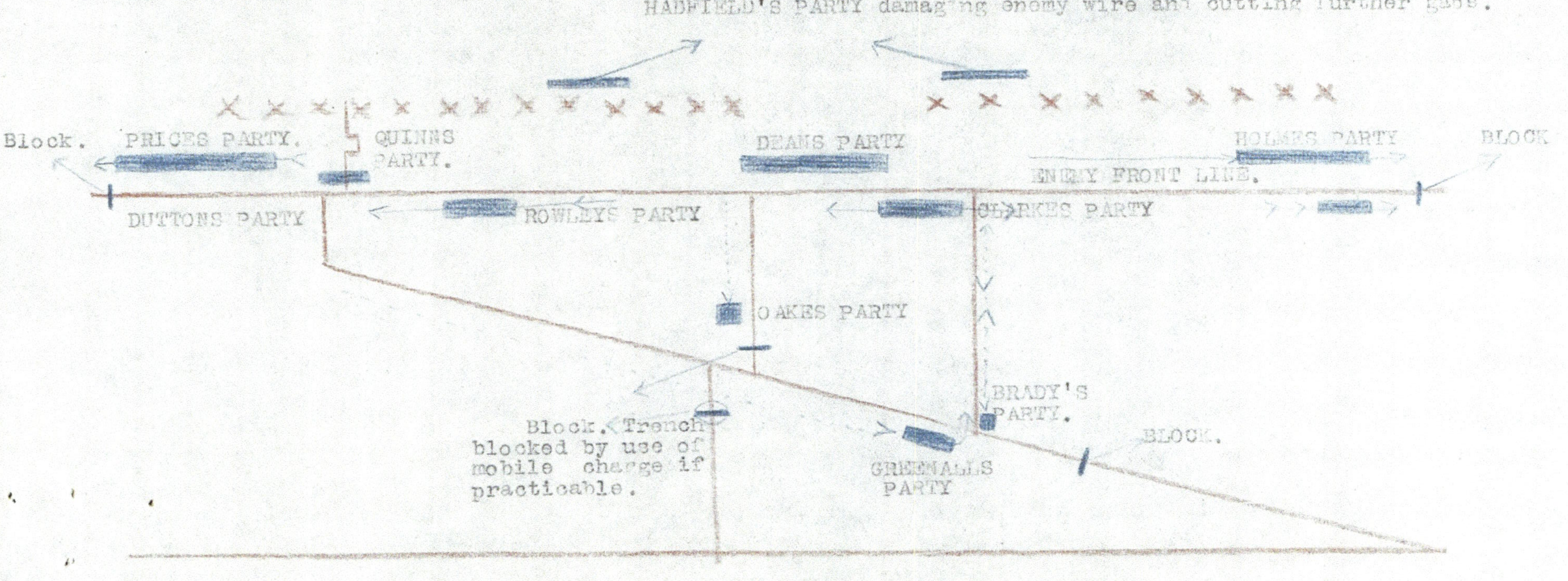

ZERO + 35.

PHASE 4.

PHASE 4. Withdrawal across N.M.L. PARAPET PARTIES last to leave enemy trenches.

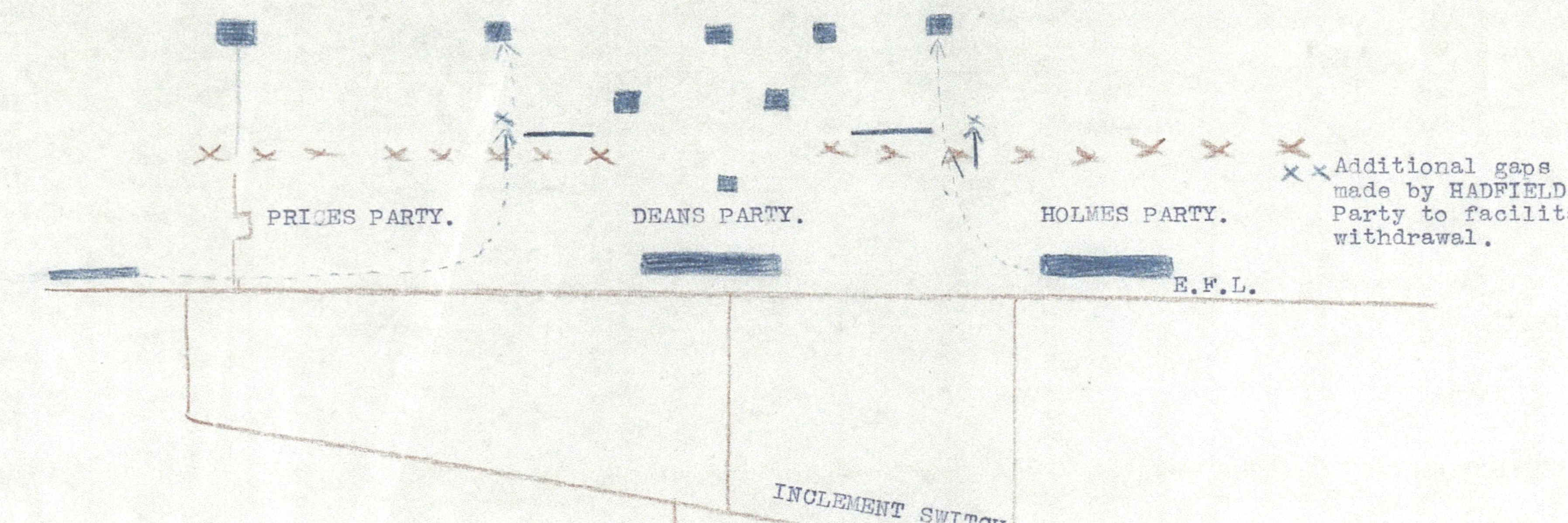

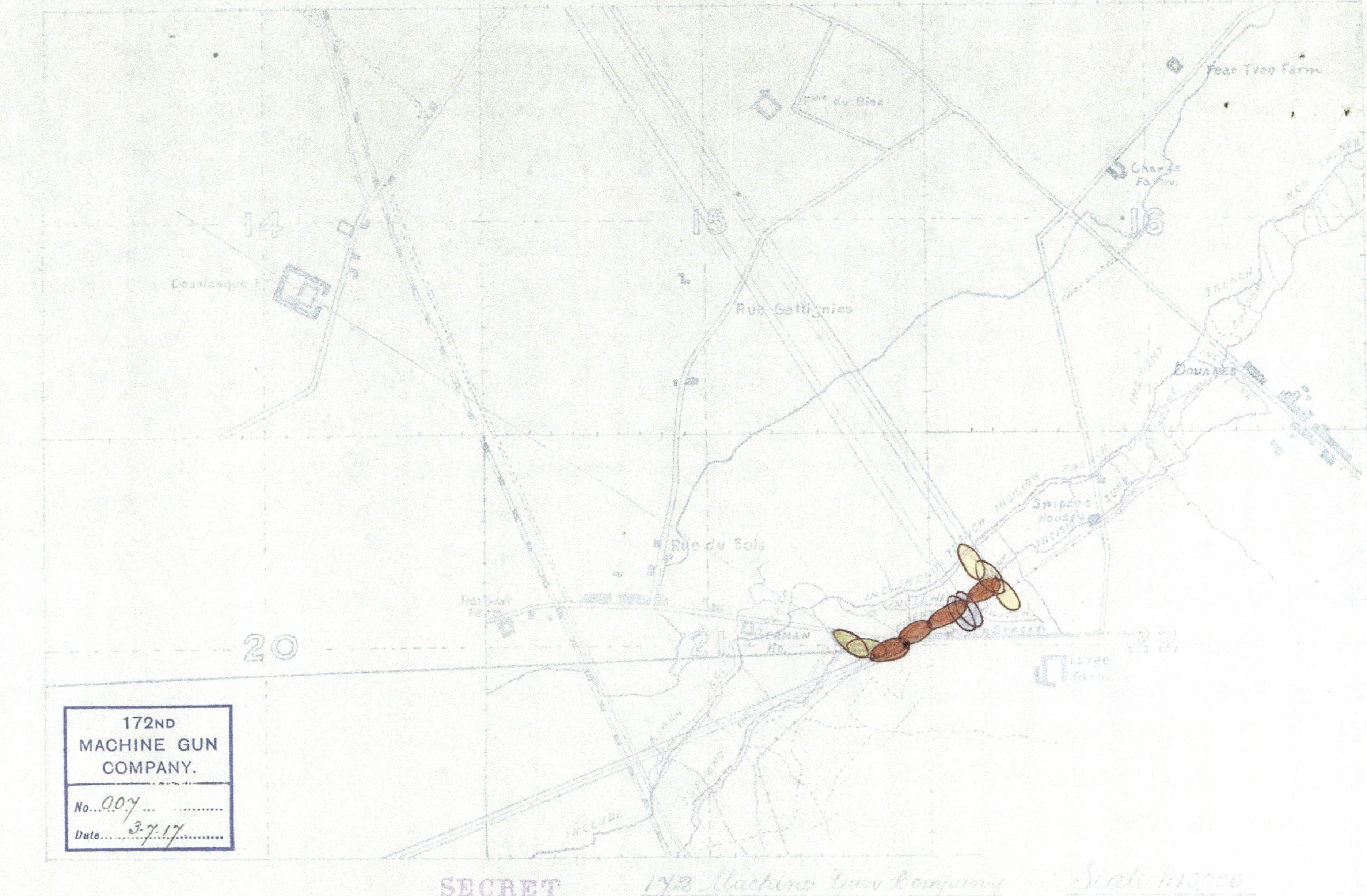
Pear Tree Farm
Fme du Bois
Chards Farm
14
15
16
Desplanque F.
Rue Gattignies
Douanes
Snipers House
Rue du Bois
Railway Farm
20
21
22
German Ho.
172ND
MACHINE GUN
COMPANY.
No. 007
Date 3.7.17
SECRET
172 Machine Gun Company
Scale 1:10,000

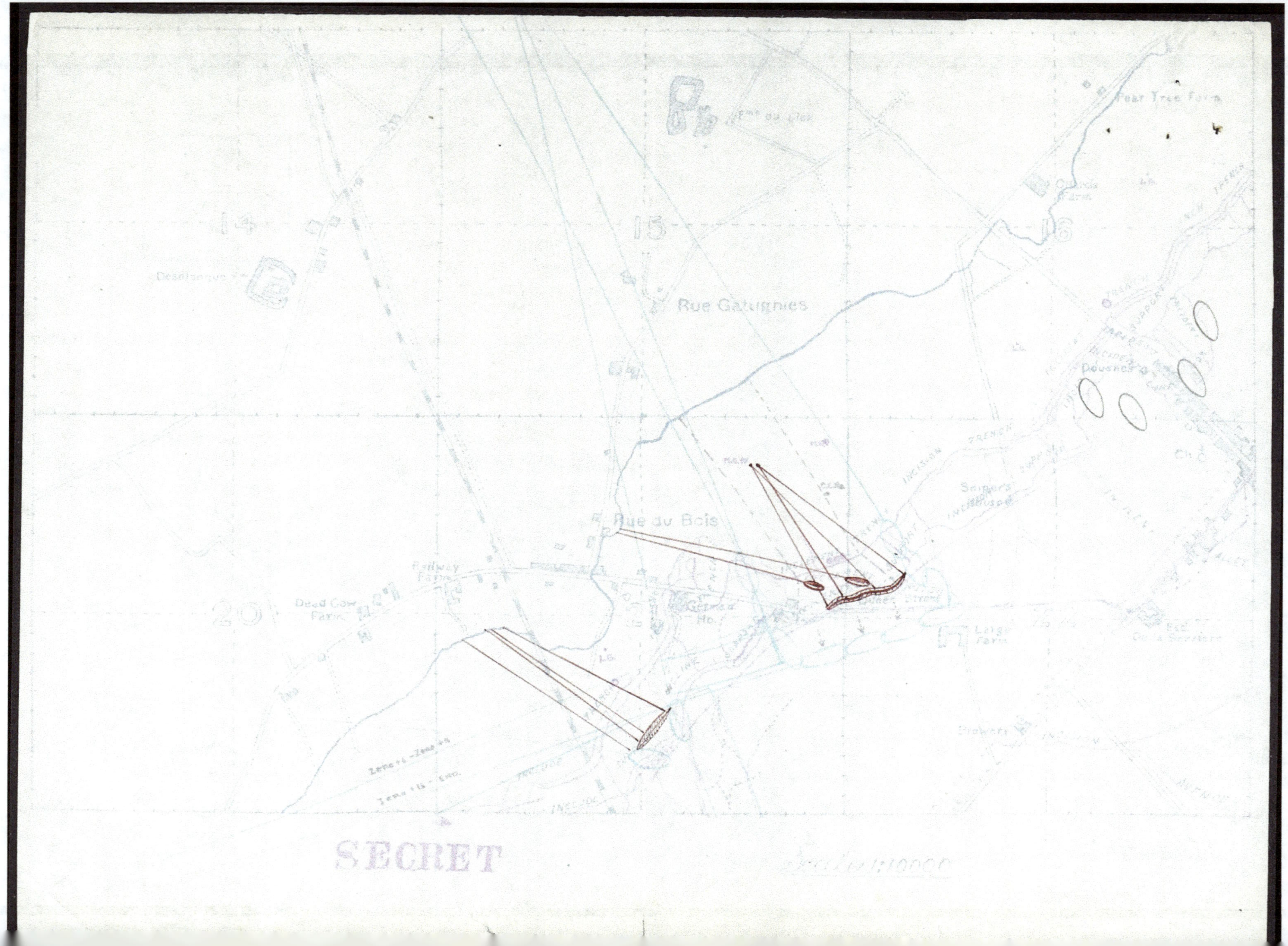

Pear Tree Farm

14

15

16

20

Desolangue

Rue Gatignies

Rue du Bois

Railway Farm

Dead Cow Farm

Snipers' Houses

Douvres

INCISION TRENCH

SECRET

Scale 1:10000

APPENDIX XVIII

REPORT ON HOSTILE BARRAGE AND EXPECTED RAID ON RUE DU BOIS SUBSECTOR NIGHT 6/7th. JULY, 1917.

1. PREPARATION. In accordance with B.M.197 dated 4/7/17, Front Line and First Supports were completely cleared from PEAR TREE GAP to RUE DU BOIS Salient. In addition all posts from RUE DU BOIS Salient and Park Row were cleared except one Lewis Gun Post on the left of PARK ROW in Front Line. The whole of PARADISE ALLEY from LILLE POST inclusive and QUEEN STREET as far as SALOP AVENUE including the whole of the ORCHARD was cleared.
Bombing Posts were posted in COWGATE, AVONDALE and WINE with protective blocks.
The Subsidiary Line between WELLINGTON AVENUE and WINE AVENUE was cleared. Instructions were also given that in event of shelling of STURT STREET and QUEENS STREET men would be put either well in front or behind out of the danger zone.
A Fighting Platoon of 1 Officer and 30 Other Ranks were ordered to be in position in N.M.L. in ditch at I.16.c.80.60 at 10.30 p.m.

2. DIVERSION. At about 9.45 p.m. enemy opened a barrage on FLAMNEGRIE SUBSECTOR.

3. BARRAGE. At 10.15 p.m. enemy opened and intense barrage on I.21.b and I.21.a. front and first support lines creeping back to second Support Line.
The Box Barrage was put on RUE DU BOIS C.T., STURT TRENCH QUEEN STREET, WINE STREET & Front Line.
The junction of SALOP AVENUE with Front Line and QUEEN STREET received an abnormal amount of attention.
The ORCHARD, PARADISE ALLEY, HAYSTACK AVENUE, WELLINGTON AVENUE and Subsidiary Line (in vicinity of railway) all received a fair amount of attention. The "Minnie" barrage was very intense, air bursts, and ground bursts being most accurate and completely demolishing certain localities, especially junctions of C.T.'s.
C.T.'s were principally dealt with by air burst "Minnies" and H.E. Shrapnel. (time fuse.)

4. AEROPLANE. An enemy aeroplane was over our lines during the whole of the operation and dropped white and red lights.

5. OUR ARTILLERY. At 10.20 p.m. our Artillery opened fire on enemy front and support lines.
The enemy barrage had not lifted from our front line when this happened.

6. L.T.M.B. & M.G.'s. At 10.25 p.m. our Light Trench Mortars and Machine Guns opened on our own trenches in area between COWGATE and WINE as previously arranged.
As soon as Box Barrage was seen to be on I.21.a. orders were given to the Machine Gun Officer to fire into this area and to form barrage across N.M.L. at this point. This was immediately carried out.

7. INFORMATION. Correct information was extremely difficult to obtain owing to the clearing of Front and Support Lines and communication trenches being barraged.
Two men trying to come overland from Bombing Block in WINE STREET were blown to bits.
At 10.40 p.m. a report was received from AVONDALE ROAD that the HUNS were on the right of WINE STREET but this has proved to be inaccurate (as far as is known.)
At about 10.50 p.m. the Boche Barrage began to slacken when green and red lights were sent up from his trenches in the vicinity of QUEER STREET.

(Continued.)

8\. PATROLS. (a) The patrol referred to in para. 1 left our trenches at 10.15 p.m. just as the barrage started. This patrol pushed out to about I.16.c.8.6. and then worked towards COWGATE. None of the enemy however were encountered or seen. This patrol returned to our trenches by orders from Battalion Headquarters by as soon as the M.G. Barrage on N.M.L. was ordered by Brigade Headquarters. This latter order however was cancelled later, but it was too late to stop the patrol coming in.

(b) As soon as barrage slackened patrols were pushed up all C.T.'s and as enemy barrage permitted them to go forward searched communication trenches, front line and ground in between including first Support.
No trace of the enemy however was found.

(c) A patrol of two Officers and 60 O.R. with 4 Lewis Guns went out into N.M.L. between AVONDALE and SALOP. N.M.L. was searched to within 20 yards of enemy wire but no trace of the enemy could be found, nor where any tracks in the long grass found.
Sergt. BICKERSTAFFE made a special note of this fact.

9\. CASUALTIES. Total Casualties as under:-

2/5th. S. Lan. R.	6	Other Ranks killed.
do.	11	" " wounded.
L.T.M.B.	5	" " "
2/4th. S. Lan. R.	3	" " "

The last named party were caught in the barrage towards KNIGHTSBRIDGE and as far as is known was a party ordered from the 5th. Coy. by the R.E. without any reference to these Headquarters.

10\. CONCLUSIONS. It would appear that the enemy did not raid these trenches and that if he intended to do so our artillery prevented him from issuing from his trenches.
It will be noted that our artillery opened before his barrage had lifted from our front line and it is almost definitely confirmed that our M.G. and L.T.M.B. fire opened before his barrage had lifted from our front line. This in itself would probably be sufficient to prevent him carrying out his designs.
From the area bombarded it is suggested that he had no intention of raiding as the photograph of his practice trenches is of the area between COWGATE and WINE. A raid on the latter area is still quite probable.
One is inclined to think however that the three missing men may have given him inaccurate information as to our intended raid and in consequence of such information he has attempted to anticipate out intentions and position of assembly.
The long range obtained by his "MINENWERFER" is the most remarkable feature of this operation.
Many of his heavy "Minnies" dropped over PARADISE ALLEY and QUEEN STREET. Assuming that he was firing from a position opposite I.21.5. it is apparent that he had his "Minenwerfer" in his front line.
This possibly explains the recent activity and exceptional amount of noise and working parties reported in his front line.
It has been reported indirectly to these Headquarters that the enemy was particularly active in his counter battery work during the operation.

Lieut.Col.,
Commanding,
2/5th. S. Lan. R.

7th. July, 1917.

REPORT ON ENTRY OF BOCHE RAIDING PARTY IN RUE DU BOIS SALIENT, NIGHT JULY 6th/7th. 1917.

Boche Party estimated 15 to 20 strong entered RUE DU BOIS Salient. Traces show two entrances at about I.21.a.98.08 and I.21.a.88.10. One party apparently went to right extremity of Salient and another to left extremity. Both parties bombed as they went, and there are numerous fuze buttons and serrated cups lying in trench besides a few bombs on parapet.

At first point of entry an automatic rifle or light gun has been in action over our parapet and it is thought a "pine-apple" gun was also brought over, as a "pine-apple" can be seen lying outside parapet. Nothing was seen of this ~~party~~ raiding party who do not appear to have gone beyond front line.

APPENDIX. XIX

S E C R E T.

Copy No. 7..

2/5th. S. LAN. R., OPERATION ORDER NO. 24.
(To be read in conjunction with
Operation Order No. 23.)

Ref. Map
Sheet 36/N.W.4
1/10,000

1. INTENTION. There will be a "Dummy" Raid on enemy's trenches opposite RUE DU BOIS Sub-sector on night 8th./9th. July, commencing at ZERO hour.

2. ACTION. (a) 2/Lt. J. CLARKE and 14 O.R. of "B" Coy. will lie up in N.M.L. until ZERO hour when they will reconnoitre INCLEMENT and INCISION TRENCHES and obtain identification if opportunity offers, returning in their own time.

(b) 2/Lt. A.R. ST.GEORGE will be at R.H.7, with one section of 6 Bombers in support to 2/Lt. CLARKE.

(c) O/C "B" Coy. with 1 Platoon and Company Stretcher Bearers will be in PARADISE ALLEY.

(d) A patrol of 1 Platoon, 30 O.R. strong, of "B" Coy. will lie up in N.M.L. at I.21.b.25.55 from 10 p.m. to 1 a.m. when they will withdraw to Subsidiary Line.

3. CLEARANCE OF TRENCHES. The whole of the Front Line, First Support and Second Support Lines will be cleared with the following exceptions:-

(a) Bombing Blocks will be established in LEITH WALK, COWGATE, WINE and WELLINGTON by O/C Coy.'s concerned.
(b) O/C "A" Coy. will man the Lewis Gun positions of LEITH WALK defensive flank.
(c) Lewis Guns required for Support Line by Brigade Defence Scheme will remain in position to co..operate with Vickers.

4. ARTILLERY. From ZERO till ZERO + 48 there will be an 18 pounder barrage onenemy trenches as under:-
From I.21.b.40.40 along Front Line to junction with INCLEMENT SWITCH, along INCLEMENT SWITCH, INCLEMENT SUPPORT, INCISION SUPPORT to Front Line at I.16.c.9.0. thence along INCIDENT TRENCH to I.16.d.30.60.
In addition single 18 pounders will deal with M.G. emplacements and Howitzers will deal with "Minnie" positions.

5. PROJECTORS. Projectors will be fired by "M" Special Coy. R.E. as under at ZERO, ~~xx~~ ZERO + 10, ZERO + 15 and ZERO + 30.

Support Line	I.16.d.20.20 to I.16.d.60.60.
Tile Factory	I.22.a.25.85.
Cross Roads	I.22.b.98.75.
Road	I.22.b.85.90.
Support Line	I.21.c.95.30 to I.21.d.16.53.

6. MACHINE GUNS. Vickers guns will fire from ZERO till, ZERO 45 as under:-

WEZ MACQUART
DISTILLERY ROAD.
LARGE FARM
INCIDENT ALLEY
C.T. from I.22.a.30.55 to I.22.a.50.05.

also two guns will fire indirect~~ix~~ from 10.30 p.m. to 1.35 a.m. to cover movements of CLARKE'S Party.

(Continued)

7 L.T.M.B. & M.T.M.B.	will not co-operate.
8. COMMUNICATION.	The Signalling Officer will arrange for communication between H.H.7 and H.[illegible].2 through H.M.10.
9. SIGNALS.	In the event of it being found necessary to postpone operations a blue rocket will be fired from H.H.7 and repeated from Battalion Headquarters. White Mortar Rockets will be sent up at ZERO + 30 and Green Very Lights at ZERO + 65.
10. CODE.	The Code laid down in Operation Order No.23 will stand good.
11. SYNCHRONIZATION OF WATCHES.	The Signalling Officer will synchronize watches at Brigade Headquarters at 6 p.m. July 8th. All Battalion watches will be synchronized at 9 p.m. at Battalion Headquarters.
12. MEDICAL ARRANGEMENTS.	The M.O. will be at R.A.P. at Battalion Headquarters
13. REPORTS.	All reports must be sent at once to Battalion Headquarters by wire or runner.
14. INTELLIGENCE OFFICER.	The Intelligence Officer will be at FME DU BIEZ from 1.30 a.m. till 3 a.m. A full report will be rendered to Battalion Headquarters at 4 a.m.
15. ZERO.	ZERO HOUR will be at 1.35 a.m. 9th. July, 1917.

R.C. Heyward
Lieutenant,
Adjutant,
2/5th. S. Lan. R.

Issued at p.m. by runner

Copy No. 1 to C/O.
" 2 to O/C "A" Coy.
" 3 to O/C "B" Coy.
" 4 to O/C "C" Coy.
" 5 to O/C "D" Coy.
" 6 to H.Q., 172nd. Inf. Bde.
" 7 to War Diary.
" 8 FILE.

APPENDIX. XX

REPORT ON DUMMY RAID NIGHT 8/9TH.
JULY, 1917,
RUE DU BOIS SUB - SECTOR.

Patrol of 1 Officer and 14 other ranks left our Front Line at I.16.d.52.20 at 11.30 p.m. and followed up ditch to I.22.a.41.96 thence to I.22.a.40.65 where an apparent gap had been located.
On reaching this portion it was found that though the wire had been considerably knocked about it had not been cut.

~~Rep~~ Previous to deciding on this gap however patrol moved between I.22.a.55.75 and I.22.a.05.30 in search of a definite gap.

The original gap was however found to be most suitable. Therefore at about 1 a.m. party commenced cutting their way through.

Good progress was made by 2/Lt. CLARKE and three other men in cutting the wire. Unfortunately however one man got hung up and in extricating himself the rattling of the wire was overheard. This occurred after cutting had proceeded for 20 minutes.

Rifle Grenades then began to fall round and about the party. The wire was still further cut but Machine Gun fire from the two salients, RUE DU BOIS and CHARDS FARM, now began to enfilade his wire and things began to get pretty warm.
Our barrage now opened and short shrapnel bursts behind the party throwing bullets into the wire caused 2/Lt. CLARKE to withdraw his party into the ditch.

Another attempt was made but to no avail and 2/Lt. CLARKE decided to withdraw with the information he had gained.
The patrol returned to our lines at 2.45 a.m. without casualties.

INFORMATION. The enemy Front Line was apparently devoid of any sign of life. No very Lights were sent up from his front line except left of LILLE ROAD and right of RUE DU BOIS and from the support line only a very few lights were sent up.
A certain number of coloured lights, red and green, were sent up from in or behind his support line. Rifle Grenades came from his Support Line and no rifle or automatic rifle fire came from his front line.

OUR BARRAGE. Except for certain 18 pdrs. bursting short as previously reported the barrage appeared satisfactory though far too thin for any definite operation in the way of a large raid.
The oil projected seemed satisfactory though the results anticipated were not realised owing probably to the very heavy rainfall the previousnight.

ENEMY BARRAGE. This was brought down very soon after our guns opened.
CHARDS FARM, COWGATE, and RUE DU BOIS Localities receiving most attention. About 50 4.2's fell round FME DU BIEZ.
Only about six "whizz-bang" guns engaged our front line.
"Minnies" were fairly active on CHARDS FARM and more so on RUE DU BOIS as far back as QUEEN STREET.
"Minnie" barrage was put on or about the centre of N.M.L. for a short time, soon after ZERO switching from there on to RUE DU BOIS.
The number of "Minnie" guns seemed to be normal and supplied with plenty of ammunition.

Lieut.Col.,
Commanding,
2/5th. S. Lan. R.

9th. July, 1917.

APPENDIX XXI

MILITARY MEDAL.

Date of Award, 20/7/17.

***

(Auty:- XI Corps Routine Order No. 1870 dated 25/7/17.)

No. 241394, L/Cpl. SAMUEL BLACKHURST. "N" Battalion.
For exemplary conduct on the night of 6/7th. July, 1917 in the .... during an intense bombardment of our trenches by the enemy, L/Cpl. BLACKHURST led the "D" Coy. stretcher bearers into the heaviest part of the barrage and succeeded in carrying in severely wounded men to safety. It was owing to this N.C.O.'s coolness that the lives of the wounded were saved as the trenches were subsequently obliterated at this point.
He has done good work on previous occasions.

***

No.241945, Rfn. JAMES HAYES. "N" Battalion.
For bravery on the night of 6/7th. July, 1917, in the .... during a hostile raid. The enemy opened an intense barrage setting a dump on fire containing a large quantity of S.A.A. Grenades. Rfn. HAYES entered the dump in which the ammunition was already exploding and threw water on the fire. He entered the dump seven or eight times before he succeeded in putting out the fire. During the whole of the bombardment which lasted two hours he acted as runner to the Company Commander, and successfully carried messages through the heaviest part of the barrage. He has done consistent good work during the last 4½ months."

***

APPENDIX XXII

2/5th. BATTALION SOUTH LANCASHIRE REGIMENT

STATEMENT
SHOWING FLUCTUATIONS OF STRENGTH

35 Officers. 808 Other Ranks

Trench Strength 31st. July, 1917 591 Other Ranks

217 Other Ranks not on Trench Strength made up as under:-

Transport and Grooms	46
Q.M. Stores	31
R.A.M.C. (Water Duties)	4
Course of Instruction	38
Hospital	4
O.R. Sergeant at Base	1
Rest Camp 1st Army	8

Detached:-

Employed at Bde and Divn	23
Town Guard ARMENTIERES	9
A.P.M.	5
L.T.M.B.	14
Signallers with M.G. Coy	2
Brigade Pioneer Coy	32
	217

APPENDIX XXIII

2/5th BATTALION SOUTH LANCASHIRE REGIMENT
****

NOMINAL ROLL OF OFFICERS, as on 31st. July, 1917.

HEADQUARTERS

Lieut-Colonel.	Owen W.L. M.C.	Commanding Officer
Major.	Brewis A	Second in Command.
Captain.	Wood R.L.	Medical Officer.
Lieut.	Hayward R.C.	Adjutant
Lieut.	Gregory H.	Quartermaster.
Lieut.	Hadfield J.L.	Bombing Officer.
2/Lieut.	West H.	Lewis Gun Officer.
2/Lieut.	Tanton L.E.	Transport Officer.
2/Lieut.	Nimmo A.A.	Intelligence Officer.
2/Lieut.	St. George A.R.	Assistant Adjutant.

"A" COMPANY

Captain	Wood R.H.	O.C. Company
2/Lieut.	Hargreaves R.	Platoon Commander.
2/Lieut.	Davis H.P.W.	Platoon Commander.
2/Lieut.	Messum A.W.	Second in Command.
2/Lieut.	Stone A.R.	Platoon Commander.

"B" COMPANY

Captain	Crowe J.A.	O.C. Company.
Lieut.	Donald T.M.	Second in Command.
2/Lieut.	Bullen H.G.	Platoon Commander.
2/Lieut.	Dean L.M.	Platoon Commander.
2/Lieut.	Clarke J.	Platoon Commander.

"C" COMPANY

Captain.	Guest E.L.	O.C. Company.
2/Lieut.	Le Mare E.B.	Second in Command.
2/Lieut.	Adams B.C.	Platoon Commander.

"D" COMPANY

Captain	Stephenson C.W.	O.C. Company.
Lieut.	Frodsham F.J.	Second in Command.
2/Lieut.	Holland W.H.E.	Platoon Commander.
2/Lieut.	Handley W.C.	Platoon Commander.

DETACHED.

Captain	Gould M.L.B.	Divisional Salvage Offier.
Lieut.	Timson H.H.	Signal Course, Dunstable, ENGLAND.
2/Lieut.	Hall W.S.	172nd Inf. Bde. Pioneer Coy.
2/Lieut.	Paul R.B.	172nd Inf. Bde. Instructor.

HOSPITAL.

Captain	Wallis A.C.
2/Lieut.	Brazener W.F.
2/Lieut.	Dickinson W.

*****

Original

28031 W3125/M2250 1000m 6/17 M.R.Co.,Ltd. (1367) Forms W3091

Army Form W. 3091.

Vol 7

Cover for Documents.

CONFIDENTIAL

Nature of Enclosures.

WAR DIARY

2/5th S LAN R

From 1/8/17

To 31/8/17

Notes, or Letters written.

WITH APPENDICES

XXIV to XXXI

Instructions regarding War Diaries and Intelligence Summaries are contained in F. S. Regs., Part II. and the Staff Manual respectively. Title Pages will be prepared in manuscript.

WAR DIARY

~~or~~

~~INTELLIGENCE SUMMARY~~

(Erase heading not required.)

Army Form C. 2118

Place	Date	Hour	Summary of Events and Information	Remarks and references to Appendices
	August	1917		
LA ROLANDERIE	1st to 2nd		In Billets. On evening of 2nd a practice gas alarm was held. The result was satisfactory	
LA ROLANDERIE	3rd		The Battalion relieved the 2/9th K.L.R in the FLAMENGRIE Subsector. The relief started at 8 p.m. and was complete by 9.25 pm. The night passed quietly. Weather very wet.	A.P. 8th 9th
TRENCHES BOISGRENIER SECTOR	4th		Weather still very wet. An enemy ammunition dump was blown up by M.T.M. shoot. The day passed quietly. During the night the Right Company patrol discovered an enemy working party opposite the BRIDOUX SALIENT. The patrol came back and the 18 pounder guns fired several rounds of shrapnel on to the working party.	
	5th to 6th		Quiet during the day.	
		12.35 am.	The enemy put over numerous gas shells on the Battalion on our left. Rattles were sounded immediately ~~sounded~~ and gas masks put on. A few gas shells were sent over the left Company Sector. We had no casualties. Gas masks were taken off after wearing them just over one hour. The gas appeared, was the used mustard oil gas.	A.P. 8th 9th

1875 Wt. W593/826 1,000,000 4/15 J.B.C. & A. A.D.S.S./Forms/C. 2118.

Army Form C. 2118

Instructions regarding War Diaries and Intelligence Summaries are contained in F. S. Regs., Part II. and the Staff Manual respectively. Title Pages will be prepared in manuscript.

WAR DIARY
~~or~~
~~INTELLIGENCE SUMMARY~~

(Erase heading not required.)

Place	Date 1917	Hour	Summary of Events and Information	Remarks and references to Appendices
TRENCHES BOIS GRENIER SECTOR	August 7th		Quiet during the day, except for some retaliation on right of SHAFTESBURY AVENUE to our M.T.M. shoot	
	8th	6.40 a.m.	Enemy commenced a systematic registration of the front and support line trenches in the centre sector. All necessary precautions were taken in case enemy attempted to raid, which he did not do. A patrol of ours went out at night and a hostile patrol was seen, but it was not possible to get into touch with the enemy.	AR. 81. G7/H
	9th	7.45 a.m.	The enemy heavily bombarded our Left and Centre Company Sectors with heavy- medium and light "Minnies". KIWI AVENUE and front and support lines in vicinity were heavily shelled for an hour. The trenches were badly damaged, a gap being blown in the front line parapet. Some 150 to 200 'MINNIES' of all calibres fell in the Centre Coy. Sector. Our artillery replied vigorously.	AR. 81. G7/H
		5.30am to 10am.	Unusual movement was observed in INDEX TRENCH. Over 100 men in steel helmets and carrying rifles were seen. Every precaution was taken in the evening.	APPENDIX XXIV

Army Form C. 2118

Instructions regarding War Diaries and Intelligence Summaries are contained in F. S. Regs., Part II. and the Staff Manual respectively. Title Pages will be prepared in manuscript.

WAR DIARY

~~or~~

~~INTELLIGENCE SUMMARY~~

(Erase heading not required.)

Place	Date 1917	Hour	Summary of Events and Information	Remarks and references to Appendices
TRENCHES BOIS GRENIER SECTOR	August 10th		Quiet during the day.	
		8.50 p.m.	At 8.50 p.m. enemy put down a heavy barrage on the sector on our left. Very little came over our sector, but expecting this to be a bluff every precaution was again taken and 1 Platoon and 2 Lewis Guns from the 4th Company were sent up PARK ROW to act as a defensive flank.	A.P. 8.G.7/1k
		10.5 p.m. to 10.15 p.m.	During this time a hurricane bombardment was put down in the vicinity of PRINCES STREET. It certainly looked as though the enemy was going to raid. This he did not do, but the next day some papers were found in the trenches which had evidently been left by the enemy. A minor operation was carried out at 12.45 am (11th) with Bangalore Torpedoes, for the purpose of getting an identification. This was not obtained.	APPENDIX XXVII A.P. 8.G.7/1k APPENDICES XXV XXVI
	11th		Quiet during the day. The Battalion was relieved by the 2/9th R.L.R. Relief carried out satisfactorily. Battalion went into billets at LA ROLANDERIE FARM – ARTILLERY FARM – CANTEEN FARM and the MILL ERQUINGHEM. Casualties during tour – Killed (1) O.R. Wounded 1 Officer, 11 OR Died of Wounds 3	

1875 Wt. W593/826 1,000,000 4/15 J.B.C. & A. A.D.S.S./Forms/C. 2118.

Instructions regarding War Diaries and Intelligence Summaries are contained in F. S. Regs., Part II. and the Staff Manual respectively. Title Pages will be prepared in manuscript.

WAR DIARY
~~or~~
~~INTELLIGENCE SUMMARY~~
(Erase heading not required.)

Army Form C. 2118

Place	Date 1917	Hour	Summary of Events and Information	Remarks and references to Appendices
LA ROLANDERIE	August 12th to 14th		In Billets. Training and Inspections. Special attention was paid to Bayonet fighting. Major A. BREWIS and 2/Lt. L. M. Dean were in charge of this training	
	15th to 18th		In Billets. A lecture was given on the 15th by Major Gillespie R.F.A on Artillery in cooperation with the Infantry. The Battalion won 9 prizes out of 18 in the Boxing Tournament. (Brigade)	A.R. 8.9/17
	19th		The Battalion relieved the 2/9th KLR in the FLAMENGRIE Sector. The relief was satisfactory and complete by 10 pm. L/C Prescott awarded Military Medal. Date of award 5/8/17.	APPENDIX XXVIII
TRENCHES BOIS GRENIER Sector	20th	2.15 am	The enemy sent over about 100 gas shells, mixed with pineapples. These shells fell in and around KIWI. We had 7 casualties. The day passed quietly. An enemy aeroplane dropped a message in our lines giving information as to R.F.C. prisoners.	A.R. 8.9/17
		9 pm	Enemy aeroplanes passed over our lines on a bombing expedition.	

1875 Wt. W593/826 1,000,000 4/15 J.B.C. & A. A.D.S.S./Forms/C. 2118.

Instructions regarding War Diaries and Intelligence Summaries are contained in F. S. Regs., Part II. and the Staff Manual respectively. Title Pages will be prepared in manuscript.

WAR DIARY

~~or~~

~~INTELLIGENCE SUMMARY~~

(Erase heading not required.)

Army Form C. 2118

Place	Date 1917	Hour	Summary of Events and Information	Remarks and references to Appendices
TRENCHES BOIS GRENIER SECTOR	August 21st		The day passed fairly quietly. There was no T.M. shoot on this sector. Wiring was started in front of strong posts. The Centre Company patrol reported having seen an enemy patrol of about 30 men. A strong patrol was immediately sent out and the right company warned, but nothing more was seen of the enemy.	A.R. 8/9/17
	22nd		Quiet day.	
		3.45 p.m.	A small enemy balloon flew over the sector and dropped behind the lines near ARTILLERY FARM	
		9 p.m.	A large number of enemy aeroplanes flew over our lines, the majority of them going well behind. Our aeroplanes dropped 6 bombs in the vicinity of LONDON BRIDGE	
	23rd		Quiet period. Orders for minor operations completed	APPENDIX XXIX
	24th	12.15 am	The enemy put up a very heavy barrage on the Battalion on our right. Our right Company right post came in for a good deal of this Barrage, about 90 "Minnies" falling in the vicinity of SAFETY ALLEY causing considerable damage and blocking the communication trench. Strombos Horns were also sounded on the right but no gas reached us	A.R. 8/9/17

1875 Wt. W593/826 1,000,000 4/15 J.B.C. & A. A.D.S.S./Forms/C. 2118.

Instructions regarding War Diaries and Intelligence Summaries are contained in F. S. Regs., Part II. and the Staff Manual respectively. Title Pages will be prepared in manuscript.

WAR DIARY

~~or~~

~~INTELLIGENCE~~ SUMMARY

(Erase heading not required.)

Army Form C. 2118

Place	Date	Hour	Summary of Events and Information	Remarks and references to Appendices
TRENCHES BOIS GRENIER SECTOR	24th	8pm	Received orders from Brigade to cancel MINOR Operations, owing to identification having been obtained on the right.	O.O. 89. [illegible]
	25th		Quiet period. The M.T.M. shooting between KIWI and COLLEGE GREEN fired 28 rounds, when the gun was knocked out by a direct hit, killing two men & wounding another. During the night our Artillery fired 12 rounds on the tramway behind the enemy's front line. The tramway seems to be constantly in use	
	26th		Received orders that we will be relieved on night 27th/28th by the 2/9th K.L.R. Quiet day. 2/9th K.L.R. Lewis Guns came up at 10pm.	
	27th		Quiet day	
		8.30pm	Relieved by 2/9th K.L.R. Relief satisfactory. Complete by 10.30pm. Battalion went into Billets at LA ROLANDERIE FARM and huts near STREAKY BACON FARM. Billets at FACTORY ERQUINGHEM given up on account of shelling whilst Battalion was in the trenches.	[illegible]
			No. 9 Platoon (2/Lt ADAMS) sent to Brigade School for training as exhibition platoon for demonstration of Platoon in offensive action	

1875 Wt. W593/826 1,000,000 4/15 J.B.C. & A. A.D.S.S./Forms/C. 2118.

Instructions regarding War Diaries and Intelligence Summaries are contained in F. S. Regs., Part II. and the Staff Manual respectively. Title Pages will be prepared in manuscript.

WAR DIARY
or
INTELLIGENCE SUMMARY
(Erase heading not required.)

Army Form C. 2118

Place	Date	Hour	Summary of Events and Information	Remarks and references to Appendices
ERQUINGHEM LA ROLANDRIE	27th.		One platoon from each Battalion in the Brigade during this training. G.O.C to select one of these platoons as Brigade exhibition platoon. Casualties during tour in trenches 8 Other ranks gassed 5 Other ranks wounded	RCLs.
	28th.		In Billets. Reequipping, Baths, Brigade Duties and working parties.	
	29th to 30th.		No special feature. Divisional Boxing Tournament held on 29th. Preceded by lecture on Bayonet Fighting by Lt. Col. CAMPBELL. "Blood on the bayonet" specially emphasized and the necessity for use of "bayonet and bullet". 240969 Cpl. LANAKEY. R. (C Coy) won Featherweight Final and 240604 Rfn TIPPING. H (A Coy) won Lightweight Final.	
	31st.		C.O. Adjutant, Senior Major, O'S.C. Companies, NCO'S and runners from companies reconnoitred posts 4–13 of H.Q. Second Line. The portion of line reconnoitred is a continuous line of trenches running from western outskirts of FLEURBAIX to RUE DU BIEZ, ERQUINGHEM, with posts (strong points) at intervals. The posts are generally in good condition but trenches in between are very dilapidated. Wire very good along whole line.	RCLs.
			Strength of Battalion 31/8/17 34 Officers 764 Other Ranks	See APPENDICES XXX and XXXI.

[signature]
LIEUT. COL.
2/5TH BATTALION SOUTH LANC. REGT.

1875 Wt. W593/826 1,000,000 4/15 J.B.C. & A. A.D.S.S./Forms/C. 2118.

APPENDIX XXIV

INTELLIGENCE REPORT.

From 6 a.m. to 6 p.m., 9th. August, 1917.

FLAMENGRIE SUBSECTOR.

Our Operations.
(A)

*****

(1) Heavy retaliation on enemy's lines for "Minnie" strafe during the morning. Retaliation was very effective as it eventually forced the enemy to quieten down considerably.

(2) M.T.M. Did not fire.

(3) SNIPERS. Quiet.

(9) AIRCRAFT. Two of our planes patrolled our lines at 11.0 a.m.

(10) GENERAL. With the exception of our artillery retaliation the day has been quiet.

Enemy Operations.
(B)

*****

(1) ARTILLERY. Has been very quiet all day. Only a few shells on our supports and Infantry posts. Shelled back areas during the afternoon.

(2) TM. Commencingat 7.45 a.m. the enemy heavily bombarded our left and centre companies sectors with heavy medium and light minnies. KIWI AVENUE and front line and supports in vicinity were heavily bombarded for an hour. The trenches are badly damaged, a gap being blown in the front line parapet. After this the bombardment ceased, but recommenced at 9.10 a.m. though not so heavily as the previous one. This continued till about mid-day. It is estimated that upwards of 80 heavy minnies were fired on this sector in addition to a large number of medium and light ones.
Commencing at 8.30 a.m. enemy also opened a heavy "minnie" bombardment on JOCK'S JOY and vicinity of SHAFTESBURY AVENUE and PRINCES STREET. This continued till about mid-day when it slackened off considerably. This part of the line has been shelled intermittently all afternoon. PRINCES STREET and SHAFTESBURY AVENUE have been badly damaged. Pineapples were distributed profusely on front line and supports during the operations. It is estimated that from 150 to 200 minnies of all calibres fell in centre company's sector.

(9) AIRCRAFT. An enemy plane flew over our lines about 10.30 a.m. and another at 5 p.m.

(10) MOVEMENT. Unusual movement observed in INDEX TRENCH between 5.30 a.m. and 10 a.m. this morning.

MOVEMENT - Contd. Over a hundred men in steel helmets and carrying rifles and bayonets were observed.
The following table shows the time, place and number of men that were observed. They were seen from BREWERY O.P.

Time.	Place.	No.	Moving	Dress.
5.30 a.m. - 6 a.m.	INDEX TRENCH.	18.	Left.	Steel helmets & Bayonets.
5.30 a.m. - 6 a.m.	INDEX ~~TRENCH~~ SUP.	15.	Left.	do.
6. a.m. - 6.30 a.m.	INDEX TRENCH.	22	Left.	do.
6 a.m. - 6.30 a.m.	INDEX SUP.	9	Left.	do.
6 a.m. - 6.30 a.m.	O.1.d.46.30.	14.	Rearwds.	Round caps
6.30 a.m. 7.30 a.m.	INDEX TRENCH.	7.	Left.	do.
6.30 a.m. - 7.30 am.	INDEX SUP.	11.	Left.	Steel Helmets
6.30 a.m. - 7.30 a.m.	INDEX TRENCH.	4.	right.	Round caps.
6.30 a.m. - 7.30 a.m	INDEX SUP.	8.	right.	do.
7.30 a.m. - 10 a.m.	INDEX SUP.	3.	right.	do.
7.30 a.m. - 10 a.m.	INDEX SUP.	5.	Left.	do.

Considerable movement was also seen in the back areas. A large number of enemy emerged from trees in O.86 and appeared to wash themselves in a corrugated iron shed at about O.86. .90.45.
At 7.20 a.m. 4 of the enemy were seen carrying timber in INDEX TRENCH and dumped it in front line between I.31.d.00.25 and I.31.d.30.35.

12. GENERAL. Enemy fairly quiet after his morning strafe. Visibility good.

APPENDIX XXV

XV 31

SECRET.

Ref maps
Sheet 36.N.W.4
1/10.000.
Sheet 36.S.W.2
1/10.000

ORDERS FOR MINOR OPERATIONS.

COPY. No. 8

NIGHT — 10th/11th AUGUST. 1917.

INFORMATION. Enemy posts have been located at:-

(a) I 26. d. 45.68.

(b) I 32. a. 49.30.

(c) I 31. d. 60.55.

(d) I 31. c. 98.10

2. INTENTION To blow gaps in enemys wire in front of above posts by means of Bangalore Torpedoes, enter his front line trench and secure identification. Bangalore Torpedoes will be blown at Zero hour.

3. DIVERSIONS. To distract enemys attention, Bangalore Torpedoes will also be blown to cut enemy wire at about:-

(e) I.26. b.78.28.

(f) I. 32. a. 58.55.

(g) I. 31. d. 78.60.

(h) O. 1. a. 62.99.

4. PARTIES. The identification parties to go into enemy front line at points indicated in para 1 and for diversions at points indicated in para 3 will be found as under:-

(a) and (e) by "B" Company.

(b) and (f) by "A" Company.

(c) and (g) by "C" Company.

(d) and (h) by "D" Company.

4. PARTIES (CONTINUED) — Each Identification and Diversion Party will consist of 10 Other Ranks who will carry out the Bangalore Torpedoes, place them in position and fire them. Diversion Parties, less two men to fire torpedoes after placing Torpedoes in position will act as covering parties to Identification Parties.

5. POINTS OF EXIT. — Points of Exit from our Front line as under:-

"B" Coy. I.26.a.95.67.
"A" Coy. I.31.b.65.28.
"C" Coy. I.31.d.15.85.
"D" Coy. I.31.c.40.40.

6. LEWIS GUNS. — Each Diversion Party will have One Lewis Gun for use when acting as covering party.

7. MACHINE GUNS. — Arrangements have been made with O.C. 172nd Machine Gun Coy to fire indirect fire to cover noise made by placing of torpedoes in position. At 12.55 (55) A.M., Machine Guns will fire on all emergency routes leading to enemy support lines.

8. ARTILLERY. — Arrangements have been made with Centre Group Artillery to fire on enemy Support line at 1.A.M., to catch enemy when he mans his [illegible] after discharge of Bangalore Torpedoes.

9. OBSERVATION. An Officer from each Compan[y] will be at a convenient pl[ace] in our front line. He will communicate by runner with Company Hqrs.

10. CODE FOR ARTILLERY. Should any Company Comman[der] need Artillery Support he will communicate direct with his covering battery by use of code word "BANGS" followed by map reference. This will be repeated to Battalion Hqrs.

11. ENTRY OF ENEMY FRONT LINE. Entry into Enemy Front line will only be effected by Identification parties i.e. at four points mentioned in para 1.

12. DRESS AND EQUIPMENT. (1) No head dress, other than cap-comforter will be worn.
(2) All ranks except Lewis Gunners will carry rifles and bayonets and two bombs.

13. POSTS IN OUR OWN LINE. All front line posts will be withdrawn at STAND-DOWN to-night. Posts in Support Line covering gaps remain in position and must be warned of light signals (See para. 14.)

14 LIGHT [SIG]NALS. A Single GREEN very light will be fired at zero hour from junction of KIWI AVENUE and STANWAY AVENUE with front line

15. ZERO. Zero hour 12-45 A.M.

R.H. Hayward.
LIEUT,
A.A.T.
2/5th BN. S. LAN. R.

10-8-1917.

ISSUED AT BY RUNNER.

No. 1 Copy to C.O.
" 2 " " O.C., "A" Coy
" 3 " " O.C., "B" Coy
" 4 " " O.C., "C" Coy.
" 5 " " O.C., D. Coy.
" 6 " " H.Q. 172nd Inf. Bde (For Information).
" 7 " " H.Q., Centre Group Artillery.
" 8 " " War Diary.
" 9 " " War Diary.
" 10 " " File.

APPENDIX XXVI

REPORT ON MINOR OPERATIONS CARRIED OUT BY "N" BATTALION ON NIGHT 10th./11th. AUGUST, 1917.

****

ORDERS. See our X.Y.32.

BANGALORE TORPEDOES. These were carried out across N.M.L. and laid in their respective positions. Owing to the bombardment on our left this operation was somewhat delayed. It was about 15 minutes after ZERO before the torpedoes were finally laid in position and an attempt made to light them.

OPERATIONS. A party of 3 N.C.O.'s and 11 O.R. left our trenches at KIWI at 11.15 p.m. with a Bangalore Torpedo which was placed in position at I.26.d.45.68 and the fuse lit about 1 p.m. The detonator exploded but failed to detonate the torpedo. This party lay up for some time close to enemy wire. It then collected the torpedo almost undamaged except the end which had been blown off. The party returned to our lines at 1.45 a.m.
A party of 20 O.R. left SHAFTESBURY AVENUE with two torpedoes and placed them in position at I.32.a.49.30 and I.32.a.58.55 respectively. Neither of the torpedoes went off, although several attempts were made to light them. The probable cause of this was wet fuses.
This party returned at 2 a.m. bringing the torpedoes with them.
A third party of 2 N.C.O.'s and 20 O.R. left our line at I.31.d.15.85 and placed a torpedo in position at I.31.d.50.56. Several attempts were made to light the fuse and it was only after some trouble that the fuse was finally lit. A very small explosion took place but a large volume of smoke rose in the air.
A party then went to examine the spot and found that the torpedo had not detonated. The torpedo was brought back to our lines, and on examination it was discovered that the detonator had exploded but had failed to detonate the H.E. This was probably due to dampness.
A fourth party from the right Company also proceeded from our lines at I.31.c.40.40. with two torpedoes. The right torpedo failed to get into position, but the other was laid in enemy's wire at I.31.c.98.10. The party were in the act of lighting it when an enemy patrol about 20 strong attacked it from the rear. One man who was lighting the fuse was seized by the head by a Boche, but his comrades jumped up and kicked the Boche in the testicles. The Boche dropped without a groan and did not move again. The party then opened fire on the enemy and one fell groaning with several bullets in him. Unfortunately our party were unable to bring back either of the wounded boche, as they were outnumbered and taken by surprise. We sustained one casualty one man being wounded. The torpedo was left in enemy wire.

ARTILLERY. Our artillery opened fire on enemy lines as arranged sweeping support line at irregular intervals with shrapnel opposite points were torpedoes were exploded.

The enemy retaliated on our support line with H.E. and Gas Shells, and put up a considerable number of Very Lights during the operations.

APPENDIX XXVII

INTELLIGENCE REPORT.

From 6 p.m. 10th. Aug. 1917 to 6 a.m., 11th. Aug., 1917.

FLAMENGRIE SUBSECTOR.

(A)
Our Operations.

1. ARTILLERY.	Fired in response to S.O.S. on our left. Shelled enemy Supports in co-operation with our minor operations.
4. M.G.	Indirect fire on enemy's back areas.
6. PATROLS.	See Special Report.
9. AIRCRAFT.	Planes thought to be ours over our lines at 10.15 p.m.
10. GENERAL.	Apart from enemy barrage on our left it has been a fairly quiet period.

(B)
Enemy Operations.

1. ARTILLERY.	At 8.50 p.m. put down a heavy barrage on RUE DU BOIS sub-sector which lasted till about 10.15 p.m. Fairly quiet on this sector. 8 whizz-bangs in KIWI SUPPORTS at 12 .45 a.m. Some 4.2s on PRINCES STREET and Front Line and Supports in vicinity.
2. T.M.	A large number of medium "minnies" on PRINCES STREET and front line and supports in vicinity from 10.5 p.m. to 10.15 p.m. A few pine-apples in KIWI at 11 p.m.
3. M.G.	Active especially in vicinity of WHITE CITY.
5. PATROLS.	See Special Report.
6. DEFENCES.	New soil thrown over parapet on left end of NEAR TRENCH.
9. AIRCRAFT.	A number of hostile aeroplanes over our lines during the night. One plane dropped redlights.
10. MOVEMENT.	Man observed looking over parapet at approx 0.2.c.40.45 OIL TRENCH. Man observed signalling at approx 0.2.c70.20.
GENERAL.	There is a Machine Gun emplacement at 0.1.a.30.47 approximately. Suspected O.P. in house 0.14.b.60.60. Light observed shining on glasses.

APPENDIX XXVIII

COPY OF D.R.O. 1278 DATED 16/8/17.

No. 241404, L/Cpl. HENRY JOHNSON PRESCOTT, "N" Bn.
South Lancs. Regt.

For devotion to duty on the night of August 5th. 1917 in the
.... Subsector S.E. of..................................
A fighting patrol came under fire and 3 men were wounded, one of whom fell into the enemy's wire. L/Cpl. PRESCOTT immediately went to the rescue. After working for some time he found he was unable to extricate the man himself, so went for assistance. He guided a party to the place and finally managed to remove the wounded man to our own lines. It was due to L/Cpl. PRESCOTT's perseverance under continuous fire that the enemy was prevented from making the wounded man a prisoner.

The G.O.C., 57th. Division congratulates the above named on the ~~rxxmxgt~~ receipt of the reward for their gallantry.

16/8/17.

APPENDIX XXIV

SECRET. Copy No. 9

Ref. Map, Sheet 36 N.W.4 1/10,000

2/5th. S. Lan. R.
ORDERS FOR MINOR OPERATION
NO.2.

Ref.No. X.Y.35.
22/8/17

1. INFORMATION. Enemy posts have been located at:-
(1) I.31.c.35.40. (3) I.26.c.98.20.
(2) I.32.c.15.90. (4) I.26.d.45.70.

2. INTENTION. To cut enemy wire in front of above posts by means of Bangalore Torpedoes, enter the front line trench and secure identification.

3. DIVERSION. To distract enemy's attention from points of entry Bangalore Torpedoes will also be exploded in enemy wire at about following points:-
(5) I.31.d.01.28. (7) I.26.c.80.01.
(6) I.32.a.46.35. (8) I.26.b.80.20.

4. PARTIES. Identification parties to enter enemy front line at points in para. 1 and diversion parties to explode torpedoes at points in para 3 will be found as under:-
(1) & (5) by "D" Coy.
(2) & (6) by "C" "
(3) & (7) by "A" Coy.
(4) & (8) by "B" Coy.
Each party will consist of 1 N.C.O. and 10 men who will carry out torpedoes and place them in position. One Sapper will be attached to each Identification Party to fire torpedoes. Diversion parties will fire their own torpedoes.
As soon as the torpedoes have exploded Diversion Parties will throw two bombs per man into enemy wire and return at once to nearest front line post where they will Stand-by.

5 EXIT. Parties will leave our front line at ZERO minus 2 hours as under:-
"D" Coy. I.31.b.40.00.
"C" " STANWAY AVENUE.
"A" " KIWI STREET.
"B" " I.26.a.97.00.

6 ARTILLERY. Arrangements have been made with Centre Group Artillery to fire on enemy Support Line at ZERO plus 15. to catch enemy when he mans the parapet.
A list of M.G. and T.M. emplacements has been handed to O/C Centre Group. These will be dealt with by howitzers on receipt of code-word "CANDLE" followed by numbers of emplacement.

(Continued.)

7. MACHINE-GUNS. Arrangements have been made with O/C 172nd. M.G.Company to fire indirect fire to cover noise made by placing of Bangalore Torpedoes in position. This will continue during the operations.

8. DISPOSITIONS. All Front Line Posts will be reduced to one Lewis Gun with team except those at COLLEGE GREEN and on right of BRIDOUX SALIENT.

9 SYNCHRONIZATION. Watches will be synchronized as under:-

Brigade headquarters.	7 p.m.	By Officer from B.H.Q.
Company H.Q.	10 p.m.	By representatives from Battn. Headquarters.

10. ZERO. Bangalore Torpedoes will be exploded at ZERO hour on night 24/25th. instant. Time to be notified later.

R.Henry Ward
Captain,
Adjutant,
2/5th. S. Lan. R.

Issued at:-

No. 1 Copy to	C/O
2	"A" Coy.
3	"B" "
4	"C"
5	"D"
6	H.Q. Centre Group R.A.
7.	H.Q. 172nd. Inf. Bde. (for information)
8.	O/C 505 F.d. Co. R.E.
9 & 10	War Diary.
11	File.

APPENDIX . XXX

2/5th Battalion SOUTH LANCASHIRE REGIMENT.

STATEMENT
SHOWING ~~FLUCTUATIONS OF~~ STRENGTH

34 Officers. 764 Other Ranks.

Trench Strength 31st August, 1917, 524 Other Ranks.

240 Other Ranks not on trench strength, made up as follows :-

Transport and Grooms.	40
Q.M. Stores.	32
R.A.M.C. (Water duties)	4
Courses of instruction.	38
Hospital.	17
O.R. Sergeant at Base.	1
Rest Camp, 1st Army.	4
Band.	21

Detached

Employed at Brigade & Div.	21
Town Guard, Armentieres.	7
A.P.M., 57th Division.	5
L.T.M.B.	13
M.G. Coy. (Signallers)	4
Brigade Pioneer Coy.	33
Total	240

------------oOo----------------

APPENDIX 

2/5th BATTALION SOUTH LANCASHIRE REGIMENT.

NOMINAL ROLL OF OFFICERS

31st August, 1917.

H E A D Q U A R T E R S.

Lieut-Colonel.	Owen, W.L. M.C.	Commanding Officer.
Major.	Brewis, A.	Second in Command.
Captain.	Wood, R.L.	Medical Officer.
Captain.	Hayward, R.C.	Adjutant.
Lieut.	Gregory, H.	Quartermaster.
Lieut.	Hadfield, J.L.	Bombing Officer.
2/Lieut.	West, H.	Lewis Gun Officer.
2/Lieut.	Tanton, L.E.	Transport Officer.
2/Lieut.	Nimmo, A.A.	Intelligence Officer.
2/Lieut.	St. George, A.R.	Assistant Adjutant.
2/Lieut.	Davies, H.P.W.	Signalling Officer.

"A" C O M P A N Y

Captain.	Donald, T.M.	O.C. Company.
Captain.	Messum, A.W.	Second in Command.
2/Lieut.	Stone, A.R.	Platoon Commander.
2/Lieut.	Hargreaves, R.	Platoon Commander.

"B" C O M P A N Y.

Captain.	Crowe, J.A.	O.C. Company.
2/Lieut.	Bullen, H.J.	Second in Command.
2/Lieut.	Dean, L.M.	Platoon Commander.
2/Lieut.	Clarke, J.	Platoon Commander.
2/LIEUT	BRAZENER. W.F.	PLATOON COMMANDER.

"C" C O M P A N Y.

Captain.	Guest, E.L.	O.C. Company.
2/Lieut.	Le Mare, E.B.	Second in Command
2/Lieut.	Wollett, J.S.	Platoon Commander.
2/Lieut.	Adams, B.C.	Platoon Commander.
~~2/Lieut.~~	~~Brazener, W.F.~~	~~Platoon Commander.~~

"D" C O M P A N Y.

Captain.	Stephenson, C.W.	O.C. Company.
Lieut.	Frodsham, F.J.	Second in Command.
2/Lieut.	Holland, W.H.E.	Platoon Commander.
2/Lieut.	Handley, W.C.	Platoon Commander.

D E T A C H E D.

Captain.	Gould, M.L.B.	Divisional Salvage Officer.
Lieut.	Timson, H.H.	Signal Course, England.
2/Lieut.	Hall, W.S.	172nd Inf. Bde Pioneer Coy.
2/Lieut.	Paul, R.B.	505 R.E. Coy.

H O S P I T A L.

Captain.	Wallis, A.C.
Captain.	Wood, R.H.

----------------oOo-----------------

mins [illegible] ORIGINAL

28031 W3125/M2250 1000m 6/17 M.R.Co.,Ltd. (1367) Forms W3091

Army Form W. 3091.

Cover for Documents.

CONFIDENTIAL

Nature of Enclosures.

WAR DIARY
2/5th S Lan R

FROM 1/9/17

TO 30/9/17

Notes, or Letters written.

WITH APPENDICES
XXII to XXVII

Instructions regarding War Diaries and Intelligence Summaries are contained in F. S. Regs., Part II. and the Staff Manual respectively. Title Pages will be prepared in manuscript.

WAR DIARY

~~or~~

~~INTELLIGENCE SUMMARY~~

(Erase heading not required.)

Army Form C. 2118

Place	Date	Hour	Summary of Events and Information	Remarks and references to Appendices
LA ROLANDERIE	SEPT^R 1st to 3rd 1917		Battalion in billets. A practice gas alarm took place on the night of the 3rd which was satisfactory	
	4th	10am 10.30am	An anti-Aircraft Battery took up a position on RUE DES ACQUETS. This battery opened fire on an enemy aeroplane. About half hr later about 100 5.9's came over in the vicinity of the A.A. Battery position. "A" Company were compelled to evacuate their huts at STREAKY BACON.	a.R.S.G.
		1pm to 1.30pm	A further 20 5.9's came over. There were no casualties. The A.A. battery evacuated their position as soon as the shelling commenced and did not return.	
			The Battalion relieved the 2/9th K.L.R in FLAMENGRIE Subsector at night. The relief passed off satisfactorily and was complete at 11pm. The Lewis Guns and Teams relieved with their platoons which lengthened the relief	a.R.S.G.
FLAMENGRIE SUBSECTOR	5th	8.15 am	A great deal of aerial activity in the early morning. One of our scout machines came down just behind Subsidiary line. The Pilot was slightly injured and the machine badly damaged. A guard	

1875 Wt. W593/826 1,000,000 4/15 J.B.C. & A. A.D.S.S./Forms/C. 2118.

Instructions regarding War Diaries and Intelligence Summaries are contained in F. S. Regs., Part II. and the Staff Manual respectively. Title Pages will be prepared in manuscript.

WAR DIARY

or

~~INTELLIGENCE SUMMARY~~

(Erase heading not required.)

Army Form C. 2118.

Place	Date	Hour	Summary of Events and Information	Remarks and references to Appendices
FLAMENGRIE SUB SECTOR	5th Sept. 1917		was posted, and the machine which had landed nose down, was camouflaged over. Lieut. Col. Owen slightly wounded by piece of shrapnel from 4.2 Howitzer whilst inspecting Lewis Gun positions in the Subsidiary Line	
	6th	1.30am	Gas shell bombardment on front line and support line from KIWI AVENUE to SHAFTESBURY AVENUE. Shells were mostly T.M's. mixed with pineapples. About 300 pineapples were sent over. Gas used appeared to be both phosgene and mustard gas. No casualties	A.R.B.G.
	7th – 9th		A quiet period. On the 8th all officers except 2 from H.Q. and one per Company attended lectures at 3 p.m. in ERQUINGHEM by the C.R.A. and C.R.E 8th Division. The subject of the lectures was the battles round YPRES on July 31st & August 16th.	
	10th		Quiet during the day. Enemy aircraft was very active during the afternoon. An enemy patrol was seen by one of our patrols, who fired on the enemy, but the enemy got away. The enemy sent gas over on the right and left of our Battalion sector, but none reached us.	A.R.B.G.

1875 Wt. W593/826 1,000,000 4/15 J.B.C. & A. A.D.S.S./Forms/C. 2118.

Instructions regarding War Diaries and Intelligence Summaries are contained in F. S. Regs., Part II. and the Staff Manual respectively. Title Pages will be prepared in manuscript.

WAR DIARY

or

~~INTELLIGENCE SUMMARY~~

(Erase heading not required.)

Army Form C. 2118

Place	Date	Hour	Summary of Events and Information	Remarks and references to Appendices
FLAMENGRIE Sub sector BOIS GRENIER	11th Sept. 1917		Generally quiet during the day, the enemy retaliation to our T. M. shoot being weak. Enemy aircraft were fairly active during the day.	
		11 pm.	A patrol of 1 N.C.O. and 15 O.R. left our line at PRINCES Street and layup in N.M.L. They suspected the presence of an enemy patrol some distance to their left so opened fire with Lewis Guns and Rifles. The enemy put up a pink light, and a light barrage of pineapples was immediately put on our trenches in the vicinity of KIWI and TRAMWAY. A machine gun barrage was also put on KIWI and COLLEGE GREEN. Our M.G's. and L.G's immediately opened fire on the gaps and in N.M.L. and rifle Grenades were also fired. Whistles were heard in enemy's line and shouting in N.M.L. A patrol examined the gaps and N.M.L as far as our wire - but no trace of enemy could be found. We had no casualties.	A.R. 8.9.
	12th		Quiet during the day. Our M.G's were firing indirect fire during the afternoon. The battalion was relieved by the 2/9th Bn. H.L.R. The relief was satisfactory and completed by	
		9.25 pm	9.25 pm. The Battalion went into billets at LA ROLANDERIE.	A.R. 8.9.

1875 Wt. W593/826 1,000,000 4/15 J.B.C. & A. A.D.S.S./Forms/C. 2118.

Instructions regarding War Diaries and Intelligence Summaries are contained in F. S. Regs., Part II. and the Staff Manual respectively. Title Pages will be prepared in manuscript.

WAR DIARY

~~or~~

~~INTELLIGENCE SUMMARY~~

(Erase heading not required.)

Army Form C. 2118

Place	Date	Hour	Summary of Events and Information	Remarks and references to Appendices
LA ROLANDERIE	13th Sept 1917		In Billets. Companies re-equipping.	
	14th & 15th		In Billets. All Officers except the Orderly Officer at B.H.Q. and as many N.C.O's as possible attended a demonstration by platoons who have been specially training, in the Attack in the Open. Brigade orders received concerning the relief by the 113th Infantry Brigade. Advance party of the 15th R.W.F. came & see the C.O. and Adjutant. Battalion orders for the relief were issued.	A.P. 8.9.
	16th		In Billets. Parade Service.	
	17th		Battalion relieved by the 15th R.W.F. Advance party consisting of the	
		Left	Adjutant, the four C.Q.M.S's and an N.C.O. from the Transport left for ESTAIRES early in the morning to arrange billets for the Battalion. The relief of the Battalion was complete by 1.30 pm.	
		1.30 pm.	A. B. & C. Companies marched to ESTAIRES where they arrived ~~~~ at 4.45 p.m. and were all settled in billets by 5.30 p.m. "D" Company who had marched from the line, having been there as 5th Company arrived in ESTAIRES at midnight. Lieut-Col. Oats arrived back from hospital	A.P. 8.9

Instructions regarding War Diaries and Intelligence Summaries are contained in F. S. Regs., Part II. and the Staff Manual respectively. Title Pages will be prepared in manuscript.

WAR DIARY
or
~~INTELLIGENCE SUMMARY~~
(Erase heading not required.)

Army Form C. 2118

Place	Date	Hour	Summary of Events and Information	Remarks and references to Appendices
ESTAIRES	18th Sept 1917		The Battalion spent the day & night at ESTAIRES.	
BUSNETTES	19th	8.30 am	The Battalion paraded at 8.30am for the march to BUSNETTES	
		9.16am	The Head of the Battalion passed the starting point CROSS ROADS-LA GORGUE following the 7/10th Bn. K.L.R. The route taken was LA GORGUE-LESTREM-CROSS ROADS Q28d-HINGES-T. ROADS W8D-GONNEHEM and thence to Billets. The Battalion arrived at Billets at 3.30pm. The marching throughout the Battalion was good.	A.R.8.1.9.
LAIRES	20th	9.15am	The Battalion left BUSNETTES and marched to its destination at LAIRES. The route taken was BAS-RIEUX-LILLERS-BOURECQ-S of. St HILAIRE-N of. AUCHY-AU-BOIS-WESTREHEM-FLEBVIN-PALFART-LAIRES The Battalion had a long halt at midday and arrived in Billets at 6p.m. The Brigadier General congratulated the Battalion on its smart appearance and fine marching.	A.R.8.1.9.
LAIRES	21st and 22nd		No training done, and the men were resting after the three days march. All Billets were cleaned up and adjustments made	A.R.8.1.9

1875 Wt. W593/826 1,000,000 4/15 J.B.C. & A. A.D.S.S./Forms/C. 2118.

Instructions regarding War Diaries and Intelligence Summaries are contained in F. S. Regs., Part II. and the Staff Manual respectively. Title Pages will be prepared in manuscript.

WAR DIARY

or

~~INTELLIGENCE SUMMARY~~

(Erase heading not required.)

Army Form C. 2118

Place	Date	Hour	Summary of Events and Information	Remarks and references to Appendices
LAIRES	23rd Sept 1917	10am	Parade Service. The 2nd/3rd Wessex Field Ambulance and the 505 Field Company R.E. also attended. The Battalion was inspected by the G.O.C. 172nd Infantry Brigade at 11.30 am.	[illegible]
	24th to 25th		Battalion Training according to programme for first week	See Appendix XXV
	26th		Draft of 140 other ranks arrived. 80 of these A.S.C. men. Remainder casuals from other units of S. Lan. R. including 2nd, 7th, 8th and 11th.	[illegible]
	27th		C.O. inspected Draft. Very good material but ASC men need further training. Special training instituted for men of draft who have not had previous service in front line trenches. Remainder with Companies.	
	28th		Battalion Sports in afternoon. Very successful.	
	29th		Training as usual. No special feature.	
	30th	9am	G.O.C. 172nd Bde. inspected Battalion in Full Marching order. Very good turnout. B Coy selected by C.O. as smartest Coy on parade.	[illegible]
		4pm	Major A. BREWIS left for England. All ranks very sorry to lose him. Strength of Battalion 30/9/17 — 33 Officers 904 Other Ranks	See Appendices XXVI & XXVII

W. C. Owen [?]
Lieut Col.
2/5th S. Lan. R.

1875 Wt. W593/826 1,000,000 4/15 J.B.C. & A. A.D.S.S./Forms/C. 2118.

APPENDIX XXXII

SECRET. Copy No. 10.

2/5th. S. LAN. R., OPERATION ORDER NO.40.

Ref.Maps,
Sheet 36 & 36A 1/40000
HAZEBROUCK 5A 1/100000

1. BATTALION RELIEF. This Battalion will be relieved by the 15th. R.W.F. on 17th. Sept. 1917.
On relief Companies will proceed independently to billets in ESTAIRES.
Relief of Battalion less "D" Company to be complete by 2 p.m.

2. RELIEF OF COMPANIES. Companies will be relieved as under:-

"A" Coy.	in billets	LA ROLANDERIE FME.	by "A"	Coy.	15 R.W.
"B" "	"	STREAKY BACON.	" "B"	"	" "
"C" "	"	LA ROLANDERIE FME.	" "C"	"	" "
"D" "	in SUBSIDIARY LINE (5th.Coy.)		" "D"	"	" "

3. RELIEF OF 5th. COY. "D" Coy. 15th. R.W.F. will proceed to LA ROLANDERIE FME. remaining there till dusk when relief of 5th. Coy. will take place.

4. GUIDES. Guides will be provided as under:-
5 Guides each from "A", "B"- "C" Coy. (i.e. 1 per platoon and 1 for Company Headquarters.)

2 Guides from Battalion Headquarters.
Report to 2/Lieut. H. WEST on Main Road at ERQUINGHEM CHURCH at 11.15 a.m. 17th. instant.
O/C "C" Coy. will also detail 3 guides to take "D" Coy. 15th. R.W.F. to LA ROLANDERIE FME.
The Transport Officer will arrange to have a guide on the main road at G.18.d.9.7. at 10.30 a.m. to show T.O. 15th. R.W.F. ~~XXXXXXXXXXXXXXXXXXXXX~~ (or representative) position of Transport Lines.
O/C "D" Coy. will send Guides at rate of one per Lewis Gun Team to report to O/C "D" Coy. 15th. R.W.F. at LA ROLANDERIE FME. at 1.30 p.m. to guide teams to trenches and 3 guides for remainder of Company to report at LA ROLANDERIE FME. 6.15 p.m.
Every guide must have a chit showing Company, Platoon and destination.

5. LEWIS GUNS. Lewis Guns, Tin Boxes, etc. of Companies in billets will be taken to Q.M.Stores by 8.30 a.m. on 17th. instant and packed under the supervision of the Lewis Gun Officer
L.G.Limbers will proceed with Companies.
Relief of 5th. Company Guns will take place during afternoon of 17th. instant and will be complete by 5 p.m.
Teams of "D" Coy. 15th. R.W.F. will leave LA ROLANDERIE FME. at 2 p.m.
After relief teams of "D" Coy. 2/5th. S.Lan.R. will remain in Subsidiary Line until Company relief is complete.

(Continued.)

6. ROUTES. Routes from billets and trenches will be as under:-
"A" Coy. LA FLAMENGRIE FME. - via Emergency Road to [illegible] - South to junction of roads at [illegible].18.b.1.[illegible] - RUE DU MOULIN - Main ERQUINGHEM-SAILLY-ESTAIRES Road
"B" Coy. STREAKY BACON - RUE DELETTREE to [illegible] - Emergency Road to RUE DU MOULIN - Main ERQUINGHEM-SAILLY-ESTAIRES Road.
"C" Coy. as for "A" Coy.
"D" Coy. RUE DES CHARLES - [illegible].23.a.7.[illegible] - Emergency Road to RUE DU MOULIN - Main ERQUINGHEM-SAILLY-ESTAIRES Road.
Battn. H.Q. as for "B" Coy.

7. ORDER OF MARCH. "A", "C" & "D" Coys. Battn. H.Q. "B" Coy. will proceed independently after relief.

8. FORMATION. By Platoons in File at 200 yards distance. Platoons will form into Companies at a convenient halt, but not before reaching FORT RAMPU.

9. BAND. The Band will join "A" Coy. as they pass through BAC ST. MAUR.

10. RECEIPTS & CERTIFICATES. Receipts for all Trench and Area Stores (including those on charge of T.O. & Q.M.) and documents, defence schemes etc. also certificates that billets, Transport Lines, Q.M. Stores, and Trenches have been handed over in a clean and sanitary condition will be obtained in triplicate.
Two copies will be sent to Battalion Headquarters immediately handing over is complete.

11. BAGGAGE & STORES. Officers Valises, Baggage, Stores, etc. will be collected by transport on night of 18th. instant and loaded under arrangements made by T.O. & Q.M.
O/C "B" Coy. will send out of the trenches all stores except Lewis Gun Boxes and accessories and a minimum number of dixies on night of 18th. instant.

12. TRANSPORT. First and Second Line Transport, (with exception of L.G. Limbers, Mess Cart and Maltese Cart, which will be loaded at Q.M. Stores on morning of 19th. instant) will proceed to ESTAIRES under arrangements made by T.O.

13. WATER SUPPLY. The Q.M. will arrange to hand over all water-tanks in billets FULL.

14. REPORTS. Reports of completion of relief will be sent by Companies in billets to Battalion Headquarters at ARTILLERY FME. O/C "B" Coy. will report completion of Lewis Gun and Company Relief to O/C FLAMENGRIE Sub-sector.

15. BILLETING PARTIES. Details of Billeting Parties will be issued later. They will meet their Companies at a point outside the Billeting Area which will be notified as soon as known.

(Continued)

18. MARCH DISCIPLINE. The strictest attention must be paid to "182nd. Infantry Brigade Standing Orders for March Discipline" copies of which have been issued to all concerned.

Captain,
Adjutant,
2/5th. S.Lan.R.

Issued through Signals:-

at /8/17.

No. 1 Copy to O/C "A" Coy.
No. 2 Copy to O/C "B" "
No. 3 Copy to O/C "C" "
No. 4 Copy to O/C "D" "
No. 5 Copy to T.O.
No. 6 Copy to Q.M.
No. 7 Copy to H.Q. 182nd.Inf.Bde. (for information.)
No. 8 Copy to O/C 15th. R.W.F.(for information.)
No. 9 File.

SECRET 2/5th Bn. S. Lan. R. COPY. No
Operation orders No 41.
Ref. maps Sept. 18th 17.
Sheet 36A 1/40.000
HAZEBROUK. 5A.

APPENDIX XXXIII

1. On wednesday 19th inst the Battalion will march from ESTAIRES to billets at BUSNETTES and LA VALLEE.

2. STARTING POINT. Cross Roads LA GORGUE (Sheet 36A. L.34 d.)

3. The head of the Battalion will pass the Starting Point at 9-16a.m following 2/10th Bn. K.L.R.

4. Order of March
Signallers and Runners
Headquarters Details.
"D" "A" "B" "C" Coys
Q.M. Personnel.
Transport.
The BAND will march at head of third Company throughout the march. Similarily Q.M. Personnel will march with rear Company.

5. ROUTE:- LA GORGUE - LESTREM - Cross Roads Q 28 d - HINGES - T Roads W 8 d - GONNEHEM - thence to Billets.

6. Intervals of 100 yards will be maintained between Companies.

7. The Battalion will fall in on the alarm post in close column of Companies at 8.30 A.M.

8. Regimental Police will march behind Transport to form rear party.

9. There will be a halt of one hour ~~for~~ mid-day rations. at 12 NOON. mid-day meal. Tea and dry rations. Dinners on arrival in billets.

10. Officers Kits will be dumped at the FACTORY by 7-30 am where T.O. will collect them.

11. Billeting parties will be held in readiness. Details will be issued later.

3.

Issued by runner at ______

R.H. Hayward Capt,
adjt,
2/5th Bn S. Lan. R.

No 1. O.C. A Coy
2. " B "
3. " C "
4. " D "
5. T.O
6. Q.M.
7. FILE

Secret. 2/5th. S. Lan. R. Operation Order No 40. Copy No.

APPENDIX XXXIV

Ref. Maps.
HAZEBROUCK 5A.
Sheet 36A. 1/40000.

19/9/17.

1. The Battalion will march from BUSNETTES to billets at LAIRES tomorrow 20th inst. with 172nd Infantry Brigade Group.

2. Starting Point. Cross Roads BAS RIEUX Sheet 36 A. V 24 b. 1.6.

3. Route. BAS RIEUX – LILLERS – BOURECQ – S of ST. HILAIRE – N of AUCHY-au-BOIS – WESTREHEM – CROSS ROADS 400 yards S of second A in FEBVIN-PALFART – thence to billets.

4. Assembly. Battalion will be ready to march off at 9.15 a.m. Parade in column of route on main road running through BUSNETTES. Head of column at Road Junction V. 14 d 9.7 facing NORTH.

5. Order of March. C – D – A – B – Transport. Headquarters, Band

5. (contd) and Q.M. Personnel will occupy same positions in line of march as today.

6. <u>Packs.</u> Packs will be dumped at same points at which they were unloaded today.
H.Q. and Band's Packs with A Coy. Q.M. Personnel Packs with B Coy.

7. <u>Motor Transport</u> Two Busses and two lorries will be at V 18 a 7.7. at 8 a.m.
The R.S.M. will detail a cyclist to meet lorries at 7.45 a.m.
2/Lt HALL will accompany lorries to LAIRES. A different route to that used by Brigade Column will be taken.

8. 100 yard intervals will be maintained between companies.

9. Halts at ten minutes to each clock hour.

10. <u>Routine</u> Reveillé 6.30 a.m.
Breakfast 7 a.m.
Dry rations for mid-day meal will be issued at Breakfast time.

10 (contd.) Dinners as usual in billets.

11 Billeting Parties composed as today with addition of 1 NCO for Battn HQ. will report to 2/Lt St George at Battn O.R. at 7.20 am. Party will proceed on foot.

Issued by Runner at 9 pm. [signature] Capt.
Adjt
2/5th Sherwd

All Companies
T.O.
Q.M.

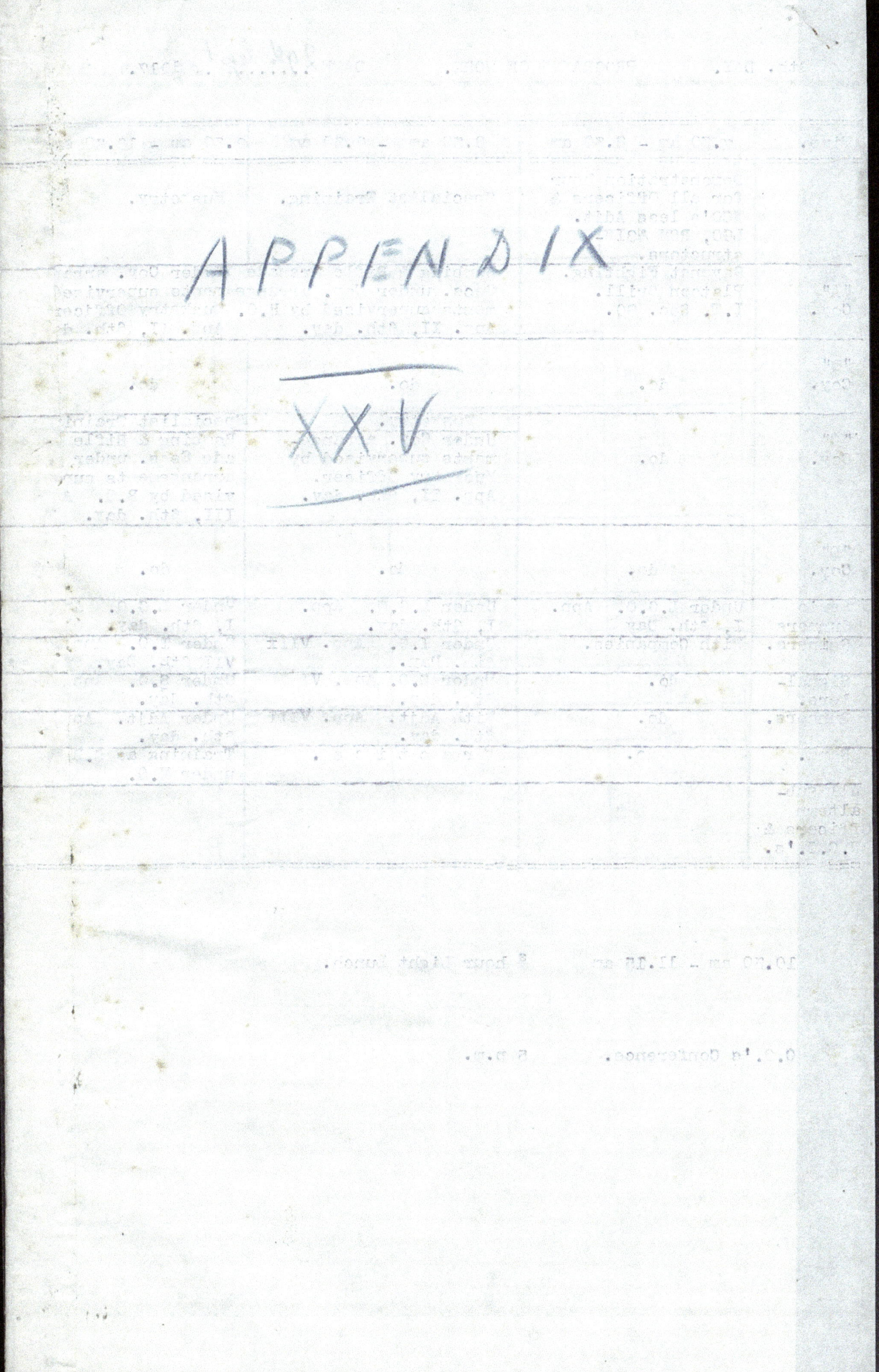
APPENDIX
XXV

6th. DAY.   PROGRAMME OF WORK.   DATE 29th Sept. 1917.   2/5th. S. LAN. R.

Time.	7.30 am - 8.30 am	8.30 am - 9.30 am	9.30 am - 10.30 am	11.15 am - 12 noon	12 - 12.30 p.m	12.30 - 12.45 pm	12.50 - 1.30 pm	
	Demonstration hour for all Officers & NCO's less Adjt. LGO, RSM &SIN-structors.	Specialist Training.	Musketry.	B a t t a l i o n	P a r a d e .			S.B.'s and Sanitary Men under M.O.
"A" Coy.	Bayonet Fighting. Platoon Drill. I.T. Sec. 80.	Bombing & Rifle Grenade Secs. under Coy. arrangements supervised by B.O. App. II, 6th. day.	Under Coy. arrangements supervised by Musketry Officer. App. II, 6th. day.	Trench to Trench Attack. App. X.	Open Attack. App. X.	Mash Past.	Foot Inspection at disposal of Coy. Commanders	
"B" Coy.	do.	do.	do.	do.	do.	do.	Range.	
"C" Coy.	do.	Musketry. Under Coy. arrangements supervised by Musketry Officer. App. II, 6th. day.	Specialist Training. Bombing & Rifle Grenade Secs. under Coy arrangements supervised by B.O. App. III, 6th. day.	do.	do.	do.	Foot Inspection at disposal of Coy Commanders	
"D" Coy.	do.	do.	do.	do.	do.	do.	do.	
Lewis Gunners	Under L.G.O. App. I, 6th. Day	Under L.G.O. App. I, 6th. day.	Under L.G.O. App. I, 6th. day.	do.	do.	do.	With Coys. except "B"	
Snipers.	With Companies.	Under I.O. App. VII 6th. Day.	Under I.O. App. VII 6th. Day.	do.	do.	do.	do.	
Signallers.	do.	Under S.O. App. VI 6th. day.	Under S.O. App. VI 6th. day.	do.	do.	do.	do.	
Runners.	do.	With Adjt. App. VIII 6th. day.	Under Adjt. App. VIII 6th. day.	do.	do.	do.	do.	
Band.	do.	P r a c t i c e .	Training as S.B.'s under M.O.	P r a c t i c e .		do.	do.	
All Subaltern Officers & N.C.O.'s.							Adjutant's Parade.	

10.30 am - 11.15 am   ¾ hour Light Lunch.

C.O.'s Conference.   5 p.m.

5th. DAY. PROGRAMME OF WORK. DATE 28th Sept. 1917. 2/5th. S. LAN. R.

Time.	7.30 am - 8.30 am	8.30 am - 9.30 am	9.30 am - 10.30 am	11.15 - 12 noon	12.15 - 12.30 p.m	12.30 - 12.45 pm	12.50 - 1.50 pm
	Demonstration hour for all Officers & NCO's less Adjt. LGO, RSM & 8 instructors.	Musketry.	Specialist Training.	B a t t a l i o n P a r a d e .			
"A" Coy.	Bayonet Fighting & Platoon Drill. (T.F Secs 78 - 79.)	Under Coy. arrangements supervised by Musketry Officer. App. II, 5th. Day.	Bombing & Rifle Grenade Secs. under Coy. arrange-ments supervised by B.O. App. III, 5th.day.	Trench to trench Attack. App. X	Open Attack. App. X.	March past.	Range.
"B" Coy.	do.	do	do.	do.	do.	do.	Foot Inspection At disposal of Coy.Commander.
"C" Coy.	do.	Specialist Training Bombing & Rifle Grenade Secs. under Coy. arrangements supervisedby B.O. App. III, 5th. day.	Musketry. Under Coy. arrangements supervised by Musketry Officer. App. II, 5th. day.	do.	do.	do.	do.
"D" Coy.	do.	do.	do.	do.	do.	do.	do.
Lewis Gunners	Under L.G.O. App. I, 5th. day.	Under L.G.O. App. I, 5th. day.	Under L.G.O. App. I, 5th. day.	do.	do.	do.	With Companies except "A" Coy.
Snipers.	With Companies.	Under I.O. App. VII, 5th. day.	Under I.O., App. VI, 5th. day.	do.	do.	do.	With Coys.
Signallers.	do.	Under S.O. App. VI 5th. day.	Under S.O. App. VI 6th. day.	do	do.	do.	do.
Runners.	do.	With Companies.	Under Adjt. App. VIII 5th. day.	do.	do.	do.	do.
Band.	do.	P r a c t i c e .	Training as S.B.'s under M.O.	P r a c t i c e .		do.	do.
All Subaltern Officers & NCO's.							Adjutant's Parade.

S.B.'s and Sanitary Man under M.O.

SPORTS. 3.30 p.m.

10.30 a.m. - 11.15 a.m. 8 hour Light Lunch.

C.O.'s Conference 6 p.m.

N I G H T W O R K.
****
(28/9/17)

CONSOLIDATION OF AN IRREGULAR SYSTEM OF SHELL HOLES.

Each Company will train as follows:-
1. One Platoon will cover Patrol. (Protection, Reconnaissance, Reporting
2. One Platoon will wire in Strong Point.
3. One Platoon will consolidate irregular system of shell-holes.

If a fourth platoon is available a C.T. will be dug back to an imaginary line.
Positions will be selected and shell-holes dug under directions of the Adjutant the previous afternoon.
Companies will dig each others shell-holes, and no reconnaissance will be made by daylight.
Message cards will be used.
Connecting files and advance guards and rear-guards will be practised march to and from billets with S.B.R. worn.

4th DAY.   PROGRAMME OF WORK.   DATE 27th Sept 1917.   2/5th Bn. S.LAN. R.

Time	7-30 - 8-30 am	8-30 am - 9-30 am	9-30 am - 10-30 am.	11-15 am - 12 noon.	12 - 12-30 p.m.	12-30 - 12-45 p.m.	12-50 - 1-30
	Demonstration hour for all Officers & N.C.Os less Adjt LGO & S Instrs.	Specialist Training.	Musketry.	Battalion	Parade.	Bn. Parade.	
"A" Coy.	Bayonet Fighting & Platoon Drill. I.T. Sec. 76 &77.	Bombing & Rifle Grenades Secs. under Coy. arrangements supervised by Bn. BO App. 111, 4th day.	Under Coy arrangements supervised by Bn. Musketry Officer. App. 11, 4th day.	Trench to Trench Attack. See App. X.	Open Attack. See App. X.	March Past.	Foot Inspection at disposal of Coy Commanders.
"B" Coy.	do	do	do	do	do	do	do
"C" Coy.	~~Musketry~~ do	Musketry. Under Coy. arrangements supervised by Battn. M.O. App. 11 4th day.	Specialist Training. Bombing & Rifle Grenade Secs. under Coy. arrangements supervised by B.O. App. 111, 4th day.	do	do	do	do
"D" Coy.	do	do	do	do	do	do	do
Lewis Gun Teams.	Under L.G.O. App. 1, 4th day.	Under L.G.O. App. 1, 4th day.	Under L.G.O. App. 1, 4th day.	do	do	do	do
Snipers.	With Companies.	Under I.O. App. V11, 4th day.	Under I.O. App. V11, 4th day.	do	do	do	do
Singallers.	do	Under S.O. App. V1, 4th day.	Under S.O. App. V1, 4th day.	do	do	do	do
Runners.	do	With Companies.	Under Adjt. App. V111, 4th day.	do	do	do	do
Band.	do	Practice.	Training as S.B's under M.O.	P r a c t i c e		do	do
All Subaltern Officers & N.C.O's.							Adjutant's Parade.

S.B's and Sanitary Men under M.O.

¾ hour Interval. Light lunch under Company arrangements.

C.O's Conference at 6-0 P.M.

3rd. DAY. PROGRAMME OF WORK. DATE 26th Sept. 1917. 2/5th. S. LAN. R.

Time.	7.30 am - 8.30 am	8.30 am - 9.30 am	9.30 am - 10.30 am	11.15 - 12 noon	12 - 12.30 p.m	12.30 pm - 12.45 pm	12.50 - 1.50
	Demonstration hour for all Officers & NCO's less Adjt. LGO, RSM & 8 instructors.	Musketry.	Specialist Training.	B A T T A L I O N	P A R A D E.		
"A" Coy.	Gas Drill. Box Helmet & Inspection Squad Drill. (I.T. Sec. 18 - 46.)	Under Coy. arrangements supervised by Musketry Officer. App. II, 3rd. Day.	Bombing & Rifle Grenade Secs. under Coy. Instructors supervised by Battn. B.O. App. III 3rd. Day.	Rapid Wiring App. IV.	Strong Point Construction Drill. App. V.	March past.	Foot Inspection. At disposal of Coy. Commander.
"B" Coy.	do.	do.	do.	do.	do.	do.	do.
"C" Coy.	do.	Specialist Training Bombing & Rifle Grenade Secs. under Coy. Instructors supervised by B.O. App. III, 3rd. day.	Musketry. Under Coy. arrangements supervised by Musketry Officer. App. II, 3rd. day.	do.	do.	do.	Range.
"D" Coy.	do.	do.	do.	do.	do.	do.	Foot Inspection at disposal of Coy. Commanders.
Lewis Gunners.	Under L.G.O. App. I, 3rd. day.	Under L.G.O. App. I, 3rd. day.	Under L.G.O. App. I, 3rd. day.	do	do.	do.	With Coys.
Snipers.	With Coys.	Under I.O. App. VIII, 3rd. day.	Under I.O. App. VII 3rd. day.	do	do.	do.	do.
Signallers.	do.	Under S.O. App. VI, 3rd. day.	Under S.O. App. VI 3rd. day.	do.	do.	do.	do.
Runners.	do.	Under Adjt. App. VIII, 3rd. day.	Under Adjt. App. VIII 3rd. day.	do	do.	do.	do.
Band.	do.	P r a c t i c e.	Training as S.B.'s under M.O.	P r a c t i c e,		do.	do.
All Subaltern Officers & NCO's.							Adjutant's Parade.

S.B.'s and Sanitary Men under M.O. Appendix IX

10.30 a.m. - 11.15 am. ¾ hour Light Lunch.

2nd. DAY. PROGRAMME OF WORK. DATE 25th Sept. 1917. 2/5th. S. LAN. R.

Time.	7.30 am - 8.30 am	8.30 am - 9.30 am	9.30 - 10.30 a.m.	11.15 am - 12 noon	12 - 12.30 pm	12.30 pm - 12.45 pm	12.50 - 1.50 pm	
	Demonstration hour for all Officers & NCO's less Adjt. LGO & 6 Instructors & RSM.	Musketry.	Specialist Training.	B a t t a l i o n	P a r a d e.			S.B.'s and Sanitary Men under M.O. Appendix IX.
"A" Coy.	Bayonet Fighting & Squad Drill. (I.T. Sec. 12 - 46)	Under Coy. arrangements supervised by Musketry Officer. App. II, 2nd. day.	Bombing & Rifle Grenade Secs. under Coy. arrangements supervised by Bn. B.O. App. III, 2nd. day.	Rapid Wiring. Appendix IV.	Strong Point Construction Drill. App. V.	March past.	Foot Inspection at disposal of Coy. Commander.	
"B" Coy.	do.	do.	do.	do	do	do.	Range.	
"C" Coy.	do.	Specialist Training Bombing & Rifle Secs under Coy. arrangements supervised by B.O. App. III 2nd. day.	Musketry. Under Coy. arrangements supervised by Musketry Officer. App. II 2nd. day.	do	do.	do.	Foot Inspection at disposal of Coy. Commander.	
"D" Coy.	do.	do.	do.	do.	do.	do.	do.	
Lewis Gunners	Under L.G.O. App. I 2nd. day.	Under L.G.O. App. I. 2nd. day.	Under L.G.O. App. I 2nd. day.	do.	do.	do.	With Coys.	
Snipers.	With Companies.	Under I.O. See App VII 2nd. day.	Under I.O. App. VII 2nd. day.	do.	do.	do.	do.	
Signallers	do.	Under S.O. App. VI 2nd. day.	Under S.O. App. VI 2nd. day.	dó.	do.	do.	do.	
Runners.	do.	With Coys.	Under Adjt. App. VIII 2nd. day.	do.	do.	do.	do.	
Band.	do.	P r a c t i c e.	Training as S.B.'s under M.O.	P r a c t i c e.		do.	do.	
All Subaltern Officers & NCO's.							Adjutant's Parade.	

10.30 am. - 11.15 am. ¾ hour. Light Lunch. under Company arrangements.

1st. DAY. PROGRAMME OF WORK. DATE 24th Sept 1917. 2/5th. S. LAN. R.

Time.	7.30 am - 8.30 am	8.30 am - 9.30 am	9.30 am - 10.30 am	11.15 am - 12 noon	12 noon - 12.30 pm	12.30 - 12.45 pm	12.50 pm - 1.50
	Demonstration hour for all Officers, & NCO's less Adjt. RSM & Instructors per Company.	Specialist Training.	Musketry.	B a t t a l i o n P a r a d e .			
"A" Coy.	Gas Drill with P.H. Helmet & Inspection Squad Drill. (I.T. Sec.18 to 46.)	Bombing & Rifle Grenade Secs. under Coy. Instructors. Supervised by B.O. See. App. III. 1st. day.	Under Coy. arrangements supervised by Battn. Musketry Officer. See App. II, 1st. day.	Rapid Wiring. See App. IV.	Strong Point Construction. Drill. See App. V.	March Past.	Range.
"B" Coy.	do.	do.	do.	do.	do.	do.	Foot Inspection at disposal of Company Commanders.
"C" Coy.	do.	Musketry. Under Coy. arrangements. Supervised by Musketry Officer See App. II, 1st. day.	Specialist Training. Bombing & Rifle Grenade Secs. under Coy. Instructors supervised by Battn. B.O. See. App III 1st.day	do.	do.	do.	
"D" Coy.	do.	do.	do.	do.	do.	do.	do.
Lewis Gunners	Under L.G.O. (1st. day App. I.)	Under L.G.O. App. I, 1st. day.	Under L.G.O. App. I 1st. day.	do.	do.	do.	With Coys.
Snipers	With Coys.	Under I.O. See App. VII, 1st. day.	Under I.O. see App. VII, 1st. day.	do.	do.	do.	do.
Signallers.	do.	Under Bn. S.O. See App. VI. 1st. day.	Under Bn. S.O. See. App. VI 1st. day.	do.	do.	do.	do.
Runners.	do.	With Companies.	Under Adjt. See App. VIII.	do.	do.	do.	do.
Band.	do.	P r a c t i c e.	Training as S.B.'s under M.O.	P r a c t i c e.		do.	do.
All. Subaltern Officers & NCO's.							Adjutant's Parade.

S.B.'s and Sanitary Men under M.O. See. App. IX.

10.30 a.m. - 11.15 a.m. Lunch will be served under Company arrangements.

2 p.m. Dinners.

APPENDIX XXVI

2/5th Battalion South Lancashire Regiment.

NOMINAL ROLL OF OFFICERS.

30th September, 1917.

HEADQUARTERS.

Lieut-Colonel	Owen, W.L. M.C.	Commanding Officer.
Major (Captain)	Brewis, A.	Second in Command.
Captain (Lieut.)	Hayward, R.C.	Adjutant.
2/Lieut.	St George, A.R.	Assistant Adjutant.
Lieut.	Gregory, H.	Quartermaster.
2/Lieut.	West, H.	Lewis Gun Offizer.
2/Lieut.	Tanton, L.E.	Transport Officer.
2/Lieut.	Nimmo, A.A.	Intelligence Officer.
2/Lieut.	Davies, H.P.W.	Signalling Officer.
2/Lieut.	Stone, A.R.	Bombing Officer.
Captain	Wood, R.L.	Medical Officer.

"A" COMPANY.

Captain (Lieut)	Donald, T.M.	O.C. Company.
Captain (2Lieut)	Messum , A.W.	Second in Command.
2/Lieut.	Hargreaves, R.	Platoon Commander.

"B" COMPANY.

Captain (Lieut)	Crowe, J.A.	O.C. Company.
2/Lieut.	Brazener, W.F.	Second in Command.
2/Lieut.	Bullen, H.G.	Platoon Commander.
2/Lieut.	Dean, L.M.	Platoon Commander.
2/Lieut.	Clarke, J.	Platoon Commander.

"C" COMPANY.

Captain (2Lieut)	Guest, E.L.	O.C. Company.
2/Lieut.	Le Mare, E.B.	Second in Command.
2/Lieut.	Woollett, J.S.	Platoon Commander.
2/Lieut.	Adams, B.C.	Platoon Commander.

"D" COMPANNY.

Captain	Stephenson, C.W.	O.C. Company.
Lieut.	Frodsham, F.J.	Second in Command.
2/Lieut.	Holland, W.H.E.	Platoon Commander.
2/Lieut.	Hall, W.S.	Platoon Commander.
2/Lieut.	Handley, W.C.	Platoon Commander.

DETACHED.

Captain	Gould, M.L.B.	C.R.E.S.O. (Director of Wks
2/Lieut.	Paul, R.B.	505 Fld Coy, R.E.

HOSPITAL

Captain (Lieut)	Wallis, A.C.

COURSES.

Lieut.	Timson, H.H.	Signal Course, Dunstaple.
Lieut.	Hadfield, J.L.	1st Army School.

APPENDIX - XXVIII

2/5th Battalion South Lancashire Regiment.

STATEMENT
SHOWING STRENGTH

30th September, 1917.

33 OFFICERS. 904 OTHER RANKS.

		Officers	Other Ranks.
(a)	On Parade.	22	705
(b)	Off Parade. (With Unit)	3	119
(c)	Detached.	8	80
	Total.	33	904

Column "B"

	Officers	Other Ranks.
Transport.	-	46
Q.M. Personnel.	1 (Q.M.)	18
Orderly Bugler.	-	1
Company Clerks.	-	4
Cooks.	-	14
Officers Cooks.	-	6
Despatch Riders.	-	2
Police.	-	7
Orderly Room Staff.	1 (Asst Adjt)	3
Canteen.	-	2
Medical Staff.	1 (M.O)	7
Sick (Off Duty)	-	7
Isolated.	-	2
Total	3	119

Column "C"

	Officers	Other Ranks
Division	-	4
Brigade.	-	7
M.G.Coy.	-	10
Hospital.	1	6
A.P.M.	-	4
Courses.	2	27
xi Corps School.	-	5
L.T.M.B.	-	9
505 Coy, R.E.	1	1
Leave.	3	4
Base.	-	1
Army School.	-	1
Trade Test.	-	1
Director of Works.	1	-
Total.	8	80

-------------oOo-------------

Instructions regarding War Diaries and Intelligence Summaries are contained in F. S. Regs., Part II. and the Staff Manual respectively. Title Pages will be prepared in manuscript.

WAR DIARY

~~or~~

~~INTELLIGENCE SUMMARY~~

(Erase heading not required.)

Army Form C. 2118

2/5 S Lanc Rgt
Vol 9

Place	Date	Hour	Summary of Events and Information	Remarks and references to Appendices
LAIRES	1917 1st October		Training. Major A. H. Schultz returned from Senior Officers Course at ALDERSHOT and took over Second in Command.	A.P. & G.
	3rd & 4th		Training. A Battalion dinner was held for the men on the afternoon of the 4th. Very heavy rain fell during the dinner, which marred the proceedings, but the men enjoyed the dinner given them, which consisted of Pork - Vegetables and Apple Sauce - Pudding and free Beer. The Battalion won 2nd place in the Brigade Signalling Competition	APPENDIX XXVIII APPENDIX XXVIII
	5th		Training. "B" Company were sent up for the Brigade Company Efficiency Test, which they won. This was most satisfactory, as it means that "B" Coy are the best Company in the Brigade. Capt. Glynn G.S.O. 3 57th Division gave a lecture in the afternoon to Officers and N.C.O's on "Instruction in the use of Pill Boxes and methods of dealing with same" illustrated by Air Photographs. Orders received that the Commander in Chief would inspect the Brigade on the 6th.	A.P. & G. APPENDIX XXVIII

1875 Wt. W593/826 1,000,000 4/15 J.B.C. & A. A.D.S.S./Forms/C. 2118.

Instructions regarding War Diaries and Intelligence Summaries are contained in F. S. Regs., Part II. and the Staff Manual respectively. Title Pages will be prepared in manuscript.

WAR DIARY

~~or~~

~~INTELLIGENCE SUMMARY~~

(Erase heading not required.)

Army Form C. 2118

Place	Date	Hour	Summary of Events and Information	Remarks and references to Appendices
LAIRES	1917 6th October		The Battalion moved off at 7.45am to be inspected by Sir Douglas Haigh. The weather was very wet and cold, but the C in C was very pleased with the outturn under adverse circumstances.	A.R. 8.9.
	7th		Weather still very wet. The Battalion attended a joint service with the 2/10th Bn K.L.R., at which the G.O.C. Division was present. At the conclusion of the service the Battalion marched past the G.O.C. Brigade Sports were cancelled owing to the bad weather.	
	8th		Training. Battalion did Trench to Trench attack in the morning. Very wet weather in the afternoon	APPENDIX XXVIII
	9th		Training in the morning which consisted of rapid wiring. The Battalion left billets at midnight to proceed to ENGUINATTE to take part in the Brigade Trench to Trench attack.	A.R. 8.9.
	10th	4.30 am.	The Battalion arrived at the Assembly Point at 4.30 am. The men had previously been issued with hot tea, rum and a buiscuit. The night was good for marching, and the weather fine. Zero hour was fixed for 5.30 am. Rain started about	APPENDIX XXIX A.R. 8.9.

1875 Wt. W593/826 1,000,000 4/15 J.B.C. & A. A.D.S.S./Forms/C. 2118.

Instructions regarding War Diaries and Intelligence Summaries are contained in F. S. Regs., Part II. and the Staff Manual respectively. Title Pages will be prepared in manuscript.

WAR DIARY

~~or INTELLIGENCE SUMMARY~~

(Erase heading not required.)

Army Form C. 2118

Place	Date	Hour	Summary of Events and Information	Remarks and references to Appendices
LAIRES	1917 10th Oct.		5 a.m. and continued steadily during the proceedings. The frontage allotted to the Brigade was about 600 yards, and the Battalion had to capture and consolidate the left half of the Second and Final objectives with the 1/9th K.L.R. on its right. The proceedings	APPENDIX XXIX
		8 a.m.	finished at 8 a.m., after which the G.O.C. Division spoke to all Officers. The men had breakfast and then marched back to Billets. In the afternoon Major Schultz and Second in Command of Companies attended a Lecture at WESTREHEM by Major Fuller D.S.O. on "Cooperation of Tanks and Infantry".	A.P.S.9.
	11th		Training. In the Afternoon the Brigade sports were held. The weather was very fine, and the sports went off very well. Tea for the men was served on the ground and the Canteen was also on the ground.	APPENDIX XXVIII A.P.S.9.
	12th		In the afternoon the Brigade Signalling Officer gave a lecture to the N.C.O.'s on the use of Pigeons in the Field. Major Schultz also lectured to the Officers and N.C.O.'s on "Cooperation of Tanks and Infantry".	A.P.S.9.

1875 Wt. W593/826 1,000,000 4/15 J.B.C. & A. A.D.S.S./Forms/C. 2118.

Instructions regarding War Diaries and Intelligence Summaries are contained in F. S. Regs., Part II. and the Staff Manual respectively. Title Pages will be prepared in manuscript.

WAR DIARY

~~or INTELLIGENCE SUMMARY~~

(Erase heading not required.)

Army Form C. 2118

Place	Date	Hour	Summary of Events and Information	Remarks and references to Appendices
LAIRES	1917 October 13th		The Battalion left billets at 7am marched to ENGUINATTE, and again carried out Brigade Trench to Trench Attack. The C.O. held a conference in the afternoon for all Officers and N.C.O's	AD 81.9
	14th		Church parade in the morning. Seven new Officers joined the Battalion for duty	
			Lieut. R.L. LEAKE from 2nd S. Lan. R.	
			2/Lieut. I.W.F. AGABEG from 2nd S. Lan. R.	
			2/Lieut. S.J. MILTON from 5th LEICESTER REGT.	AD 81.9
			2/Lieut. P.F. QUINTON from 5th LEICESTER -"-	
			2/Lieut. J.G. HALL from 4th LEICESTER -"- T.F.	
			2/Lieut. W.H. FARMER from 1/5th LEICESTER -"- T.F.	
			2/Lieut. A.C. CASTLE from 4th LEICESTER -"- T.F.	
			Received orders that expected move had been postponed for 3 days.	
	15th		The Battalion trained in the morning. The G.O.C. Brigade was present at the Operations. The Adjutant and Assistant Adjutant attended a conference at Brigade in the afternoon when points on the issue of Operation Orders was discussed.	APPENDIX XXVIII

Instructions regarding War Diaries and Intelligence Summaries are contained in F. S. Regs., Part II. and the Staff Manual respectively. Title Pages will be prepared in manuscript.

WAR DIARY

~~or INTELLIGENCE SUMMARY~~

(Erase heading not required.)

Army Form C. 2118

Place	Date	Hour	Summary of Events and Information	Remarks and references to Appendices
LAIRES	1917 Octbr 16th		Training. Lecture by Capt. Wade M.G.C. to all Officers and N.C.Os	A.R. 8.9
	17th		The day was spent in preparing for the move on the 18th.	
LAIRES	18th	8.15	The Battalion left LAIRES, and marched to Billets in the RENESCURE area. The march was approximately 17 miles. A midday halt was made at 12.50 pm till 2 p.m., when the men had a hot meal. Packs were taken off here, and dumped on the road where motor lorries had to bring them along to the billeting area. The Battalion arrived in the RENESCURE area at 4.45 pm and were all in billets at 5.30 pm. Only half the packs were brought by motor lorry, the remainder arriving the next morning.	APPENDIX XXV XXXI A.R. 8.9
RENESCURE	19th		The Battalion left billets at 10.30 am - there being some delay owing to the fact that ~~all~~ packs arrived just before starting. The Battalion marched to the embussing point, and embussed at 12.30 noon, & proceeded to PROVEN. PROVEN was reached at 4.45 p.m. where the Battalion debussed and marched to camp about 2 miles away. The camp consisted of tents and "bivvies".	A.R. 8.9

1875 Wt. W593/826 1,000,000 4/15 J.B.C. & A. A.D.S.S./Forms/C. 2118.

Instructions regarding War Diaries and Intelligence Summaries are contained in F. S. Regs., Part II. and the Staff Manual respectively. Title Pages will be prepared in manuscript.

WAR DIARY

or

~~INTELLIGENCE SUMMARY~~

(Erase heading not required.)

Army Form C. 2118

Place	Date	Hour	Summary of Events and Information	Remarks and references to Appendices
PROVEN	1917 October 20th to 23rd		In Camp. Practice Assemblys were held. Gas Drill and Physical training were also carried out, with games in the Afternoon.	A.P. 8.9
	25th		Major A.H. Schultz, 3 Officers and 54 Other Ranks left for the XIV Corps Reinforcement Camp - HERZEELE	
	24th	2 pm.	Moved from PRIVETT CAMP to PRATTLE CAMP - PROVEN AREA	A.P. 8.9
	25th		In Camp. Inspections etc. Weather very bad.	
	26th	6 pm.	Received orders from Brigade to prepare for a sudden move.	
		9 pm.	Orders came from Brigade that the battalion would entrain from PROVEN STATION at 1 a.m. on the 27th. The Battalion left PRATTLE CAMP at 11.30 pm. Entrain at PROVEN Station for ELVERDINGHE. The transport proceeded by road.	A.P. 8.9
ELVERDINGHE	27th	3 a.m.	The Battalion arrived at BRIDGE CAMP and men 'got down' as soon as possible. During the day, inspection of S.A.A. gas appliances, rifles etc. Weather fine and cold.	
	28th	8 a.m.	The C.O. Adjutant and Company Commanders went up the line to reconnoitre. C.O. also attended Commanding Officers Conference at Brigade Headquarters.	A.P. 8.9

1875 Wt. W593/826 1,000,000 4/15 J.B.C. & A. A.D.S.S./Forms/C. 2118.

Instructions regarding War Diaries and Intelligence Summaries are contained in F. S. Regs., Part II. and the Staff Manual respectively. Title Pages will be prepared in manuscript.

WAR DIARY
or
INTELLIGENCE SUMMARY
(Erase heading not required.)

Army Form C. 2118

Place	Date	Hour	Summary of Events and Information	Remarks and references to Appendices
ELVERDINGHE	1917 October 29th		Capt. Guest and the Asst. Adjt. reconnoitred MARSUIN CAMP accompanied by 2 H.Q. Runners. The M.O. visited the Medical Relay Post at GALLWITZ FARM and the A.D.S. at FUSILEER FARM. Company Officers also went to reconnoitre various points. The T.O. and Q.M. reconnoitred tracks for taking pack animals. The C.O. Adjutant and all available Officers visited Brigade Headquarters and examined raised map of Divisional Front. C.O's conference for Officers in the evening.	A.R. 8. 9.
	30th		The Adjutant - Bombing Officer and Company Commanders reconnoitred various points. Lieut HARGREAVES and 2 N.C.O's went on a reconnoitring patrol in the evening.	A.R. 8. 9.
	31st		Signalling Officer - Bombing Officer and Capt. E.L. Guest went reconnoitring.	
		9.30 pm	At 9.30 p.m. enemy aeroplanes bombed the camp severely, causing several casualties in the Camp, but only 1 Casualty in this Unit. Several horses were also killed - including one of our riders.	A.R. 8. 9
			Strength of Battalion. Officers 39. Other Ranks 913.	App. XXXII / XXXIII

D.J. Oakes [signature]
Lieut. Col.
2/5th S. Lan. R.

1875 Wt. W593/826 1,000,000 4/15 J.B.C. & A. A.D.S.S./Forms/C. 2118.

APPENDIX
XXIX

Copy No.......

BRIGADE TRENCH TO TRENCH ATTACK.

2/5th. S. Lan. R, Preliminary Orders.

Ref. Maps,
BOMY, 1/20,000
THEROUANNE 1/40000

4th. Oct., 1917.

1. The Battalion will take part in a Brigade Practice Trench to Trench Attack which will take place at dawn 10th. instant. The March to Special Manoeuvre Area will be on 9th. instant, and assembly for assault on night 9/10th. instant.

2. Company Commanders and Signalling Officer went over the ground on 3rd. instant.

3. There will be two objectives:-
   (a) Enemy Front and Support Lines.
   (b) Line from about R.22.b.30.75 to 23.a.80.20.

4. The frontage allotted to the Brigade is about 600 yards.

5. The 2/10th. K.L.R. will capture and consolidate the First Objective on the whole frontage.
This Battalion will capture and consolidate the left half of the Second and Final Objectives with the 2/9th. K.L.R. on its Right.
The 2/4th. S. Lan. R. less one Company will be in Brigade Reserve and will form a Defensive Flank on the Left after the capture of the Second objective.

6. One Company of 2/4th. S. Lan. R. will represent barrage, garrison enemy strong points etc.

7. The barrage will be represented by flags and will move forward as under:-
Z to Z plus 12   100 yards in 4 minutes.
Z plus 12 onwards 100 yards in 6 minutes.

8. The Battalion will assemble on a three Company frontage. Each Company's frontage 100 yards. Order of Companies from Left A.B.C. "D" Company will be in reserve and will follow 200 yards in rear of last wave of "B" Company.

9. Machine Guns have been allotted definite tasks by Brigade.

10. Three Trench Mortars will be attached to the Battalion to deal with Strong Points etc.
"D" Coy. will find necessary carrying parties for these.

11. Dress:- Fighting Kit as laid down.

12. Action of Lewis Guns.
   (a) When the Final objective has been captured the barrage will move on to a line in which 60 disappearing targets have been constructed. Men representing barrage will act as markers to manipulate targets.
   (b) When barrage advances Lewis Guns will push forward in to shell holes to cover consolidation.
   (c) Targets will be raised once or several times to represent counter attacks.
   Lewis Guns will open fire immediately on these targets.

Continued.

13. Precautions.
(a) As soon as Companies have assembled Rifles and pouches will be examined and O.'s C. Coys. will report to Battn. H.Q. in writing that magazines and pouches are empty.
(b) No ball ammunition will be carried except for Lewis Guns.
(c) Lewis Guns will be carried forward without magazine on the gun. Magazines will be placed on guns when they push forward into shell holes.

14. 2/Lt. A.A. NIMMO will act as "Marking-out" Officer to the Battalion with Capt. A. W. MESEUM as Assistant. Necessary rope, pickets, distinguishing marks etc. will be prepared and ready by 8th. instant.

15. Further details will be issued when received.

16. Transport Arrangements will be notified later.

R.C. Hayward
Captain,
Adjutant,
2/5th. S. Lan. R.

No. 1 Copy to O/C "A" Coy.
2 " to O/C "B" "
3 " to O/C "C" "
4 " to O/C "D" Coy.
5 " 2/Lt. NIMMO.
6 " H.Q. 172nd. Inf. Bde. (for information.)
7 & 8 Spare.

BRIGADE TRENCH TO TRENCH ATTACK.

(October 9/10th. 1917)

* * *

Ref.Maps,
BOMY
1/20,000.
THEROUANNE.
1/40,000.

9/10/17.

In continuation of preliminary orders dated 4/10/17.

1. The Battalion will march direct from billets to ENGUINATTE, via FLECHIN.

2. The Battalion Starting Point will be the Cross Roads X.28.b.6.5. The order of march will be:- A B C D. The Battalion will move off at ~~11.30 p.m.~~ 12 midnt. The head of the Leading Company will pass the Brigade Starting Point, Brigade Headquarters, FLECHIN, at ~~[illegible]~~ 1.07 a.m. 10th. instant.

3. ROUTE. Direct Road FLECHIN to ENGUINATTE.

4. ADVANCE PARTIES. O.'s C. Coys. will send out the necessary advance parties to reconnoitre their positions, to mark them out and to meet their Companies on arrival at ENGUINATTE CHURCH to guide them into position.
The Advance Parties will report to 2/Lieut. A.A.NIMMO at Battn. H.Q. at 8.30 p.m.
Two Platoon Commanders, C.S.M., and 1 Platoon Sergt. per Coy. and Captain E.L. GUEST will report to Major A.H. SCHULTZ at 8 a.m. on the 9th. instant at Battn. H.Q. ready to proceed to reconnoitre Battalion H.Q. and Advance Battalion Report Centres.

5. TRANSPORT. The Company Cookers will proceed with their Coys. Water-carts will also accompany the Battalion. These must be filled before starting. Seven pack animals with pack saddles will also accompany the Battalion.

6. BRIGADE DUMP. The Brigade Dump will be on the road at R.11.b.9.8. The Advanced bBrigade Dump will be at sunken road at R.17.a.6.4.

7. SUPPLIES FOR FIRING LINE. Supplies for the firing line will be drawn from the Advanced Brigade Dump by Carrying Parties, who will deliver whenever needed. O.'s C. Coys. will always give written demands before sending parties to draw from this Dump.

8. CARRYING PARTIES.
(a) O/C "B" Coy. will detail one N.C.O. and 2 men to report to Staff Captain at point R.11.b.9.8. one hour before ZERO.
(b) Transport Sergeant and 7 pack animals with pack-saddles will report to Staff Captain at point R.11.b.9.8. one hour before ZERO.
(c) One Officer and 10 men from "D" Coyx. will report to B.H.Q. at 5 a.m. on morning 10th. instant, and move with B.H.Q. when it goes forward. This party will be reserved for carrying from advanced Bde. Dump to wherever Battalion needs supplies.

(Continued.)

9. SIGNAL COMMUNICATION & CO-OPERATION OF AIRCRAFT.

Communication will be maintained by:-

(a) Telephone.
(b) Fullerphone.
(c) Visual.
(d) Runners.

The following will be the H.Q. report Centres:-

Original Battle H.Q.	Advanced Report Centre.
R.11.b.2.5.	R.17.a.9.2.

Ground Signal Panels and Ground Signal Strips will be exposed at original Battle H.Q. from ZERO onwards. At ZERO plus 30 and again at ZERO plus 150 minutes a contact patrol machine will be in the area.
Flares will be lit when called for by the aeroplanes.
Flares should be lit in groups of 3, at intervals of about 100 yards.

10. SYNCHRONIZATION OF WATCHES.

All watches will be synchronized two hours before ZERO, ~~[illegible]~~.

11. BALL AMMUNITION.

All arrangements for shooting with ball ammunition have been cancelled.

12. ACTION OF LEWIS GUNS.

Reference Preliminary Orders dated 4/10/17, delete sub-paras. (c) & ([illegible]) of para. 12. and substitute for sub-para. (b) of para. 13 "No ball ammunition will be carried."

13. ZERO.

ZERO HOUR will be 5.30 a.m. on the 10th. instant.

[signature]

2/Lieutenant,
Asst. Adjutant,
2/8th. S. Lan. R.

No. 1 Copy to O/C "A" Coy.
2 " O/C "B" "
3 " O/C "C" "
4 " O/C "D" "
5 " C.O.
6 " H.Q., 172nd. Inf. Bde. (for information.)
7 " Q.M. & T.O.
8 & 9 Spare.

ADMINISTRATIVE ARRANGEMENTS.
IN CONNECTION WITH
BRIGADE "TRENCH TO TRENCH ATTACK"
Oct. 9/10th. 1917.

1. MEALS. Dinners will be at 7 p.m. on the 9th. instant in Billets.
Hot Drinks Hot Tea and a Biscuit will be served at 4 a.m. on the 10th. instant prior to the attack.
Breakfast At termination of the Attack.
Water Carts will be filled before starting. Water Bottles will be filled.

2. TRANSPORT. The T.O. will detail one animal with driver to report to the O/C 172nd. Light T.M. Battery at 1 p.m. on the 9th. instant at the Headquarters of the 172nd. L.T.M.Battery PALFART to assist in drawing the L.T.M.Battery's handcarts to ENGUINATTE. Each animal will be equipped with the necessary harness and drag ropes.

3. STORES. The Q.M. will hand over the following at Q.M. Stores to T.O. at 3.30 p.m. 9th. instant.

20 large screw pickets.
10 Coils of barbed wire.

These will be dumped at sunken road at R.17.a.6.4. by 6.30 p.m. 9th. instant.
The Bombing Officer will hand over the following to T.O. at 3.30 p.m. 9th. instant, at Q.M. Stores.

10 Boxes of S.A.A.
5 Boxes of Mills Grenades.

These will be dumped at point R.11.b.9.8. by 6.30 p.m. 9th. instant.

4. RATIONS. 1 Officer & 12 men from the 172nd. L.T.M.B. will bring their rations and hand them over to our Cookers, and will draw their cooked rations at breakfast on the 10th. instant.
Rations for Headquarters personnel will be cooked in "D" Company's Cooker.

A. P. St. George

2/Lieutenant,
Asst.Adjutant,
2/5th. S.Lan.R.

Copy No.......

2/5th. S. LAN. R. OPERATION ORDER
NO.1.

Ref. Maps,
THEROUANNE &
BERGUENEUSE
1/40,000.

****

3/10/17.

1. INFORMATION.	The enemy is holding line ENQUIN-FLECHINELLE and our Scouts have reported that he has formed strong points on the Eastern Edge of Woods lying North of BERQUIGNY.
2. INTENTION.	The Battalion has been ordered to clear this wood.
3. INSTRUCTION.	At 7.30 a.m. on 4th. instant the Battalion will leave LAIRES by road running through X.22.c. to Cross-roads at X.21.b.7.3. - thence by road running North to BERQUIGNY to Road Junction X.3.d.99.20.
4. ADVANCE GUARD. Capt. MESSUM. 2 Platoons "A" Company.	Advance Guard will pass Road Junction at X.28.b.1.3. at 7.30 a.m.
5. ORDER OF MARCH. Main Body.	"A" Coy. less 2 platoons, "B", "C" "D".
6. DEPLOYMENT.	The Battalion will deploy on a line running due North from X.3.d.99.20.
7. FRONTAGE.	The frontage allotted to the Battalion is from road junction at X.3.d.99.20 to point on road at X.3.b.99.80. This frontage will be equally divided between the four Companies.
8. DISTRIBUTION.	Order of Companies from LEFT A B C D. Three Platoons of each Company will form the Firing Line. One Platoon in Reserve. Line of Scouts 250 yards in advance.
9. FORMATION.	Formation in accordance with Brigade Circular dated 22 /9/17.
10. DIRECTION.	The advance through the wood will be on a bearing of 103° Magnetic. The Left will direct.
11. CONSTRUCTION OF STRONG POINTS.	Immediately after the capture of the wood Strong Points will be constructed at suitable points inside the wood, to break up any counter attacks which may develop. Reserve Platoons will construct these if not thrown into the Firing Line.
12. REPORTS.	Battalion H.Q. will be with Reserve Platoon of "B" Coy.

R.Kay Ward
Captain,
Adjutant,
2/5th. S.Lan.R.

Issued at 6 p.m. by runner.
No. 1 Copy to O/C "A" Coy.
No. 2 " to O/C "B" "
No. 3 " to O/C "C" "
No. 4 " to O/C "D" "
No. 5 " to 172nd. Inf. Bde. (for information.)
No. 6 " File.

APPENDIX
XXVIII

50 - 1.50 p.

t Inspect at dis- al of Coy. manders.

do.

nge.

ot Inspect- on at dis- osal of Coy. ommanders.

nder L.G.O. xcept "C" Coy.

With Coys.

With S.O. xcept "C" Coy.

With Coys.

do.

Adjutant 's Parade.

S.B.'s and Sanitary Men under M.O. for instructions

11th. DAY. PROGRAMME OF TRAINING. DATE. 5th. Oct. 1917

2/5th. S. LAN. R.

Time.	7.30 - 8.30 am	8.30 am - 9.30 am	9.30 am - 10.30 am	11.15 - 12 noon.	12 noon - 12.30	12.30 - 12.45 p.m.	12.50 - 1.50 p.
	Demonstration hour for all O.'s & NCO's less Asst. Adjt. RSM & 2 Instructors per Coy.	Specialist Training.	Musketry.	B a t t a l i o n	P a r a d e.		
'A' Coy.	Bayonet Fighting.	Bombing & Rifle Grenade Secs. under Coy. arrangements supervised by B.O.	Under Coy. arrangements supervised by Musketry Officer.	Trench to Trench Attack. formation of defensive flank App. XI.	Open attack. App. X.	March past.	Foot Inspection at disposal of Coy. Commanders.
"B" Coy.	do.	do.	do.	do.	do.	do.	do.
"C" Coy.	do.	Musketry. Under Coy. arrangements supervised by Musketry Officer.	Specialist Training. Bombing & Rifle Grenade Secs. under Coy. arrangements supervised by B.O.	do.	do.	do.	Range.
"D" Coy.	do.	do.	do.	do.	do.	do.	Foot Inspection at disposal of Coy. Commanders.
Lewis Gunners.	Under L.G.O. App. I.	Under L.G.O. App. I.	Under L.G.O. App. I.	do.	do.	do.	Under L.G.O. except "C" Coy.
Snipers.	With Companies.	Under I.O. App. VII.	Under I.O. App. VII.	do.	do.	do.	With Coys.
Signallers.	With Coys.	Under S.O. App. VI.	Under S.O. App. VI.	do.	do.	do.	With S.O. except "C" Coy.
Runners.	do.	With Companies.	Under Adjt. App. VIII.	do.	do.	do.	With Coys.
Band.	do.	P r a c t i c e.	Under M.O. Training as S.B.'s. App. IX.	do.	do.	do	do.
All Subaltern O.'s & N.C.O.'s.				do.	do.	do.	Adjutant 's Parade.

S.B.'s and Sanitary Men under M.O. for Instructions

10.30 am - 11.15 a.m. ¾ hour Light Lunch.

C.O.'s Conference 3.15 p.m. (All Officers & N.C.O.'s.)

Place X.28.a.8.8.

32

CO

4/11/17

S.B.'s and Sanitary Men under M.O. for instruction.

10th. DAY. PROGRAMME OF WORK. DATE 4th Oct ....1917. 2/5th. S. LAN. R.

Time.	7.30 am - 8.30 am	8.30 am - 9.30 am	9.30 am - 10.30 am	11.15 am - 12.noon.	12.30 pm - 12.45 pm	12.50 p.m. - 1.50 pm.
	Demonstration hour for all Officers & NCO's less Asst.Adj RSM, CSM's & 2 Instructors per Coy.	Musketry.	Specialist Training.	B a t t a l i o n P a r a d e.		
"A" Coy.	Company Drill. I.T. Secs. 85 - 86 & 46.	Under Coy. arrangements supervised by Musketry Officer. App. III.	Bombing & Rifle Grenade Secs. under Coy. arrangements supervised by B.O. App. III.	Wood Fighting. Appendix XIII.	March Past.	Foot inspection at disposal of Coy. Commanders.
"B" Coy	do.	do.	do.	do.	do.	Range.
"C" Coy.	do.	Specialist Training Bombing & Rifle Grenade Secs. under Coy. arrangements supervised by B.O. App. III.	Musketry. Under Coy. arrangements supervised by Musketry Officer. App. II.	do.	do.	Foot Inspection at disposal of Coy. Commanders.
"D" Coy.	do.	do.	do.	do.	do.	do.
Lewis Gunners	Under L.G.O. App. I.	Under L.G.O. App. I.	Under L.G.O. App. I.	do.	do.	Under L.G.O. Except "B" Coy.
Snipers.	With Companies.	Under I.O. App. VII.	Under I.O. App. VII.	do.	do.	With Coy.
Signallers.	do.	Under S.O. App. VI.	Under S.O. App. VI.	do.	do.	Under S.O. Except "B" Coy.
Runners.	do.	With Companies.	Under Adjt. App. VIII.	do.	do.	With Companies.
Band.	do.	P r a c t i c e.	Under M.O. Training as S.B.'s.	do.	do.	do.
All Subalterns Officers & NCO's				do.	do.	Adjutant's Parade.

S.B.'s and Sanitary Men under M.O. for instruction.

CANCELLED SEE BELOW

10.30 am. - 11.15 am Light Lunch.

Training from 7.30 a.m. - 10.30 a.m. will be Wood Fighting. See Operation Order No. 1 attached. Draft will attend.

C.O.'s Conference All Officers & N.C.O.'s. 3.15 p.m. X.28.a.9.8.

9th. DAY. PROGRAMME OF TRAINING. DATE Oct. 3rd. 1917. 2/5th. S. LAN. R.

Time.	7.30 am - 8.30 am	8.30 am - 9.30 am	9.30 am - 10.30 am	10.30 - 11.15	11.15 - 12 p.m.	12 pm - 12.30 pm	12.30 pm - 12.45	12.50 - 1.30.	
	Demonstration hour for all Officers & NCO's less A/Adjt. R.S.M. & 2 Instruct-ors per Company.	Specialist Training.	Musketry.	Lunch	Battalion	Parade	Battn. Parade.		S.B.'s and Sanitary Men under M.O.
"A" Coy.	Bayonet Fighting.	Bombing & Rifle Grenade Secs. under Coy. arrangements supervised by Battn B.O. App. III.	Under Coy. arrangements supervised by Battn. Musketry Officer. App. II.	do.	Trench to Trench Attack with T.M. Co-operation. App. XI.	Open Attack. Artillery Formation. App. V.	March past.	Range.	
"B" Coy.	do.	do.	do.	do.	do.	do.	do.	Foot inspection at disposal of Company Commanders.	
"C" Coy.	do.	Musketry. Under Coy. arrangements supervised by Bn. Musketry Officer App. II.	Specialist Training. Bombing & Rifle Grenade Secs. under Coy. arrangements supervised by Bn. B.O. App. III.	do.	do.	do.	do.		
"D" Coy.	do.	do.	do.	do.	do.	do.	do.	do.	
Lewis Gunners	Under L.G.O. App. I.	Under L.G.O. App. I.	Under L.G.O. App. I.	do.	do.	do.	do.	Under LGO except A Coy.	
Snipers	With Companies.	Under I.O. App. VII.	Under I.O. App. VII.	do.	do.	do.	do.	With Coys	
Signallers.	do.	Under S.O. App. VI.	Under S.O. App. VI.	do.	do.	do	do.	Under S.O. except A Coy	
Runners.	do.	With Coys.	Under Adjt. App. VIII.	do.	do.	do.	do.	With Coys	
Band.	do.	Practice.	Train'g as S.B.'s under M.O.	do.	do.	do.	do.	do.	
All Subaltern Officers NCO's.								Adjutants Parade.	

C.O.'s Conference .... p.m. All Officers & N.C.O.'s.

Place and time to be notified later.

PROGRAMME OF TRAINING Date 2nd. October, 1917. 2/5th. S. LAN. R. 8th. day.

Time	7-30.am - 8-30.am	8-30.am - 9-30.am	9-30.am - 10-30.am	11.15 - 12 noon	12 - 12.30 pm	12.30 pm - 12.45 pm	12.50 - 1.50 pm
	Demonstration for all Officers and NCO's less A/Adjt R.S.M. C.S.M.'s & 2 Instructors per Company	Musketry	Specialist Training.	B a t t a l i o n	P a r a d e .		
"A" Coy	Company Drill. I.T. Secs. 81 to 84 and 46	Under Coy. Arrangements supervised by Batt. Musketry Off. App. 11	Bombing and Rifle Grenade Secs. under Coy arrangements supervised by Batt. B.O. App. 111	Trench to trench attack with T.M. co-operation. App. XI.	Open Attack. Artillery Formation. App. X.	March past.	Pay at disposal of Coy. Commander.
"B" Coy	do.	do.	do.	do.	do.	do.	do.
"C" Coy	do.	Specialist Training Bombing and Rifle Grenade Secs under Coy. arrangements supervised by Batt. B.O. App. 111	Musketry Under Coy. arrangements supervised by Batt. Musketry Officer App. 11.	do.	do.	do.	do.
"D" Coy	do.	do.	do.	do.	do.	do.	Range.
Lewis Gunners	Under L.G.O. App. 1	Under L.G.O. App. 1.	Under L.G.O. App. 1.	do.	do.	do.	Under L.G.O. except "D" Company.
Snipers	With Coys.	Under I.O. App. VII.	Under I.O. App. VII.	do.	do.	do.	With Coys.
Signallers	do	Under S.O. App. VI.	Under S.O. App. VI.	do.	do.	do.	Under S.O. except "D" Company.
Runners	do	With Coys	Under Adjt. App. VIII.	do	do.	do.	With Coys.
Band.	do.	P r a c t i c e.	Training as S.B.'s under M.O. App. IX.	do.	do.	do.	do.
All Subalterns Officers & NCO's							Adjutant's Parade.

S.B.'s and Sanitary Men under M.O. for instruction.

C.O.'s Conference 2-15.p.m. All Officers & N.C.O's

Place X.28.a.8.8.

10.30 - 11.15 a.m. ¾ hour Light Lunch.

CO
1/10/17

PROGRAMME OF TRAINING. DATE [illegible] 1917. 2/5th. E. LAN. R. 7th. DAY.

Time.	7.30 am - 8.30 a.m.	8.30 am - 9.30 am	9.30 am - 10.30 am	11.15 - 12 noon	12.15 - 12.30 pm	12.30 - 12.45 pm	12.50 - 1.30 pm
	Demonstration hour for all Officers & NCO's less Adjt. RSM 2 instructors per Coy	Specialist Training	Musketry.	B a t t a l i o n Parade.		Battn. Parade.	
"A" Coy.	Bayonet Fighting.	Bombing & Rifle Grenade Secs. under Coy. Instructors supervised by Bn. B.O. App. III.	Under Coy. arrangements supervised by Battn. Musketry Officer. App. II.	Trench to Trench Attack with T.M. Co-operation. App. XI.	Open Attack & Artillery Formation. App. X.	March-past.	Foot Inspection at disposal of Coy. Comndrs.
"B" Coy.	do.	do.	do.	do.	do.	do.	do.
"C" Coy.	do.	Musketry Under Coy. arrangements supervised by Battn. Musketry O. App. II.	Specialist Training. Bombing & Rifle Grenade Secs. under Co. Instructors supervised by Battn. B.O. App. III.	do.	do.	do.	Range.
"D" Coy.	do.	do.	do.	do.	do.	do.	Foot Inspection at disposal of Coy Commanders.
Lewis Gunners	Under L.G.O. App. I	Under L.G.O. App. I	Under L.G.O. App. I.	do.	do.	do.	Under L.G.O. Except "C" Coy.
Snipers	With Companies.	Under I.O. App. VII	Under I.O. App. VII	do.	do.	do.	With Coys.
Signallers.	do.	Under S.O. App. VI	Under S.O. App. VI	do.	do.	do.	Under S.O. except "C" Coy.
Runners	do.	With Companies.	Under Adjt. App. VIII.	do.	do.	do.	With Coys.
Band.	do.	P r a c t i c e.	Training as S.B.'s under M.O. App. IX.	do.	do.	do.	do.
All Subaltern Officers & NCO's							Adjutant's Parade.

S.B.'s and Sanitary Men under M.O. for instruction.

C.O.'s Conference 5 p.m. All Officers & N.C.O.'s.

Place Field X 28 a 8.8.

10.30 - 11.15 a.m. 3/4 hour Light Lunch.

2/5th. Sth. Lancs. Regt.

TRAINING PROGRAMME 3rd. WEEK, 1st. DAY, 8th. OCTOBER, 1917.

Time.	9 a.m. - 10 a.m.	10 a.m. - 12.30 p.m.	12.30 p.m. - 1 p.m.	5.30 p.m. -
	All Officers & N.C.Os less 1 Gas NCO per Coy. Sergt. Harper & C.Q.M.S.'s on Battn. Parade Ground. C.O.'s Parade.	Battalion Trench to Trench Attack & Consolidation.	March past.	All Officers & N.C.O.'s including Gas N.C.O.'s for Gas Drill. Parade under 2/Lieut. H. West. Field next to Q.M.'s Office.
"A" Coy.	Bayonet Fighting - C.S.M. W. Kitto. Company Drill - Sergt. Harper & C.Q.M.Sergts. Gas Drill under Coy Gas N.C.O. ½ hour to be spent on each subject.	do.	do.	
"B" Coy.	do.	do.	do.	
"C" Coy.	do.	do.	do.	
"D" Coy.	do.	do.	do.	

Reveille. 6 a.m.

Breakfast. 6.45 a.m.

Dinners. 1 p.m.

ALL RANKS will be dressed and equipped as laid down for active operations.

2/5th. Sth. Lancs. Regt.

TRAINING PROGRAMME 3rd. WEEK. 2/3rd. DAY, 9/10th. OCT. 17.

Time.	9 a.m. - 10.30 a.m.	Afternoon.
	Rapid Wiring. Whole Battalion. will attend.	March to Manoeuvre Area. Bivouac for the Night. Assembly at Dawn. Brigade Trench to Trench Attack. Return to Billets.

Reveille. 7 a.m.

Breakfast. 7.30 a.m.

Dinner. ---

ALL RANKS will be dressed and equipped as laid down for Active Operations.
Detailed Orders to follow.

TRAINING PROGRAMME.

(11/10/17)

Coy.	8 a.m. - 9 a.m.	9 a.m. - 10 a.m.	10 a.m. - 11 a.m.	11 a.m. - 12 noon	12 noon - 1 p.m.	Afternoon.
"A"	Lecture for all Officers, N.C.O.'s & Sergeants on the ATTACK.	Attack Practice.	Gas Drill.	Company Drill & Platoon Drill.	Lecture on "Attack in Depth."	B R I G A D E S P O R T S.
"B"		Lecture on "Attack in Depth."	Attack Practice	Company Drill & Platoon Drill.	Gas Drill.	
"C"		do.	Company Drill & Platoon Drill.	Attack Practice	do.	
"D"		do.	Company Drill & Platoon Drill.	Gas Drill.	Attack Practice.	

SECRET. APPENDIX XXX

Copy No....8...

2/5th. S. LAN. R., OPERATION ORDER NO.43.

Ref.Map,
HAZEBROUCK 5A
1/100,000

16/10/17.

1. INFORMATION.	The 172nd. Infantry Brigade will accompany the 57th. Division which is being transferred to FIFTH ARMY (XIV Corps).
2. MOVE.	The Battalion will leave present billets at LAIRES on Thursday, 18th. inst. and will march to RENESCURE Area with 172nd. Brigade Group.
3. STARTING POINT.	Starting Point:- Railway Crossing in ESTREE BLANCHE on N.W. side of town on ESTREE BLANCHE-THEROUANNE Road. The Battalion will pass the Starting Point at 10.27 a.m. following 2/9th. K.L.R.
4. ROUTE.	ESTREE BLANCHE - BLESSY - MAMETZ - ROQUETOIRE - BELLECROIX to RENESCURE Area. The Signalling Officer is responsible for the Route.
5. TIME OF STARTING.	The Battalion will assemble in Column of Route with head of column at Cross Roads X.28.b.6.4. ready to move off at 8.15 a.m.
6. ORDER OF MARCH.	The Order of March on 18th. instant will be Signallers B - C - D - A - Transport. Band will march with their Company, H.Q. detailed will be attached to leading Company and Q.M. Personnel to Rear Company. This will apply throughout the march to new concentration area.
7. ROUTE TO STARTING POINT.	Route to Starting Point:- LAIRES - CUHEM - FLECHINELLE - ESTREE BLANCHE. The head of Battalion will not pass through CUHEM until 2/9th. K.L.R. have cleared the Cross Roads in that village.
8. REAR PARTY.	Sergeant HARRISON and two men of Regimental Police will form Rear Party under Orders of Second-in-Command.
9. BILLETING PARTY.	Billeting Party will consist of Assistant-Adjutant, Four C.Q.M.S.'s, N.C.O. for H.Q., N.C.O. for Transport, N.C.O. for Q.M. Personnel. This Party will proceed by bus. Details will be issued later.
10. BLANKETS.	Transport will be provided for blankets which must be rolled up and tied in bundles of TEN and dumped outside Company H.Q. by 6.30 a.m. H.Q. and Transport Blankets will be dumped at Q.M. Stores. Each bundle must have a label showing name of Company etc. One man per Company will be detailed to accompany blankets and act as loading party.
11. BAGGAGE.	Officers' Valises, Mess-Baskets, Dixies etc. will be dumped by 7 a.m. at same places as blankets.

(Continued.).

12. PACKS. Unless orders to the contrary are issued packs wil be carried on the man.

13. BILLETSM All billets, horse lines & stables, must be left in an absolutely clean and sanitary condition. All latrines rubbish pits etc. must be filled in before billets are vacated.
A certificate as to cleanliness of billets and filling in of latrines etc. will be rendered by O.'s C. Coys. Q.M., T.O., & Sigs. Officer for H.Q. by 7.15 a.m. on 18th. instant.
The M.O. will arrange to inspect billeting areas before departure of Battalion.

14. MARCH DISCIPLINE. Attention is directed to 172nd. Inf. Bde. Standing Orders for March Discipline which must be ~~xxxxxxxx~~ strictly adhered to. Distances of 100 yards will be maintained between Companies on the march.

15. REPORTS. Repotts during march to head of column.

R.E. Hay Ward

Captain,
Adjutant,
2/5th. S.Lan.R.

issued by Runner at:- 11.50 a.m.

No. 1 Copy to O/C "A" Coy.
No. 2 " " O/C "B" "
No. 3 " " O/C "C" "
No. 4 " " O/C "D" "
No. 5 " " Q.M.
No. 6 " " T.O.
No. 7 " " Signalling Officer.
No. 8 & 9 War Diary.
No. 10 Office.
No. 12 & 12. Spare.

APPENDIX XXXI

War Diary

SECRET.

To - O.'s C. "A", "B", "C" & "D" Coys. Ref.No. X.Y.52.
Q.M.
T.O.
Signalling Officer.

With reference to Operation Order No.43 dated 16/10/17:-

1. On night of 18th. October, the Battalion will be billeted at ~~WARDRECQUES~~. RENESCURE (CASSEL ROAD AREA)

2. Packs will be carried on the man. Ground Sheets correctly folded. Steel Helmets on back of packs secured by Supporting Straps.

3. Transport will march in rear of Battalion in order:-
   Limbers.
   Water Carts.
   Field Kitchens.
   Mess Cart.
   Medical Cart.

4. The halt for dinners will be from 12.50 p.m. - 2 p.m.

5. Blankets will all be dumped in the Village Square (opposite Estaminet AU CHEVAL BLANC and NOT at Company Headquarters. C.Q.M.S.s will supervise the loading of blankets on to motor lorries.

6. The Billeting Party will report to the Assistant Adjutant on the Village Square at 8 a.m. They will proceed on motor lorries and will meet the Billet Warden at ~~WARDRECQUES Church~~ the Mairie RENESCURE at 11 a.m.

7. On arrival in billets the Signalling Officer will detail two cyclists to report to Brigade Headquarters. A third Orderly will be sent who will return to Battalion Headquarters after ascertaining location of Brigade Headquarters.

8. The Signalling Officer will arrange to get Brigade Time before 8 a.m. on 18th. instant and give same to the Adjutant.

9. The R.S.M. will detail a N.C.O. to be at Town Square, FLECHIN at 8 a.m. 18th. instant to guide motor lorries to LAIRES.

10. The move on 19th. instant will be by motor bus. Transport will be brigaded. Detailed Orders will be issued later.

R.C. Hayward

Captain,
Adjutant,
2/5th. S.LAN.R.

16/10/17.

APPENDIX XXXII

2/5th Battalion South Lancashire Regiment.

NOMINAL ROLL (OFFICERS)

31st OCTOBER, 1917.

HEADQUARTERS.

Lieut-Colonel	Owen, W.L. M.C.	Commanding Officer.
Major	Schultz, A.H.	Second in Command.
Captain	Hayward, R.C.	Adjutant.
2/Lieut	St Goerge, A.R.	Asst. Adjutant.
Lieut	West, H.	Lewis Gun Officer.
Lieut	Dean, L.M.	Intelligence Officer.
Lieut	Davis, H.P.W.	Signalling Officer.
Lieut	Frodsham, F.J.	Bombing Officer.
Lieut	Gregory, H.	Quartermaster.
Lieut	Tanton, L.E.	Transport Officer.
Captain	Wood, R.L.	Medical Officer.

"A" COMPANY.

Captain	Wallis, A.C.	O.C. Company.
Captain	Donald, T.M.	Second in Command.
Lieut	Hargreaves, R.	Platoon Commander.
Lieut	Leake, R.L.	Platoon Commander.
2/Lieut	Castle, A.C.	Platoon Commander.

"B" COMPANY.

Captain	Crowe, J.A.	O.C. Company.
Lieut	Bullen, H.G.	Second in Command.
Lieut	Brazener, W.F.	Platoon Commander.
2/Lieut	Clark, J.	Platoon Commander.
2/Lieut	Farmer, W.H.	Platoon Commander.

"C" COMPANY.

Captain	Guest, E.L.	O.C. Company.
Captain	Messum, A.W.	Second in Command.
2/Lieut	Woollett, J.S.	Platoon Commander.
2/Lieut	Adams, B.C.	Platoon Commander.
2/Lieut	Milton, S.J.	Platoon Commander.
2/Lieut	Hall, J.G.	Platoon Commander.
Lieut	Timson, H.H.	

"D" COMPANY.

Captain	Stephenson, C.W.	O.C. Company.
Lieut	Agabeg, J.W.	Second in Command.
2/Lieut	Handley, W.C.	Platoon Commander.

DETACHED.

Lieut	Le Mare, E.B.	XIV Corps Reinforcement Camp. (Instructor)
Lieut	Hall, W.S.	172nd Bde Pioneer Coy.
Lieut	Paul, R.B.	505 Coy, R.E.
2/Lieut	Stone, A.R.	172nd Bde L.T.M.B.

COURSES.

Lieut	Hadfield, J.L.	General Course.
Lieut	Nimmo, A.A.	ditto
Lieut	Holland, W.H.E.	Lewis Gun Course.
2/Lieut	Quinton, P.F.	General Course.

APPENDIX XXXIII

2/5th Battalion South Lancashire Regiment.

STATEMENT
SHOWING STRENGTH
....

31st OCTOBER, 1917.

BATTALION STRENGTH :- 39 Officers 913 Other Ranks.

With Unit:-

"A" Company	141	Other Ranks
"B" Company	151	ditto
"C" Company	144	ditto
"D" Company	141	ditto
"Headquarters"	93	ditto
"Transport"	45 ~~[illegible]~~	ditto
"Q.M. Stores"	26	ditto
Total	741	

Detached:-

Bde and Division	19	Other Ranks
Hospital	9	ditto
A.P.M. (57th Div.)	6	ditto
Leave	5	ditto
Courses	6	ditto
Bde Pioneer Coy	22	ditto
M.G. Company	10	ditto
XI Corps School	5	ditto
Bde L.T.M.B.	8	ditto
505 Coy, R.E.	1	ditto
Corps Rein. Camp	55	ditto
Draft at Rein. Camp	22	ditto
Trade Test	2	ditto
Army School	1	ditto
Base	1	ditto
Total	172	

...............oOo...............

Instructions regarding War Diaries and Intelligence Summaries are contained in F. S. Regs., Part II. and the Staff Manual respectively. Title pages will be prepared in manuscript.

WAR DIARY
or
~~INTELLIGENCE SUMMARY.~~
(Erase heading not required.)

Army Form C. 2118.

2/5th S. Lanc. Regt. 30.11.17

Vol 10

Place	Date 1917.	Hour	Summary of Events and Information	Remarks and references to Appendices
ELVERDINGHE	NOV.R 1st	-	The Battalion at BRIDGE CAMP. All the men had gas appliances inspected, and preparing for the following day's move.	
ELVERDINGHE and PILKEM	2ND.	-	The Battalion (less 4 officers and 132 Other Ranks) moved to HUDDLESTON. CAMP, which is situated about half a mile east of YSER Canal. Took over the camp from 2/6th Bn K.L.R. Heavy bombardment by enemy during the night, (especially about 12pm. to 1-30 am) on forward areas, including a great number of Gas Shells, but fortunately area occupied by Battalion was not affected. Also a couple of our 8in hows. caused us much annoyance as our huts ~~had~~ had anything but solid foundations, and the guns were only 30 yards away. Detailes still at BRIDGE CAMP.	A.P.G.
ELVERDINGHE and PILKEIM.	3RD.	-	At HUDDLESTON CAMP. Carrying parties found, and all parties returned without having any casualties. Some consolidation had been done by our troops but some difficulty experienced owing to state of ground. Enemy artillery active again during the night, especially with gas shells, but did not affect our camp. Details still at BRIDGE CAMP.	A.P.G.

D. D. & L., London, E.C. (A7001) Wt. W1771/M2031 750,000 5/17 Sch. 52 Forms C2118/14

(2)

WAR DIARY
~~or~~
~~INTELLIGENCE SUMMARY.~~

(Erase heading not required.)

Army Form C. 2118.

Instructions regarding War Diaries and Intelligence Summaries are contained in F. S. Regs., Part II. and the Staff Manual respectively. Title pages will be prepared in manuscript.

Place	Date	Hour	Summary of Events and Information	Remarks and references to Appendices
	1917 NOV		at HUDDLESTON CAMP. The C.O., adjt, and M.O. reconnoitred forward areas including front line at BESACE FARM.	
ELVERDINGE and PILKEIM.	4TH	—		
		2-30pm.	Battalion moved from HUDDLESTON CAMP to MARSOUIN FARM CAMP, about 3/4 mile further forward ~~towards~~ South East of LANGEMARCK. Took over from 2/4th Bn. S. Lan. R. The camp consisted of ground sheet bivouacs and low "elephant" bivvies.	APPENDIX. XXXIV
		4 P.M.	At night almost the whole battalion on carrying parties under R.E's. Carrying duckboards forward for tracks. The work commenced about 4 pm and last party returned about 3. a.m. 5th inst — 10 casualties —	
		10 P.m.	Enemy were shelling tracks heavily in vicinity of LANGEMARCK. Lieut HARGREAVES and 2 N.C.O'S reconnoitred MEMLING FARM with a view to intended raid. They reported that it was strongly held by enemy who had consolidated by linking up shell holes. Patrol went out at 10 pm. and returned 12-30 am without casualties.	
		—	Details at BRIDGE CAMP.	
	5TH	1. AM	Orders received that Battalion had to take over from 2/4th Bn. S. Lan. R. in support at EAGLE TRENCH.	
		9.30am.	C.O went to Brigade re projected raid on MEMLING FARM.	
		2-30pm.	Battalion left MARSOUIN FARM Camp and relieved 2/4th Bn. S. Lan. R. in EAGLE TRENCH AREA. The relief was completed by 4-30 pm. No casualties although tracks were shelled with H.E.	APPENDIX XXXV

C. 789.

D. D. & L., London, E.C. (A8004) Wt. W1771/M2031 750,000 5/17 Sch. 52 Forms C2118/14

(3)

Army Form C. 2118.

WAR DIARY
or
~~INTELLIGENCE SUMMARY.~~
(Erase heading not required.)

Instructions regarding War Diaries and Intelligence Summaries are contained in F. S. Regs., Part II. and the Staff Manual respectively. Title pages will be prepared in manuscript.

Place	Date	Hour	Summary of Events and Information	Remarks and references to Appendices
	1917 NOV 5th (Contd)		and Shrapnel whilst Companies were going up. Dispositions in EAGLE TRENCH area were two companies about 400 yards forward of H.Q. of Battalion in line. These Companies (A+B) accomodated in shell holes, remaining two companies in EAGLE TRENCH where there were a few shelters. Battalion H.Q in "Pill-box" at DOUBLE COTTS which is about 1000 yards E. of remains of LANGEMARCK. H.Q. personnel accomodated in EAGLE TRENCH and round about "Pill-Box". Great difficulty ~~was~~ experienced in keeping lines to forward companies intact but visual very useful, Lucas Lamps used. Two forward companies held for counter-attack purposes - Two Coys in EAGLE TRENCH occupy defensive position. During night enemy ~~was~~ again busy sending over gas shells. Details at BRIDGE CAMP.	A.P.89
LANGEMARCK and ELVERDINGHE.	6th	6.AM	Our artillery opened barrage in conjunction with Army on our right, which was attacking on PACHENDALE RIDGE. Continued firing until 6-50 am, but artillery covering attacking troops kept up barrage until 12 noon. From 6 am to 8 am the barrage was intense and from 8 am to 12 noon Second rate of barrage fire. There was a good deal of hostile retaliation throughout the morning - our Casualties 2 O.Ranks Killed, 3 O.Ranks wounded.	A.P.89.

D. D. & L., London, E.C. (A7001) Wt. W1771/M2031 750,000 5/17 Sch. 52 Forms C2118/14

Instructions regarding War Diaries and Intelligence Summaries are contained in F. S. Regs., Part II. and the Staff Manual respectively. Title pages will be prepared in manuscript.

WAR DIARY

~~or~~

~~INTELLIGENCE SUMMARY.~~

(Erase heading not required.)

Army Form C. 2118.

Place	Date NOVR	Hour	Summary of Events and Information	Remarks and references to Appendices
LANGEMARCK and ELVERDINGHE.	6th. (Contd)		Lieut Hargreaves and raiding party spent day in vicinity of BESACE FARM studying the ground in readiness for night.	A.B.G.
		2. P.m.	Confirmation received that a battalion of West Riding Regt. would relieve us on night 7th/8th Nov. – Guides sent to Rear Brigade H.Q. in readiness for incoming Unit.	
		7.20 P.m.	Lieut HARGREAVES and Party went out to raid MEMLING FARM, Party returned to our lines at 10-30 am, and reported that Bosche had evacuated the farm. Enemy not as active as usual with gas shells during the night. Details at BRIDGE CAMP.	
LANGEMARCK. BOESINGHE and ELVERDINGHE.	7th.		The Battalion was relieved by West Riding Regt – relief completed by 8 P.m. – about 12 pm to 4 P.m. Bosche heavily shelled the tracks leading to EAGLE TRENCH and also shelled several Batteries, causing a few casualties to the West Ridings., but fortunately things were much quieter when we came out of the line, Relief completed by 8 P.m. Our casualties during relief – NIL. The Battalion arrived at BOESINGHE STATION about 9.30 P.m. and bivouaced at the Station for the night. Details at BRIDGE CAMP	APPENDIX XXXVI A.B.G.

D. D. & L., London, E.C. (A8003) Wt. W1771/M2031 750,000 5/17 Sch. 52 Forms C2118/14

(5)

WAR DIARY

or

~~INTELLIGENCE SUMMARY.~~

(*Erase heading not required.*)

Army Form C. 2118.

Instructions regarding War Diaries and Intelligence Summaries are contained in F. S. Regs., Part II. and the Staff Manual respectively. Title pages will be prepared in manuscript.

Place	Date NOVR	Hour	Summary of Events and Information	Remarks and references to Appendices
BOESINGHE.	8th.		Details joined Battalion about 12 noon from BRIDGE CAMP. Battalion had orders to be ready to entrain at BOESINGHE Station at 2-30 pm, but did not actually entrain till 6 pm. Battalion arrived at AUDRUICQ at 1. am. 9.11.17.	
BOESINGHE. AUDRUICQ. LANDRETHUN and YEUSE.	9th.		Transport left BOESINGHE Station at 3. am. Battalion marched from AUDRUICQ to billets, arriving in billets at 7.30. am. Packs had been dumped at NIELLES just over half-way between Audruicq and Landrethun. A. B. C. Coys and Batt: H.Q. at LANDRETHUN. D. Coy and Transport at YEUSE, a small village about 2 Kilometres from Landrethun.	
		5 pm.	Major A.H. SCHULTZ and Party (Total of 6. officers, 148. other Ranks) arrived from Divisional Reinforcement Camp, HERZEELE.	[illegible]
LANDRETHUN and YEUSE	10th.		The day was spent in resting, cleaning up billets etc.	
LANDRETHUN and YEUSE.	11th.		Company Commanders reconnoitred training grounds. Church Services also held.	[illegible]

D. D. & L., London, E.C. (A8001) Wt. W1771/M2031 750,000 5/17 Sch. 52 Forms C2118/14

(6)

Army Form C. 2118.

WAR DIARY

~~INTELLIGENCE SUMMARY.~~

(Erase heading not required.)

Instructions regarding War Diaries and Intelligence Summaries are contained in F. S. Regs., Part II. and the Staff Manual respectively. Title pages will be prepared in manuscript.

Place	Date NOVR	Hour	Summary of Events and Information	Remarks and references to Appendices
LANDRETHUN and YEUSE	12th		Training Commenced. Programme of training similar to training carried out at LAIRES.	APPENDIX XXXVII
-do-	13th		Major A.H. SCHULTZ went on 4 days course (Senior Officers musketry Course) at NORTBECOURT. Training carried out according to programme.	
-do-	14th		Training carried out according to programme	
-do-	15th		The Battalion went to GUEMY and fired on the range. Owing to the late arrival of targets and ammunition etc "D" Coy were not able to fire the full practice, and "A" Coy did not fire, as the ground was being used by the 170th Brigade. The practices fired by "B" Coy and "C" Coy was grouping and application at 100 yards.	[signature]
-do.	16th		Training carried out according to programme. A room in the MAIRIE was ~~lent~~ lent for a reading and writing room which seemed to be a boom for the troops. Canteen also doing good business	

D. D. & L., London, E.C. (A7001) Wt. W1771/M2031 750,000 5/17 Sch. 52 Forms C2118/14

(7)

Army Form C. 2118.

WAR DIARY
or
INTELLIGENCE SUMMARY.

(Erase heading not required.)

Instructions regarding War Diaries and Intelligence Summaries are contained in F. S. Regs., Part II. and the Staff Manual respectively. Title pages will be prepared in manuscript.

Place	Date NOV[R]	Hour	Summary of Events and Information	Remarks and references to Appendices
LANDRETHUN and YEUSE	17th.		Training carried out as per programme.	
- do -	18th.		Major A.H. SCHULTZ returned from Course at NORTBECOURT. Lieut-Col. W.L.OWEN. M.C. on leave. Church Parades in the morning and Battalion Sports held in the afternoon, which were a success, there being a good many entries for the various events. — C.O. inspected all N.C.O'S.	ap.9
- do -	19th.		Training as per programme. Major A.H. Schultz and asst. adjt went to meet the Brig. General to reconnoitre the RECQUES WEST training area.	
- do -	20th.	10 a.m.	Battalion inspected by G.O.C. 172nd Infantry Brigade	
- do -	21st.		Battalion went to RECQUES WEST Training area. Two Coys were on the Range and Two Coys practised the new "Leap-frog" form of attack. In the afternoon all officers from Company Commanders upwards were to have gone to the XVIII Corps Commanders lecture at NORDAUSQUES, but owing to the non-arrival of the motor lorry, they did not go.	ap.9

D. D. & L., London, E.C. (A5001) Wt. W1771/M2031 750,000 5/17 Sch. 52 Forms C2118/14

Army Form C. 2118.

Instructions regarding War Diaries and Intelligence Summaries are contained in F. S. Regs., Part II. and the Staff Manual respectively. Title pages will be prepared in manuscript.

WAR DIARY
or
~~INTELLIGENCE SUMMARY.~~
(Erase heading not required.)

Place	Date	Hour	Summary of Events and Information	Remarks and references to Appendices
	NOV^R.			
LANDRETHUN and YEUSE	22ND.		Training as usual. Lieut. SAWYER from 172nd BDE came and gave the Officers the points brought forward by the Commander, XVII Corps in his lecture.	
-do-	23rd.		Battalion at Baths. In the afternoon C.O., inspected "A" Coy in full marching order.	
-do-	24th.		Battalion went to RECQUES WEST training area and practised "Leap frog" form of attack. Attack was carried out on a 3 Company frontage. At the conclusion of the attack, the Divisional Commander, G.O.C., 172nd Bde, spoke to all officers, Platoon Sergeants and Section Commanders. The Divisional Commander laid emphasis on the fact that in an actual attack the number of "Leap frogs" would not be so numerous as those carried out in practise.	
-do.	25th.		Church Parades in the morning. In the afternoon an inter-platoon paper chase was held, which was won by No. 12 Platoon, "C" Company.	

D. D. & L., London, E.C.
(A8001) Wt. W1771/M2031 750,000 5/17 Sch. 52 Forms C2118/14

Army Form C. 2118.

WAR DIARY

~~INTELLIGENCE SUMMARY.~~

(Erase heading not required.)

Instructions regarding War Diaries and Intelligence Summaries are contained in F. S. Regs., Part II. and the Staff Manual respectively. Title pages will be prepared in manuscript.

Place	Date	Hour	Summary of Events and Information	Remarks and references to Appendices
LANDRETHUN and YEUSE	Nov. 1917 26th 27th		Training carried out according to programme	A.P.S.G.
	28th		Major A.H. Schultz Capt. to attend a four day XVIII Corps Conference at BOLLEZEELE. Capt. J.A. Crowe took over Command of the Battalion. The Battalion marched to the RECQUES WEST Training area. On arrival at the area the men had dry rations. The assembly was carried out on tapes which had been laid down for the purpose, Zero hour being at 1.30 p.m. After the attack the men had tea from the kitchens which had been brought up to the ground. As soon as it was dusk, the men fell in for a practice Assembly. The Battalion arrived back in Billets about 7 p.m. when they were issued with hot tea and rum.	APPENDIX XXXVIII A.P.S.G.
	29th 30th		Training carried out according to programme.	

J.A. Crowe. Capt.
Captain
Commanding
1/5th N. S. Lan. R.

D. D. & L., London, E.C. (A5001) Wt. W1771/M2031 750,000 5/17 Sch. 52 Forms C2118/14

APPENDIX XXXIV

To - O.'s C. "A", "B", "C" & "D" Coys.
Sigs. Officer for H.Q.
Q.M. (for information.)

1. The Battalion will move from HUDDLESTON CAMP to MARSOUIN FARM CAMP to-morrow 4th. Nov. Exact time of move will be notified later.

2. Route:- Along road from HUDDLESTON CROSS ROADS to C.14.a.72.85 - thence along TrackBto C.8.c.80.95.

3. Order of March:- Headquarters - A - B - C - D Coys.

4. Dress:- Battle Order with greatcoats rolled.

5. Blankets rolled in TEN'S and labelled will be deposited in Q.M. Stores by 10 a.m.

6. Cookers will accompany the battalion and will be on the road at about C.8.a.85.00. They must be placed so that the road is not blocked.

7. Company Commanders will proceed to MARSOUIN CAMP TO reconnoitre Company areas reaching there at 11.30 a.m. 2/Lt. DEAN will represent H.Q.

8. Lewis Gun equipment and panniers will be carried on the man. Lewis Gunners may wear great-coats.

(Sgd) R.C. Hayward

Captain,
Adjutant,
2/5th. S.Lan.R.

3/11/17.

SECRET. APPENDIX XXXV 152/7.

To - O.'s C. "A", "B", "C" & "D" Coys. Sigs.Officer,
Q.M. (for information.)

1. The Battalion will relieve the 2/4th. S.Lan.R. in EAGLE TRENCH Areato-day 5/11/17.

2. The 2/9th. K.L.R. will take over MARSOUIN FARM CAMP.

3. Battalion will leave MARSOUIN FARM CAMP in order A - B - C - D - H.Q.

4. Starting Point:- Point where Tramsway Crosses 5 CHEMINS EST - PILKEM MILL Road.

5. Route:- 5 CHEMINS EST - PILKEM MILL Road to TRACK "A". Thence along Track "A".

6. Formation:- By Platoons at 200 yards distance.

7. Leading Platoon of "A" Coy. will pass Starting Point at 1.45 p.m.

8. Guides from 2/4th.S.Lan.R. are being arranged to meet Companies at DROP HOUSES (about U.29.a.43.90.)

9. It is hoped to issue two Battle rations per man also extra water (either in patrol cans or water bottles) before the Battalion leaves camp. If this cannot be done .arrangements will be made to issue at EAGLE TRENCH.

10. All ranks will carry the unexpended portion of day's ration and full water-bottles.

11. Ref. paras. 4 & 5. The route is left to discretion of O.'s C. Coys. if they wish to vary it after this morning's reconnaissance.

12. Companies will report completion of relief by use of Company Code Name (i.e. FIGURES, COLLEEN, ADVO and COMP respectively.) Time of completion to be given.

(Sgd) R.C. Hagwara

Captain,
Adjutant,
2/5th. S.Lan.R.

5/11/17.

APPENDIX XXXVI

SECRET. Copy No......

2/5th. S. LAN. R., OPERATION ORDERS No.46.

Ref.Maps,
Sheet BIXSCHOOTE
& ST.JULIEN,
1/10,000
HAZEBROUCK,
5A, 1/100,000.

1. The Battalion will be relieved in EAGLE TRENCH AREA on night 7/8th. NOV. by a battalion of the West Riding Regiment.

2. On relief the Battalion will proceed to NIELLE by rail, entraining on night 7/8th. instant at BOESINGHE (NEW) Station. Details of entraining arrangements will be issued later.

3. The head of incoming battalion will pass STRAY FARM at 4 p.m. or possibly earlier, following the Lancs. Fusiliers which will relieve 2/4th. S.Lan.R. in Front Line.

4. Guides have already been detailed and reported to Staff Captain to-day.

5. Routes in:- Tracks "A" and "B".
Routes Out:- Stracks "A" and "B" to BARD'S CAUSEWAY - BOESINGHE Road - thence North to BOESINGHE Station.
It may be necessary to use one track only in order to avoid clashing with 2/4th. S.Lan.R. Should this be so, details will be issued later.

6. Formation:- East of the Canal.
Companies will move by platoons at 100 yards distance.

7. Platoon Commanders will march in REAR of their platoons, the platoon SERGEANT will lead.

8. An Officer will be detailed to bring up the rear of each Company.

9. In event of casualties during relief, great care must be taken to ensure that no wounded are left behind. Should any man be unfortunately killed, his pay-book, identity disc and personnel belongings will be collected by his platoon Commander and sent to Q.M.

10. Dispositions with sketch of Company area must be carefully handed over on relief. Copies of pamphlet "Enemy Defences" with secret map attached, will also be handed over.

11. Completion of relief will be reported by visual, confirmed by runner to present Battalion Headquarters, using same code-words as for last relief.

12. Transport less S.A.A. and Grenade wagon will entrain with the Battalion also all details at present at BRIDGE CAMP. The Asst. Adjutant, Q.M. & T.O. will issue necessary orders for above.

13. Officers' valises will go by road with A.S.C. Transport.

14. The Q.M. will arrange for a meal to be issued from Cookers at BOESINGHE Station.

15. ACKNOWLEDGE.

(Sgd) R.C. Howard
Captain & Adjutant,
2/5th. STH. Lancs. Regt.

No.1 Copy to O/C "A" Coy.
2 O/C "B" "
3 O/C "C" "
4 O/C "D" "
5 Q.M. Asst.Adjt. & T.O.
6 file

APPENDIX XXXVII

17th. DIV. PROGRAMME OF WORK. Date. 30th. Nov. 1917. 2/5th. S. Lan. R.

(FRIDAY)

Time.	8.15 - 9 a.m.	9 a.m. - 10 a.m.	10 a.m. - 10.45 a.m.	Break. 10.45-11.15	11.15 - 1 p.m.	2 p.m. - 3.15 p.m.	2.30 p.m - 3.30.
"A" Coy.	Platoon Comdrs. Inspection and March to Training Area by Coys App. D. Attention is drawn to S.S. 143 and to retention of Section formations.	Musketry. App. B. 30 yds. Range.	10 mins. P.T. App. G. Deploy. App. F.	Break.	Assembly commencing with troops in defensive position	March past.	Recreational Training with assistance of P.T. Instructors.
"B" Coy.	do.	Musketry. Nos. 1, 2 & 3 L.G.'s Revolver Practice App. B. S. & M. Course.	Intensive Digging. App. F	do.	do.	do.	30 yds. Range.
"C" Coy.	do.	Musketry. App. B.	10 mins. P.T. App. G. Deployment, App. F.	do.	"Leap-frog" attack. Wood near [illegible]	do.	C.O.'s Inspection. Massed Coy. Parade. Dinners 1 p.m. Inspection 2 p.m.
"D" Coy.	do.	Musketry. App. B.	10 mins. P.T. App. G. Intensive Digging App. F.	do.	do.	do.	Defaulters' Parade.
Special Lewis Gun Class.	With Platoons.	With Companies.	Under L.G.O.	do.	With Coys.	With Coys.	With Coys.
Signallers.	do.	Under S.O.	Under S.O.	do.	Special exercise under SO	H.Q. Signallers with H.Q. Coy.	do.
H.Q. Patrol.	do.	Physical Exercises.	Under Patrol-Leader.	do.	Special exercise under Patrol Leader	With H.Q.Coy.	do
Runners.	do.	With Coys.	Under C.S.M. KITTS.	do.	With Coys.	H.Q. Runners with H.Q. Company.	do.
H.Q. Intelligence Section.	do.	Under I.O.	Under I.O.	do.	Special exercise under IO	With H.Q. Coy.	do.
S.B.'s and Res. S.B.'s	do.	Physical Exercises.	With Companies.	do.	Under M.O.	With Coys.	do.
Band.	Inspection by R.S.M. (Play 7.45 a.m. - 8.15 a.m.)	Break.	Physical Exercises.	do.	Practice.	Play March Past	Play retreat and for ½ hr. in village square.
All Subaltern Officers & NCO's.							"B" Coy. under Adjt. and RSM. Drill and Communication Drill.

Dinners 1.00 p.m.
Teas. 5.00 p.m.

Inter-platoon Knock-out Competition (Platoon Commanders playing.)
No....... Platoon v. No....... Platoon.
Platoon Commanders foot-rubbing Inspection after tea.

Musketry Instruction will be carried throughout as a DRILL and on the Time Saving (out of the line) principle.

16th. DAY. PROGRAMME OF WORK. Date 29th. Nov. 1917.

(THURSDAY) 2/5th. S.Lan.R.

Time	8.15 a.m - 9 a.m.	9 a.m. - 10 a.m.	10 a.m. - 10.45 a.m.	10.45 - 11.15	11.15 - 1 p.m.	1 p.m. - 1.15	2.30 - 3.30pm.
"A" Coy.	Platoon Commanders' Inspection, and March to Training Area by Companies. App. D. Attention is drawn to B.M.1922, para. 1, and to retention of sections for formation.	Musketry. (App B)	10 mins. B.F. App. G. Deployment App. F.	Break.	Coy. Tactical Scheme. "Leap-frog" attack. Wood near 57.50.73.	March past.	Defaulters' Parade. [illegible]
"B" Coy.	do.	Musketry. (App B)	10 mins. B.F. App. G. Intensive Digging App. E	do.	do.	do.	Recreational Trainingwith assistance of PT Instrctrs.
"C" Coy.	do.	Musketry. Nos. 1 2 & 3 L.G.'s. Revolver Practice B & B. Course. App. B.	Deployment App. F.	do.	Assembling commencing with troops in defensive position	do.	30 yds. Range
"D" Coy.	do.	Musketry. App. B. 30 yds. Range.	10 mins. B.F. App. G. Intensive Digging App. E.	do.	do.	do.	~~C.O.'s Inspection. Massed Coy Parade. Dinners 1 p. Inspection Sym~~ Tactical Exercise
Special Lewis Gun Class.	With Platoons.	With Coys.	Under L.G.O.	do.	With Coys.	With Coys.	With Coys.
Signallers.	do.	Under S.O.	Under S.O.	do.	Special Exercise under SO	H.Q. Signallers with H.Q. Coy.	do.
H.Q. Patrol.	do.	Physical Exercises	Under Patrol Leader.	do.	Special Exercise under Patrol Leader.	With H.Q. Coy.	do
Runners.	do.	With Companies.	Under C.S.M. KITTS.	do.	H.Q. Runners with H.Q.Coy.	H.Q. Runners with H.Q. Coy.	do.
H.Q. Intelligence Section.	do.	Under I.O.	Under I.O.	do.	Special Exercise under I.O.	With H.Q. Coy.	do.
S.B.'s and Res.S.B.'s	do.	Physical Exercises.	With Companies.	do.	Under M.O.	With Coys.	
Band.	Inspection by S.O. (Play 7.45 - 8.15)	Break.	Physical Exercises.	do.	Practice.	Play March past	Play Retreat & ½ hr. in Village Square.
All Subaltern Officers & NCO"s.							"A" Coy. under Adj. ARSM. Drill & Communication Drill.

* Platoon Commanders Lecture to their Platoons On Trench Feet, pointing out particularly that Trench Feet are a disciplinary and not a medical matter.

Dinners 1.30 p.m.
Teas. 5.30 p.m.
Inter-platoon Knock-out Competition. (Platoon Commanders playing)
No......... platoon v. No...... Platoon.
Platoon Commanders' Feet-rubbing Inspections after tea.
Musketry Instruction will be carried throughout as a DRILL and on the Time-saving (out of the line) principle.

15th. DAY. PROGRAMME OF WORK. 23rd Nov. 1917. 8/5th. S. LAN. R.

(WEDNESDAY.)

ins.	9.15 - 12 a.m.	11.30 a.m. - 12.30 pm	12.30 pm - 4.30 p.m.	5.30 p.m.	
A" Coy.	March to Training Area [illegible] WEST.	Explanation by Company Commanders and Platoon Commanders.	Batt. Practice Attack with M.G. & L.T.M.B. co-operating followed by Conference and Teas.	Assembly Practice at Dusk. Battalion Scheme. March back to billets.	
B" Coy.	do.	do.	do.	do.	
C" Coy.	do.	do.	do.	do.	
D" Coy.	do.	do.	do.	do.	
Special Lewis Gun Class.	With Platoons.	With Platoons.	With Platoons.	With Platoons.	
Signallers.	do.	All Signallers playing their respective roles in Practice Attack.		With Companies.	
.G. ATROL.	do.	With Platoons.	With Platoons.	With Platoons.	
unners.	do.	HQ Runners playing their respective roles in Practice Attack.		With Companies.	
.O. Intelligence Section.	do.	With Platoons.	With platoons.	With Platoons.	
.B.s & es. S.B.s.	do.	Under M.O. As many as are required playing their respective roles in practice attack.		With Companies.	
and.	do.	March with Battalion to [illegible] WEST Area and back.			

Dry Rations. 12 p.m.
Dinners from Kitchens,4p.m.

Inter-platoon Knock,out Competition. (Platoon Commanders playing.)
No....... platoon v. No........ Platoon.

Platoon Commanders' Feet-rubbing Inspection after tea.

14th. DAY. PROGRAMME OF WORK. Date 27th. Nov. 1917 2/5th. S. Lan. R.

TUESDAY.

Time.	8.15 a.m. - 9 a.m.	9 a.m. - 10 a.m.	10 a.m. - 10.45 a.m.	10.45 - 11.45 am	11.15 - 1 p.m.	1 p.m. - 1.15	2.30 - 3.30 p.m.
"A" Coy.	Platoon Commanders' Inspections, and march to Training Area by Companies. App D. Attention is drawn to H.H.1922, para. 1. and to retention of section formations.	Musketry, Nos. 1, 2 & 3 L.G. Section Revolver Practice App B. B. & B. Course.	Intensive Digging. App. E.	Break.	Assembly commencing with troops in defensive positions.	March past.	C.O.'s Inspection. Massed Coy. Parade Dinners 1 p.m. Inspection 3 p.m. to D
"B" Coy.	do.	Musketry. 30 yds. Range. App. B.	10 mins. B.F. App. G. Deployment. App. F.	do.	do.	do.	Defaulters' Parade.
"C" Coy.	do.	Musketry. App. B.	B.F. 10 mins. App. G. Intensive Digging App. E.	do.	"Leap-frogging" Woodnear S.F.50.75.	do.	Recreational Training with assistance of B.T. Instructors.
"D" Coy.	do.	Musketry. App. B.	10 mins. B.F. App. G. Deployment, App. F.	do.	do.	do.	30 yds. Range. to A
Special Lewis Gun Class.	With Platoons.	With Companies.	Under L.G.O.	With Coys. do.	With Coys. do.	With Coys. do.	With Coys.
Signallers.	do.	Under S.O.	Under S.O.	do.	Special Exercise under S.O.	H.Q. Signallers with H.Q. Company	do.
H.Q. Patrol.	do.	Under CSM KITTS.	Under Patrol Leader.	do	Special Exercise under Patrol Leader	With Company.	do.
Runners.	do.	With Companies.	Under CSM KITTS.	do	With Coys.	H.Q. Runners with H.Q. Coy.	do.
H.Q. Intelligence Section.	do.	Under I.O.	Under I.O.	do	Special Exercise under I.O.	With H.Q. Coy.	do.
S.B.'s & Reg. S.B.s	do.	Physical Exercises.	With Companies.	do	Under M.O.	With Coys.	do.
Band.	Inspection by S.O. (Play 7.45 a.m. - 8.15 a.m.)	Break.	Physical Exercises.	do.	Practise.	Play March past.	Play Retreat and for ½ hr. in Village Square.
All Subaltern Officers & NCO's.							"B" Coy. under Adjt. & R.S.M. for Drill and Communication Drill.

Dinners ... 1.30 p.m.
Teas. ... 5.30 p.m.
Inter-platoon Knock-out Competition (Platoon Commanders playing.)
No........ Platoon v. No........ Platoon.
Platoon Commanders Feet-rubbing Inspection after tea.

Musketry instruction will be carried throughout as a DRILL and on the time saving (out of the line) principle.

15th. DAY. PROGRAMME OF WORK. DATE:- 26/11/17. 2/5th. S. Lan. R.

MONDAY.

Time.	8.15 - 9 a.m.	9 a.m. - 10 a.m.	10 am - 10.45 a.m.	10.45 - 11.15	11.15 - 1 p.m.	1 p.m. - 1.15	2.30 - 3.30 p.m.	
"A" Coy.	Platoon Commanders' Inspection, and march to Training Area by Companies. Appd. D. Attention is drawn to S.M.1922 para. 1, and to retention of section formations.	Musketry. App. B.	10 mins. B.F. App. G. Intensive Digging. App. F.	Break.	Coy. Tactical Schemes. "Leap-frog" attack-Wood near S.F.50.73	March past.	30yds. Range.	Platoon Commanders Lecture to their Platoons on Trench Feet pointing out particularly, that Trench Feet are a disciplinary and not a medical matter.
"B" Coy.	do.	Musketry. App. B.	10 mins. B.F. App. G. Deployment. App. F.	do.	do.	do.	C.O.'s Inspection. Massed Coy. Parade. Dinners 1 pm. Inspection 2pm	
"C" Coy.	do.	Musketry. App. B. 30 yards Range.	10 mins. B.F. App. G. Intensive Digging. App. F.	do.	Assembly commencing with troops in defensive position	do.	Defaulters' Parade.	
"D" Coy.	do.	Musketry. App.B. Nos. 1, 2 & 3. L.G.'s Revolver Practice. B.& B. Course.	Deployment. App. F.	do.	do.	do.	Recreational Training with assistance of P.T. Instructors	
Special L.Gun Class.	With Platoons.	With Companies.	Under L.G.O.	do.	With Coys.	do.	With Coys.	
Signallers.	do.	Under S.O.	Under S.O.	do.	Special Exercise under SO.	H.Q. Sigs. with H.Q.Coy.	do.	
H.Q. Patrol.	do.	Physical Exercises	Under Patrol Leader.	do.	Special Exercise under Patrol Leader.	With H.Q. Coy.	do.	
Runners.	do.	With Companies.	Under C.S.M. KITTS.	do.	With Coys.	H.Q. Runners with H.Q.Coy.	do.	
H.Q. Intelligence Section.	do.	Under I.O.	Under I.O.	do.	Special Exercise under IO.	With H.Q. Coy.	do.	
Band.	Inspection by SO. (Play 7.45 a.m. - 8.15 a.m.)	Break.	Physical Exercises and Games.	do.	Practice.	Play March Past.	Plat retreat & for 1hr. in Village Sq.	
S.B.'s & Reg.S.B.s	do.	Physical Exercises	With Companies.	do.	Under M.O.	With Coys.	With Coys.	
All Subaltern Officers & NCO's.							"C"coy. under Adjt. & RSM Drill and Communication Drill	

Dinners..........1.30 p.m.
Teas............5.30 p.m.
Inter-platoon Knock-out Competition (Platoon Commanders Playing.)
No.........Platoon v No..........Platoon.
Platoon Commanders' Feet-rubbing Inspection after tea.

Musketry Instructions will be carried throughout as a DRILL and on the Time-saving (out of the line) principle.

<u>19th. DAY.</u> PROGRAMME OF WORK. DATE...24th. NOV. 1917. 8/Bn. S. LAN. R.

Time.	9.15 - 9.30 a.m.	9.30 - 10 a.m.	10 a.m. - 11.30 a.m.	11.30 - 1 p.m.	1.45 p.m.		2.30 - 3.30 p.m.
"A" Coy.	Platoon Commanders' Inspection & March to Training Area [illegible] (1)	Explanation by Company Command-ers and Platoon Commanders.	Instruction by Observation whilst "C" & "D" Coys. practice "Leap-Frogging."	Companies "Leap_Frogging" as laid down in Training Pamphlet S.S.[illegible]	March past.	Assembly Practice. Battalion Scheme.	Defaulters' Parade.
"B" Coy.	do.	do.	do.	do.		do.	do
"C" Coy.	do.	do.	Companies "Leap-Frogging" as laid down in Training Pamphlet S.S.[illegible]	Instruction by Observation whilst "A" and "B" Coys. practice "Leap_Frogging."		do.	do.
"D" Coy.	do.	do.	do.	do.		do.	do.
Special Lewis Gun Class.	With Platoons.	With Platoons.	With Platoons.	With Platoons.		With Platoons.	do.
Signal-lers.	do.	All Signallers playing their respective		roles in Practice Attack.		With Coys.	do.
M.G. PATROL.	do.	With Platoons.	With Platoons.	With Platoons.		With Platoons.	do.
Runners.	do.	M.G. Runners playing their respective		roles in Practice Attack.		With Coys.	do.
H.Q. In-telligence Section.	do.	With Platoons.	With Platoons.	With Platoons.		With Platoons.	do.
[illegible] Res. [illegible]	do.	Under M.O.	As many as are required playing	their respective rolls in practice attack		With Companies.	do.
Band.	do.	March with Battalion to [illegible] area and		back.			do.
All Sub-altern Officers & NCO's.							

Dinners. 1 p.m.

Teas. 4 p.m.

Inter-platoon Knock_out Competition. (Platoon Commanders playing.) No........ Platoon v. No........ Platoon.

Platoon Commanders foot-rubbing Inspection after tea.

Sunday, 12 noon. C.O.'s Inspection. H.Q. Coy.

Afternoon.

Inter_platoon paper chase and Cross_country run. To be organised by Lieut. H. [illegible] [illegible] and 4 [illegible]'s.

11th. DAY. PROGRAMME OF WORK. DATE 23rd. NOV 1917. 2/4th. E. LAN. R.

Time.	8.15 - 9 a.m.	9 a.m. - 9.45 a.m.	9.45 - 10.45 a.m.	10.45 - 11.15	11.15 - 1 p.m.	1 p.m. - 1.15 pm	2.30 - 3.30
"A" Coy.	Platoon Commdrs. Inspection and March to Training Area by Coys. Attention is drawn to R.O. 1922 par.1	Musketry. 80 yds. Range.	Wiring.	Break.	Coy. Tactical Scheme.	March past.	Defaulters' Parade at disposal of Coy. Commanders. Games etc.
"B" Coy.	do.	Musketry, Nos. 1 2 & 3 L.G.'s. Revolver Practice.	Wiring.	do.	do.	do.	80 yds. Range.
"C" Coy.	do.	Musketry.	Coy. Drill.	do.	do.	do.	C.O.'s Inspection. Massed Coy. Parade. Dinners 1 p.m. Inspection 2 p.m.
"D" Coy.	do.	Musketry.	Coy. Drill.	do.	do.	do.	Defaulters' Parade. At disposal of Coy. Commanders. Games, etc.
Special Lewis Gun Class.	With Platoons.	With Companies.	Under L.G.O.	do.	do.	do.	With Coys.
Signallers.	do.	Under S.O.	Under S.O.	do.	[handwritten: With Coy] Special exercise under SO.	[handwritten: With Coy] H.Q. Signallers with H.Q.Coy.	do.
Patrol.	do.	Physical Exercises.	Under Patrol Leader.	do.	Special exercise under Patrol Leader	With H.Q. Coy.	do.
Runners.	do.	With Coys.	Under C.S.M. KIPPS.	do.	H.Q. Runners under R.O. *	H.Q. Runners with H.Q. Coy.	do.
H.Q. Intelligence Section.	do.	Under I.O.	Under I.O.	do.	Special exercise under I.O.	With H.Q. Coy.	do.
S.B.'s and Res. S.B.s	do.	Physical Exercises.	With Companies.	do.	Practice.	With Coys.	do.
Band.	do. (Play 7.45 - 8.15 a.m.)	Break.	Physical Exercises.	do.	Under B.M.	Play March Past.	do.
11 Subaltern Officers & NCO's.							"A" Coy. under Adjt. & R.S.M. Drill and Communication Drill.

Dinners. 1.30 p.m.

Teas. 5.30 p.m.

Inter-platoon Knock-out Competition. (Platoon Commanders playing.) No....... Platoon v. No......... Platoon.

Platoon Commanders feet-rubbing Inspection after tea.

* To be exercised in conjunction with Coy. Scheme.

War Diary

War Diary

13th. DAY. PROGRAMME OF WORK. DATE 22nd. NOV. 1917. [illegible] LAN. R.

Time.	8.15 a.m. - 9 a.m.	9 a.m. - 9.45 a.m.	9.45 a.m. - 10.45 a.m.	10.45 - 11.15	11.15 - 1 p.m.	1 p.m. - [illegible]	[illegible] - [illegible] pm
*A Coy.	Platoon Commanders' Inspection, and March to Training Area by Companies. Attention is drawn to [illegible] part 1.	Musketry.	Coy. Drill.	Break.	Coy. Practice Scheme.	March past.	Defaulters' Parade. At disposal of Coy. Commanders. Sergeants.
B Coy.	do.	Musketry.	Coy. Drill.	do.	do.	do.	do.
C Coy	do.	Musketry. Nos. 1, 2 and 3 L.G.'s. Revolver Practice.	Wiring.	do.	do.	do.	30 yds. Range.
D Coy.	do.	Musketry	Wiring. 30 yds. Range.	do.	do.	do.	C.O.'s Inspection. Massed Coy Parade. Dinners 1 p.m. Inspection [illegible]
Special Lewis Gun Class.	With Platoons.	With Coys.	Under L.G.O.	do.	With Coys.	With Coys.	With Coys.
Signallers.	do.	Under S.O.	Under S.O.	do.	Special Exercise under SO	H.Q. Signallers with H.Q. Company.	do.
H.Q. PATROL.	do.	Physical Exercises.	Under Patrol Leader.	do.	Special Exercise under Patrol Leader.	With H.Q. Coy.	do.
Runners.	do.	With Companies.	Under S.O. [illegible]	do.	H.Q. Runners under S.O. *	H.Q. Runners with H.Q. Coy.	do.
H.Q. Intelligence Section.	do.	Under I.O.	Under I.O.	do.	Special Exercise under I.O.	With H.Q. Coy.	do.
[illegible]	do.	Physical Exercises.	With Companies.	do.	Practice.	With Coys.	
Band.	(Play 7.45 - 8.15)	Break.	Physical Exercises.	do.	Under S.O.	Play March Past.	Play Retreat, [illegible] hr. in Village Square.
All Subalterns Officers & NCO's.							[illegible] Coy. under Adjt. [illegible] Drill and Communication Drill.

Platoon Commanders Lecture to their Platoon on Trench Feet, pointing out particularly that Trench Feet are a disciplinary matter and not Medical.

Dinners. 1.30 p.m.

Teas. 5.30 p.m.

Inter-platoon Knock-out Competition. (Platoon Commanders playing.)
No......... Platoon v. No......... Platoon.

Platoon Commanders Foot-rubbing Inspections after Tea.

* To be exercised in conjunction with Company Scheme.

War Diary

9th. DAY. PROGRAMME OF WORK. DATE. 21st. NOV. 1917. 2/4th. R. [illegible] R.

Time.	9.15 - 9.30 am	9.30 a.m.-10 a.m.	10 a.m. -11.30 a.m.	11.30 a.m. - 1 p.m.	1.15 p.m.	7.30 p.m.
"A" Coy.	Platoon Commanders' Inspection and March to Training Area -- BECOURT WEST. Battalion Parade:- 9.45 a.m.	B a t t a l i o n T r a i n i n g. Explanation by Coy. Commanders and Platoon Commanders.	Companies "leap-frogging" as laid down in Training Pamphlet S.S.1322.	Instruction by observation whilst "C" & "D" Coys. practice "leap-frogging."	March past.	Assembly Practice. Company Scheme.
"B" Coy.	do.	do.	do.			do. Defaulters' Parade.
"C" Coy.	do.	do.	Instruction by observation whilst "A" and "B" Coys. practice "leap-frogging."	Leap-frogging" as laid down in Training Pamphlet, S.S.1322.		do.
"D" Coy.	do.	do.	do.	do.		do.
Special Lewis Gun Class.	With Platoons	With Platoons.	With Platoons.	With Platoons.		With Platoons.
Signallers.	do.	All Signallers playing their respective		roles in Practice Attack.		With Coys.
H.Q. PATROL.	do.	With Platoons.	With Platoons.	With Platoons.		With Platoons
Runners	do.	All Runners playing their respective		roles in Practice Attack.		With Coys.
H.Q. Intelligence Section.	do.	With Platoons.	With Platoons.	With Platoons.		With Platoons.
C.S.M.'s and Reserve N.C.O.'s.	do.	Under H.Q. As many as required		playing their respective roles in Practice Attack.		with company
Band.	do.	March with Battalion to BECOURT WEST		Area and back.		
All Subaltern Officers & NCO's.						

Transport. C.O.'s Inspection. 2 p.m.

Dinners 2 p.m.

Teas. 5 p.m.

Inter-platoon Knock-out Competition (Platoon Commanders playing.)
No......... Platoon v. No......... Platoon.

Platoon Commanders' Foot-rubbing Inspection after Tea.

War Diary

8th. [illegible]. PROGRAMME OF WORK. DATE 20th. [illegible] 1917.

[illegible]

Time.	8.15 a.m.- 9 a.m.	9 a.m. - 9.45 a.m.	9.45 a.m. - 10.45 a.m.	10.45 - 11.15 am	11.15 - 1 p.m.	[illegible]	[illegible]
"A" Coy.	Platoon Commanders' Inspections, and march to Training Area by Companies. Attention is drawn to S.O. [illegible] para 1.	Musketry, Nos. 1, 2 & 3 L.G. Section Revolver Practice.	Wiring.	Break.	Coy. Tactical Schemes.	[illegible]	[illegible] Inspection. [illegible]
"B" Coy.	do.	Musketry. 30 yds. Range.	Wiring.	do.	do.	do.	[illegible] Parade, [illegible] Commanders. [illegible]
"C" Coy.	do.	Musketry.	Coy. Drill.	do.	do.	do.	do.
"D" Coy.	do.	Musketry.	Coy. Drill.	do.	do.	do.	30 yds. Range.
Special Lewis Gun Class.	With Platoons.	With Companies.	Under [illegible]	do.	do.	do.	With Coys.
Signallers.	do.	Under S.O.	Under S.O.	do.	Special Exercise under [illegible]	[illegible]	do.
[illegible] Patrol.	do.	Under [illegible]	Under Patrol Leader.	do.	Special exercise under Patrol Leader.	With [illegible]	do.
Runners.	do.	With Companies.	Under [illegible]	do.		[illegible]	do.
Bn. Intelligence Section.	do.	Under [illegible]	Under I.O.	do.	Special exercise under I.O.	With [illegible]	do.
[illegible]	do.	Physical Exercises.	With Companies.	do.	Under [illegible]	[illegible]	do.
Band.	do.	Break.	Physical Exercises.	do.	Practice.	[illegible]	[illegible]
All Subaltern Officers & NCO's.							[illegible]

DINNERS. 1.?0 p.m.
TEAS. 6.00 p.m.
Inter-platoon Knock-out Competition (Platoon Commanders' Playing)
"..........." Platoon v. "..........." Platoon.

Platoon Commanders Foot-rubbing Inspection after tea.

War Diary

7th. DAY. ~~PROGRAMME OF WORK.~~ DATE 19/12/[illegible]. 2/5th. [illegible] L.[illegible]. R.

Time.	[illegible] - 7 a.m.	9 a.m. - 9.45 a.m.	9.45 a.m. - 10.45 a.m.	10.45 - 11.15	11.15 - 1 p.m.	1 p.m. - 1.15	2.30 - 4.30 p.m.
"A" Coy.	Platoon Commanders' Inspection, and march to Training Area by Companies. Attention is drawn to [illegible] 1910, para. 3.	Musketry.	Company Drill. Preceded by ½ hour's Physical Drill.	Break.	Coy. Tactical Scheme.	March past.	30 yds. Range.
"B" Coy.	do.	Musketry.	Company Drill. Preceded by ½ hour's Physical Drill.	do.	do.	do.	C.O.'s Inspection. Massed Coy. Parade. Dinners 1 p.m. Inspection 2 pm.
"C" Coy.	do.	Musketry. 30 yards Range.	Wiring.	do.	do.	do.	Defaulters' Parade. At disposal of Coy. Commanders etc.
"D" Coy.	do.	Musketry. Nos. 1, 2 & 3 [illegible] Revolver Practice.	Wiring.	do.	do.	do.	do.
Special L. Gun Class.	With platoons.	With Companies.	Under L.G.O.	do.	With Coys.	do.	With Coys.
Signallers.	do.	Under S.O.	Under S.O.	do.	Special Exercise under SO.	C.O. Sigs. with H.Q. Coy.	do.
H.Q. Patrol.	do.	Physical Exercises.	Under Patrol Leader.	do.	Special Exercise under Patrol Leader.	With H.Q. Coy.	do.
Runners.	do.	With Companies.	Under [illegible]	do.	H.Q. Runners under S.O. [illegible]	Coy. Runners with H.Q. Coy.	do.
H.Q. Intelligence Section	do.	Under I.O.	Under I.O.	do.	Special Exercise under I.O.	With H.Q. Company.	do.
Band.	do. (Play 7.[illegible] a.m. - 8.15 a.m.)	Break.	Physical Exercises and Games.	do.	Practice.	Play March Past.	Play retreat, and for ½ hr. in Village Square.
[illegible]'s & [illegible]'s	do.	Physical Exercises.	With Companies.	do.	Under [illegible]	With Coys.	With Coys.
All Platoon Officers N.C.O's.							H.Q. Coy. under Adjt. & R.S.M. Drill & Communication Drill.

Platoon Commander's Lecture to their Platoons on Trench Feet, pointing out particularly, that Trench Feet are a disciplinary and not a medical matter.

Dinners. 1.[illegible] p.m.
Teas. 5.[illegible] p.m.
Inter-platoon Knock-out Competition (Platoon Commanders Playing.)
No.......... Platoon v. No............ Platoon.
Platoon Commanders' Foot-rubbing Inspection after Tea.

* To be exercised in conjunction with Coy. Scheme.

6th. DAY. PROGRAMME OF WORK. 17th. NOV. 1917. 2/5th. S. LAN. R.

Time.	8.15 a.m. - 9 a.m.	9 a.m. - 10 a.m.	10 a.m. - 11 a.m.	11 - 11.30 a.m.	11.30 - 1 p.m.	1 p.m. - 1.15 p.m.	2.30 p.m. - 3.30 pm
"A" Coy.	Platoon Commanders' Inspection and March to Training Area by Companies.	Company Drill.	Training by Sections in their respective arms supervised by their Platoon Cdrs.	Break.	Platoon Tactical Exercise and march back to Battn. Parade Ground.	March past.	Range.
"B" Coy.	do.	do.	do.	do.	do.	do.	Defaulters Parade Foot Inspections at disposal of Coy. Commanders. Games etc.
"C" Coy.	do.	do.	do.	do.	do.	do.	do.
"D" Coy.	do.	do.	do.	do.	do.	do.	do.
Special Lewis Gun Class.	With platoons.	Under L.G.O.	Under L.G.O.	With Coys.	With Coys.	With Coys.	With Coys.
Snipers.	do.	Under I.O. Physical Training	Under I.O.	do.	do.	do.	do.
Signallers.	do.	Under S.O.	Under S.O.	do.	All Signallers Special Exercise.	With H.Q. Coy.	do.
Runners.	do.	~~XXXXXXXXXXXXX XXXXXXXXXX~~ Under S.O. Lecture.	Games and Physical Drill.	do.	H.Q. Runners. Special Exercise.	~~With RUNNERS~~ With. H.Q. Company.	do.
Band.	do.	Physical Drill and Games.	Practice.	do.	Under H.Q. S.M. Drill and instructions.	Play March past.	do.
S.B.'s and Reserve S.B.'s.	do.	Stretcher Drill.	Physical Drill andGames.	do.	do.	With Coys.	
All Subalterns officers & NCO's.							"B" Coy. under Adjt. R.S.M. Drill and Communication Drill.

March to and from Parade Grounds will be carried out in Box Helmets and P.H. Helmets respectively.

PROGRAMME OF WORK. DATE .... 2/5th. S. LAN. R.

Time.	8.15 a.m. - 9 a.m.	9 a.m. - 10 a.m.	10 a.m. - 11 a.m.	11 - 11.30	11.30 - 1 pm.	1 p.m. - 1.15 p.m.	2.30 p.m. - 3.30 p.m.
"A" Coy.	Platoon Commanders Inspection & March to Training Area by Companies.	Platoon Drill.	Physical Training and Games. Bombers will do their Special Exercises.	Break.	Platoon Tactical Exercise & March back to Bn. Parade Ground.	March past.	Defaulters' Parade. Foot Inspection at disposal of Coy. Commanders. Games etc.
"B" Coy.	do.	do.	do.	do.	do.	do.	do.
"C" Coy.	do.	do.	do.	do.	do.	do.	do.
"D" Coy.	do.	do.	do.	do.	do.	do.	Range.
Special Lewis Gun Class.	With Platoons.	With Platoons.	Under L.G.O.	With Coys.	With Coys.	With Coys.	With Coys.
Snipers.	do.	do.	Under I.O.	do.	do.	do.	do.
Signallers.	do.	Under S.O. Physical Drill and Games.	Under S.O.	do.	H.Q. Signallers Special Exercise	With H.Q. Coys.	do.
Runners.	do.	With Platoons.	Games and Physical Drill.	do.	H.Q. Runners Special Exercise	H.Q. Runners with H.Q. Company.	do.
Band.	do.	Physical Drill and Games.	Practice.	--	Under M.O. S.B. Drill and Instruction.	Play March Past.	do.
S.B.'s & Reserve S.B.'s.	do.			--	do.	With Coys.	do.
All Subaltern Officers & NCO's.							"A" Coy. Under Adjt R.S.M. Drill and Communication Drill.

4th. DAY. PROGRAMME OF WORK. 15th. NOV. 1917. 2/5th. S. LAN. R.

Time.	8.15 am - 9 a.m.	9 a.m. - 10 a.m.	10 a.m. - 11 a.m.	11 a.m. - 11.30 a.m.	11.30 a.m. - 1 p.m.	1 p.m. - 1.15	2.30 - 3.30 pm
"A" Coy.	Platoon Commanders' Inspection and March to Training Area by Companies.	Platoon Drill. Inspection of Small Box Respirators by Brigade Gas N.C.O. on Training Ground.	Training by Sections in their respective arms, under their Platoon Commanders.	Break.	~~Platoon Tactical~~ Exercises & March back to Battalion Parade Ground.	March past.	Defaulters Parade. Foot Inspection at disposal of Coy. Cdrs. Games etc.
"B" Coy.	do.	Platoon Drill.	do.	do.	do.	do.	Inspections of S.B.R.'s by Bde. Gas N.C.O in Billets.
"C" Coy.	do.	do.	do.	do.	do.	do.	Range.
"D" Coy.	do.	do.	do.	do.	do.	do.	Defaulters Parade. Foot Inspection at disposal of Coy. Cdrs. Games etc.
Special Lewis Gun Class.	With Platoons.	Under L.G.O.	Under L.G.O.	With Coys.	With Coys.	With Coys.	With Coys.
Snipers.	do.	With Platoons.	Under I.O.	do.	do.	do.	do.
Signallers.	do.	Under S.O. for Squad Drill and Rifle Exercises.	Under S.O.	do.	H.Q. Signallers Special Exercise	With H.Q. Coy.	do.
Runners.	do.	With Platoons.	Games and Physical Drill.	do.	H.Q. Runners Special Exercise	H.Q. Runners with H.Q. Coy.	do.
Band.	do.	Squad Drill and Rifle Exercises.	Practice.	--	Under M.O. S.B. Drill.	March past.	do.
S.B.'s & Coy. Res. S.B.'s.	do.	With Platoons.	Stretcher Drill.	--	do.	With Coys.	do.
All Subaltern Officers & N.C.O.s							"D" Coy. under Adjt. R.S.M. Drill and Communication Drill.

3rd. DAY. PROGRAMME OF WORK. 14th. NOV. 1917. [illegible]/8th. S. Lan. R.

Time.	8.15 am - 9 a.m.	9 a.m. - 10 a.m.	10 a.m. - 11 a.m.	11 - 11.30 a.m.	11.30 - 1 p.m.	1 p.m. - 1.15 p.m.	2.30 pm - 3.30 pm.
"A" Coy.	Platoon Commanders' Inspection. Inf. Training, [illegible].	March to Training Area. Squad Drill and Rifle Exercises.	Physical Training and [illegible].	Break. All ranks should be encouraged to take a [illegible] to eat during break.	Platoon Tactical Exercise & March back to Billets.	[illegible]	Defaulters Parade. Foot Inspections at disposal of Coy. Cmdrs. Games etc.
"B" Coy.	do.	do.	do.	do.	do.	do.	Ditto.
"C" Coy.	do.	do.	do.	do.	do.	do.	Defaulters Parade. Foot Inspection at disposal of Coy. Cmdrs. Games etc.
"D" Coy.	do.	do.	do.	do.	do.	do.	do.
Special Lewis Gun Class.	With Platoons.	With Platoons.	Under L.G.O.	With Coys	With Coys.	With Coys.	With Coys.
Snipers.	do.	do.	Under I.O. Physical Training.	do.	do.	do.	do.
Signallers.	do.	Under S.O. for Squad Drill and Rifle Exercises.	Under S.O. Physical Training.	do.	S.O. Signallers Special Exercise.	With H.Q. Coy.	do.
Runners.	do.	With Platoons.	[illegible] and Physical Drill. [illegible]	do.	[illegible] Special Exercise.	[illegible] With H.Q. Coy.	do.
Band.	do.	Physical Drill. [illegible]	Squad Drill.	—	[illegible]	[illegible]	do.
S.B.'s & Hon. [illegible]	do.	Stretcher Drill.	Physical Drill.	—	do.	With H.Q. Coy.	do.
All Subaltern Officers & NCO's.							"C" Coy. Under Adjt. & R.S.M. Drill & Coy. Drill.

Dinners. 1.30 pm

Teas. 5.30 pm

March to and from Parade Grounds will be carried out in Box Helmets and P.H. Helmets respectively.

Football etc. etc. 5 Platoon v 1 Platoon

APPENDIX XXXVIII

War Diary

Copy No.....8.

2/[illegible]th. [illegible] OPERATION ORDER No.

Ref. Map,
[illegible] EAST Training Area.
1/20,000,
(Special.)

[illegible]

May 27th, 1917.

1. (a) The [illegible]nd. Infantry Brigade will attack on 28th. instant on a two Battalion frontage.
(b) The Battalion will be Left Assaulting Battalion with 2/4th. [illegible] on the Right, and the 2nd. Battalion [illegible]shire Regiment (Imaginary) on the left.

2. The Battalion will attack on a three Company frontage. Each Company on a one Platoon frontage.

RIGHT.	"A" Company.
CENTRE.	"B" "
LEFT.	"D" "
RESERVE.	"C" "

Two platoons of "C" Company under an Officer will act as skeleton enemy, and carry out a counter-attack after final objective is taken. These platoons will wear soft caps.

3. Battalion Boundaries:-
RIGHT. A line from A.10.d.[illegible] to A.10.a.[illegible].
LEFT. From A.10.d.[illegible] along road to A.10.a.[illegible].00 thence to A.9.b.[illegible], above road inclusive.
Company Boundaries:-
Between Right and Centre Companies:-
Line A.10.d.[illegible] - A.10.a.[illegible] thence to A.9.b.[illegible].
Between Left and Centre Companies:-
Line A.10.d.[illegible] - A.10.a.[illegible] thence to A.9.b.[illegible].

4. Compass Bearing of Attack:- 313° magnetic.

5. ASSEMBLY.
(a) Approximate line of assembly will be line from A.10.d.[illegible] to A.10.d.[illegible].
(b) A defensive position will be taken up and occupied for half an hour before assembly takes place. Companies on same frontage as for attack. Leading Platoons about [illegible] yards forward of line of assembly.
(c) The Intelligence Officer will mark out with tape all lines of assembly, also guide lines for those platoons whose defensive position is forward of line of assembly.
(d) Supporting Platoons of Front Line Companies will assemble first, and afterwards front platoons will assemble in rear.
(e) Reserve Company will assemble in rear of centre Company in Artillery Formation of half platoons.
(f) Each Company will assemble on a frontage of 100 yards.

6. OBJECTIVES.

(a) Leading Platoons will take strong points etc. as detailed below. Second platoons will "leap-frog" leading platoons and capture the line of first objective from A.10.c.[illegible] to A.4.d.[illegible].
(b) There will be a "pause" of 10 mins. in the barrage on line of first objective, when third and fourth platoons will close up to the barrage and leap-frog the two leading waves.
(c) Third platoons will capture defensive positions detailed below. Fourth platoons will capture and consolidate the final objective which is a line from A.9.b.[illegible] to A.10.a.[illegible].
(d) Objectives for leading platoons (see para. a)

RIGHT Company.	[illegible] about A.10.c.[illegible].
CENTRE COMPANY.	Large dug-out system represented by [illegible] at A.10.c.[illegible].
LEFT Company.	Shell-holes and Defences at A.10.c.[illegible] to A.10.c.[illegible].

P.T.O.

6. - Continued.
(c) Objectives for third platoons (see para.5) Defensive positions approximately on a line 150 yards forward of First Objective.

7. The Barrage will move at rate of 50 yards in 2 minutes with a ten minutes pause on First Objective. Barrage will be represented by flags and drums.

8. Four Machine Guns will be attached to the Battalion. They will take up a defensive position before assembly. On capture of final objective they will form two lines of fire between Jumping-off line and objective. The Officer in charge of machine-guns will select positions, and report when these have been taken up.

9. Two Light Trench Mortars will be attached as under for dealing with enemy strong points, pill-boxes, etc.
1 Mortar to Centre Company. 1 Mortar to Left Company.

10. Dress & Equipment as laid down for operations when in the line as far as stores are available.

11. Signalling Arrangements.
(a) The Signalling Officer will arrange for communications in accordance with SS 148 including visual, runner relays etc.
(b) Battn. H.Q. will be at hut at A.18.b.25.60, where all reports will be sent.
(c) Forward Command Post will be at Butts at A.18.c.9.[illegible].
(d) The Signalling Officer will establish the Forward Command Post as soon as possible, but Battn. H.Q. will not move forward until permission is obtained from Brigade H.Q.

12. Contact Aeroplanes.
(a) A contact aeroplane (imaginary) will fly over the front at ZERO plus 1½ hours and ZERO plus 3 hours.
(b) Flares will be lit in bunches of 3 to 5 when called for by aeroplane.
(c) The Signalling Officer will arrange for ground panel and strips for signalling to contact aeroplane.

13. Watches will be synchronized at 10 a.m.

14. Medical Arrangements.
(a) The R.A.P. will be at Battalion H.Q.
(b) Companies will evacuate their own wounded as far as Company H.Q. The M.O. will arrange for collection from Company H.Q. back, and for evacuation to A.D.S. at [illegible].
(c) Two Stretcher Bearers per Company will report to the M.O. at Battalion H.Q. at 10.30 a.m.

15. CONSOLIDATION.
(a) All men except snipers and observers will consolidate ground captured. Digging will be carried out on the "Intensive" system.
(b) Platoon Strong Points will be sited and dug in chequerwise formation. Supporting Strong Points covering gaps between those of Front Line platoons.

16. Every Section will have its sniper and observer detailed. The duty of these men is to cover consolidation and kill Bosche.

17. (a) Situation Reports showing progress made and position of leading troops will be sent in half hourly.
(b) Message Cards will be issued to Officers and N.C.O.s down to Platoon Commanders.

18. Zero Hour will be notified later.

(Continued.)

19. (a) All rifles and pouches will be examined on completion of assembly and a report in writing rendered to Battalion H.Q. that no N.C.O. or man is in possession of any ball ammunition.
(b) The Officer i/c Skeleton Enemy will also render a similar report.
(c) Lewis Guns and magazines will also be examined and included in certificate called for in para. (a)

20. Casualty returns will be rendered as under:-
(a) Estimated as soon as possible.
(b) Accurate as soon as possible.
(c) All Officers by name immediately.
(d) Casualties will be notifed as often as they are 25 or over.

R.C. Heyward
Captain,
Adjutant,
2/5th. S.Lan.R.

No. 1 Copy to O/C "A" Coy.
2 " to O/C "B" "
3 " to O/C "C" "
4 " to O/C "D" "
5 " to Intelligence Officer.
6 " to H.Q. 172nd. Inf.Bde. (for information.)
7 " to File.
8 " War Diary.

APPENDIX XXXIX

2/5th. Battn. Sth. Lancs. Regiment.

STATEMENT
SHOWING STRENGTH.
***

30th. Novbr. 1917.

BATTALION STRENGTH. 40 Off. 969 O.Ranks.

WITH UNIT:-

"A" Company.	181.
"B" Company.	173.
"C" Company.	182.
"D" Company.	183.
Headquarters.	76.
Transport.	46.
Q.M. Stores.	30
	871.

DETACHED.

Bde. & Division.	14.
Hospital.	7.
A.P.M. (57th. Divn.)	4.
Leave.	21.
Courses.	27.
M.G.Coy.	7.
XI Corps School.	3.
Bde. L.T.M.B.	12.
Trade Test.	1.
Army School.	1.
Base.	1.
	98.

APPENDIX XL

2/5th. Battalion South Lancashire Regt.

NOMINAL ROLL
(OFFICERS)

30th. Nov. 1917.

Headquarters.

Lieut.Col.	OWEN W.L. M.C.	C.O.
Major.	SCHULTZ A.H.	Second-in-C.
Captain	HAYWARD R.C.	Adjutant.
2/Lieutenant	ST. GEORGE A.R.	Asst.Adjutant.
Lieutenant	WEST H.	L.G. Officer.
Lieutenant	DEAN L.V.	Intell. Officer.
Lieutenant	TIMSON H.H.	Siggs. Officer.
Lieut.	GREGORY H.	Quartermaster.
2/Lieutenant	CASTLE A.C.	Transport Officer.
Captain	WOOD R.L.	M.O.

"A" Company.

Captain	WALLIS A.C.	O/C Company.
Captain	DONALD T.M.	2nd.in.C. Coy.
Lieutenant	HARGREAVES R.	Platoon Commander.
Lieutenant	LEAKE R.L.	do.
Lieutenant	DAVIS H.P.W.	do.
2/Lieutenant	MARTIN A.J.	do.

"B" Company.

Captain	CROWE J.A.	O/C Company.
Lieutenant	BULLEN H.G.	2nd.in.C. Coy.
Lieutenant	BRAZENER W.F.	Platoon Commander.
2/Lieutenant	CLARKE J.	do.
2/Lieutenant	FARMER W.H.	do.
2/Lieutenant	NOTLEY A.C.	do.
2/Lieutenan	RAGG C.W.	do.

"C" Company.

2/Lieutenant	MILTON S.J.	O/C Company.
2/Lieutenant	WOOLLETT S.J.	2nd.in.C. Coy.
Lieutenant	LE MARE E.R.	Musketry Officer.
2/Lieutenant	HALL J.G.	Platoon Commander.

"D" Company.

Captain	STEPHENSON C.W.	O/C "D" Company.
Lieutenant	FORDSHAM F.J.	2nd.in.C. Coy.
Lieutenant	HOLLAND W.H.F.	Platoon Commander.
Lieutenant	AGABEG J.W.	do.
2/Lieutenant	HANDLEY W.C.	do.
2/Lieutenant	RUSSELL C.A.	do.

COURSES.

2/Lieutenant	MARTIN G.J.	Musketry.
Lieutenant	HADFIELD J.L.	General.
Lieutenant	NIMMO A.A.	do.
2/Lieutenant	QUINTON P.J.	do.
Captain	MESSUM A.W.	do.
2/Lieutenant	ADAMS B.C.	do.

DETACHED.

2/Lieutenant	STONE A.R.	L.T.M.B.

HOSPITAL.

Captain	GUEST E.L.	(Sick)

Instructions regarding War Diaries and Intelligence Summaries are contained in F. S. Regs., Part II. and the Staff Manual respectively. Title Pages will be prepared in manuscript.

WAR DIARY
or
~~INTELLIGENCE SUMMARY~~
(Erase heading not required.)

Army Form C. 2118

2/5 S Lancs R
Vol 11

Place	Date 1917	Hour	Summary of Events and Information	Remarks and references to Appendices
LANDRETHUN & YEUSE	Dec 1st		The Battalion marched to RECQUES WEST training area and carried out the "Leap-frog" attack. Major A.H. Schultz returned from the XVIII Corps Conference. Major Schultz informed us that the Battalion had been transferred to the XIV Corps at 10 a.m. this morning	
	2nd		Church parades in the morning. Four men per platoon were granted leave to CALAIS for the day.	
	3rd		Training carried out according to programme. Capt. J.A. Crowe went to CAMIERS to see a demonstration of Machine Gun Firing. Information received that the Brigade would move on the 8th.	
	4th		Training carried out according to programme. In the afternoon Major Schultz, A/Adjutant and Company Commanders went to the RECQUES WEST training area where the Brigade Major, and reconnoitre the ground for the Brigade practice attack. Information received that the Brigade would move a day earlier, viz: the 7th and transport on the 6th. First move to the HERZEELE AREA	

1875 Wt. W593/826 1,000,000 4/15 J.B.C. & A. A.D.S.S./Forms/C. 2118.

Instructions regarding War Diaries and Intelligence Summaries are contained in F. S. Regs., Part II. and the Staff Manual respectively. Title Pages will be prepared in manuscript.

WAR DIARY
or
INTELLIGENCE SUMMARY
(Erase heading not required.)

Army Form C. 2118

Place	Date Dec	Hour	Summary of Events and Information	Remarks and references to Appendices
LANDRETHUN & YEUSE	1917 5th		The Battalion went to RECQUES WEST area to Cooperate in the Brigade Scheme. The Battalion acted as reserve Battalion. The C.O. being on leave and Major Schutty not available, Capt. C.W. Stephenson was i/c Battalion. News received that Lieut R Hargreaves had been awarded the Military Cross, and 241171 Sergt. Gorman W of "D" Company and 241565 Rifleman Trevitt J. of "A" Coy the Military Medal (Authority D.R.O. 1754 dated 27th November 1917) for gallantry and devotion to duty in action. All surplus stores etc. were sent to No. 4 billet LOSTRAAT. Baggage wagons left today.	AR 8/9 APPENDIX XLI
	6th		All Officers, and as many NCO's as possible attended demonstration at NORDAUSQUES by Lieut Col. Leroy G.S.O. XVIII Corps. Preparations made for moving at 4 a.m. on the 7th.	
	7th		The Battalion left LANDRETHUN at 4 a.m. and marched to AUDRUICQ station, and entrained for PROVEN. Arrived PROVEN 12.25 pm and marched to HERZEELE AREA, to billets, where they arrived at 4 p.m. then chiefly in billets, but a few in tents	AR 8/9 Appendix XLII

1875 Wt. W593/826 1,000,000 4/15 J.B.C. & A. A.D.S.S./Forms/C. 2118.

Instructions regarding War Diaries and Intelligence Summaries are contained in F. S. Regs., Part II. and the Staff Manual respectively. Title pages will be prepared in manuscript.

WAR DIARY
or
INTELLIGENCE SUMMARY.
(Erase heading not required.)

Army Form C. 2118.

Place	Date 1917	Hour	Summary of Events and Information	Remarks and references to Appendices
HERZEELE	8th Dec		The men were resting after the previous days journey.	
			C.O. held a conference for all Officers in the evening.	
	9th		Church parades cancelled owing to inclement weather.	
	10th		Men proceeded to Baths, and during the day washed their own clothing under Regimental arrangements.	
			C.O. held a conference for Company Commanders in the morning.	
	11th		G.O.C. 172nd Infantry Brigade inspected Companies in the latest form of training, and afterwards gave them a short lecture. "C" & "B" Companies were granted a holiday on the 13th for their good work.	
	12th		Training carried out in the morning. A fire broke out in the afternoon about 4.15 pm. in one of "A" Company's barns. Cause of fire is up to the present unknown. Feared loss of a lot of equipment. Barn completely destroyed	
	13th		The C.O, four Company Commanders and Lt. Nimmo proceeded to the ELVERDINGHE AREA to reconnoitre. They returned in the evening.	
	14th		Training carried out. Football and games taking place in the afternoon.	

D. D. & L., London, E.C. (A8001) Wt. W1771/M2031 750,000 5/17 Sch. 52 Forms C2118/14

Army Form C. 2118.

Instructions regarding War Diaries and Intelligence Summaries are contained in F. S. Regs., Part II. and the Staff Manual respectively. Title pages will be prepared in manuscript.

WAR DIARY
or
INTELLIGENCE SUMMARY.
(Erase heading not required.)

Place	Date 1917	Hour	Summary of Events and Information	Remarks and references to Appendices
HERZEELE	Dec. 15th		Training in the morning. Capt. R.L. WOOD. R.A.M.C.(T) left the battalion to join the 2/2nd Wessex Field Ambulance. His place was being taken by 1/LIEUT. T.B. MARSDEN from the 2/2nd Wessex (M.O.R.C.) U.S.R. A Divisional Boxing Tournament was held at ROUSBRUGGE, the Battalion winning 4 events out of 5 for which they entered.	ARS 19
	16th		Parade services in the morning. Preparing for next days move in the afternoon.	
	17th		The Battalion paraded at 7.15 am. and marched to HERZEELE station and entrained for PROVEN. At PROVEN the battalion again entrained for BOESINGHE. The battalion arrived at BOESINGHE at 1.30 pm. and marched to BOESINGHE No 1 Camp, which proved to be a good camp. Shortly after arrival a BOSCHE aeroplane was brought down one of the planes falling in our camp. During the afternoon officers reconnoitred the Corps Defence Line at GROYTERZALE FARM. "A" & "B" companies were warned to be ready to proceed at 10 minutes notice. "C" & "D" companies at ½ hours notice. The Battalion being "A" Battalion and the battalion in Brigade Support.	APPENDIX XLIII + XLIV
	18th		The C.O. Major A.H. Schultz and Adjutant reconnoitred the Corps Defence Line and located Infantry Posts. There was no shelling of tracks.	ARS 19

D. D. & L., London, E.C. (A8001) Wt. W1771/M2031 750,000 5/17 Sch. 52 Forms C2118/14

Army Form C. 2118.

Instructions regarding War Diaries and Intelligence Summaries are contained in F. S. Regs., Part II. and the Staff Manual respectively. Title pages will be prepared in manuscript.

WAR DIARY
or
INTELLIGENCE SUMMARY.

(*Erase heading not required.*)

Place	Date 1917	Hour	Summary of Events and Information	Remarks and references to Appendices
BOESINGHE	Dec 19th		Officers again reconnoitred the Corps Defence Line. Training carried out in the morning.	
	20th		Training in the morning. Very hard frost and misty. C.O. attended conference at Brigade H'qurs in the evening.	[illegible]
	21st		Misty and hard frost. C.O. Adjutant and Company Commanders started off for the line but owing to the mist rising only went as far as BABOON CAMP, and saw the Battalion who were about to go up the line	
	22nd		Change in the weather and slight thaw. The C.O. had a conference of Company Commanders in the morning. In the afternoon the C.O. Adjutant and M.O. visited the battalion who had just come out of the line. Company Commanders also visited their opposite numbers at 4.15 p.m. The BOSCHE put down a heavy barrage in front, several S.O.S. lights were sent up from our line. The C.O. gave orders for everyone to "stand by". The barrage began to slacken down after about 3/4 of an hour. No information had been received at 5.45 pm as to what had taken place. The BOSCHE barrage appeared to be heavy.	[illegible]

D. D. & L., London, E.C.
(A8001) Wt. W1771/M2031 750,000 5/17 Sch. 52 Forms C2118/14

Army Form C. 2118.

Instructions regarding War Diaries and Intelligence Summaries are contained in F. S. Regs., Part II. and the Staff Manual respectively. Title pages will be prepared in manuscript.

WAR DIARY
or
INTELLIGENCE SUMMARY.
(Erase heading not required.)

Place	Date	Hour	Summary of Events and Information	Remarks and references to Appendices
BOESINGHE	1917 Dec 23		C.O. Adjutant and 4 Company Commanders visited the sector which the battalion was ultimately to occupy. It was ascertained that the previous evening the BOSCHE raided the sector and captured two posts at TURENNE CROSSING.	[illegible]
			Training was in progress during the morning.	
	24th		The Officers and Sergeants had their Xmas dinner, which was much appreciated in both cases. At 10.30 pm the C.O. interviewed all Officers and N.C.Os who were proceeding to the line in advance of the battalion. The O/C platoons of odd numbers and 2nd i/c of platoons of even numbers proceeded to the line to reconnoitre position and meet battalion on arrival.	
	25th		The men had their Xmas dinner and every endeavour was made to provide a good meal. The dinner was a success. The G.O.C. 172nd Infantry Brigade visited the men whilst dinner was in progress and conveyed to the men his Xmas greetings. The Battalion left BOESINGHE CAMP at 3.15 pm and proceeded to the line arriving at EGYPT HOUSE about 6 pm. On the way up personnel of Headquarters were obliged to leave the tracks and proceed across the open for some distance owing to enemy shelling.	[illegible] XLV

D. D. & L., London, E.C. (A8001) Wt. W1771/M2031 750,000 5/17 Sch. 52 Forms C2118/14

Army Form C. 2118.

WAR DIARY
or
INTELLIGENCE SUMMARY.
(Erase heading not required.)

Instructions regarding War Diaries and Intelligence Summaries are contained in F. S. Regs., Part II. and the Staff Manual respectively. Title pages will be prepared in manuscript.

Place	Date 1917	Hour	Summary of Events and Information	Remarks and references to Appendices
HOUTHULST FOREST RIGHT. SUB SECTOR.	Oct 26	1.30am	Rear Battalion H'qurs established at PASCAL. FARM, part of H'qurs remaining at EGYPT HOUSE as forward H'qurs. During the afternoon BOSCHE put down a heavy barrage on right Division and also sent a few shells on our line causing 3 casualties. On the night 26/27th ~~we~~ carried out a ~~raid~~ reconnoitring patrol on TURENNE CROSSING, Lt. HARGREAVES and his patrol along with B & C Companies taking part.	AR8G
			Casualties: 3 O.Ranks wounded by Machine Gun fire.	
			Major Schultz arrived at PASCAL FARM.	
	27th		C.O. went to Brigade and at night went over in "no man's land" in a white patrol suit. A Barrage was put down between EGYPT HOUSE and PASCAL FARM. Just before the enemy barrage commenced, 2 green lights, which was a BOSCHE signal for annihilating fire, were sent up. The enemy had obviously seen a patrol of ours dressed in white and a carrying party and was under the impression that we were forming up for an attack. After about 20 minutes 2 red lights were sent up by the enemy and his barrage immediately slackened down.	AR8G
			"B" & "C" Coys were relieved by "B" & "D" Companies of 2/4th S. Lan R. and proceeded to BABOON CAMP.	APPENDIX XLVI

D. D. & L., London, E.C. (A5001) Wt. W1771/M2031 750,000 5/17 Sch. 52 Forms C2118/14

Army Form C. 2118.

Instructions regarding War Diaries and Intelligence Summaries are contained in F. S. Regs., Part II. and the Staff Manual respectively. Title pages will be prepared in manuscript.

WAR DIARY
or
INTELLIGENCE SUMMARY.
(Erase heading not required.)

Place	Date 1917	Hour	Summary of Events and Information	Remarks and references to Appendices
	Dec 28th		The G.O.C. 172nd Infantry Brigade visited B.H.Q about 2.15am. The C.O left for Bde H'qrs at 5am. 'D' Coy which was in reserve was relieved by 'A' Coy which was in support. Relief was satisfactory.	
	29th		C.O. still at Brigade. Everything quiet during morning. At 5.7pm the BOSCHE put up a very heavy barrage along our whole front and our S.O.S. was sent up on the right company front. About 40 Bosche raided our left company No 5 post. They advanced from a small wood but were driven off by M.G and Rifle fire when within about 10 yards. Our artillery opened out immediately our S.O.S. went up and continued until 6.5 pm. The raid was repulsed by M.G & Rifle fire. One Bosche N.C.O. brought in belonging to 148th Infy Battn. 'A' Company 2/4th relieved 'D' Coy 2/4. S.L.R. 'C' Coy 2/4 S.L.R. relieved 'D' Company 2/5th S.L.R. 'D' Company 2/5th S.L.R. relieved 'B' Coy 2/4 S.L.R in front line.	
	30th		Our artillery carried out a shelling stunt for 12 hours. At 8pm a raid was carried out on TURENNE CROSSING by 'B' & 'C' Coys. 'B' Coy took up the Right position and 'C' Coy the left position. Result of Raid:- We advanced our line about 200 yards on the attacked positions. 2/Lt. BARNETT and 2/Lt HALL were killed and 17 other ranks [illegible] 13 Other ranks were wounded. One prisoner was captured belonging to the 148th Infy Regt.	APPENDIX XLVII

D. D. & L., London, E.C. Forms C. 2118/14

Instructions regarding War Diaries and Intelligence Summaries are contained in F. S. Regs., Part II. and the Staff Manual respectively. Title pages will be prepared in manuscript.

WAR DIARY
or
INTELLIGENCE SUMMARY.
(Erase heading not required.)

Army Form C. 2118.

Place	Date	Hour	Summary of Events and Information	Remarks and references to Appendices
	31st		The Battalion was relieved by 2/4th S. Lancs. Regt. in the line. Relief was carried out satisfactorily.	
			W. [illegible] Lt. Col Commanding 2/5 Bn. S. Lan. R	

D. D. & L., London, E.C.
(A7001) Wt. W1771/M2631 750,000 5/17 Sch. 52 Forms C2118/14

War Diary

APPENDIX XLI

SECRET. Copy No....6

2/4th. BN. S. LAN. R., OPERATION ORDER NO.6.

****

Reference:-
Attd. Sketch Map of
Area and
Map "A", 1/10,000

30th. Nov. 1917.

1\. INFORMATION. The offensive will be resumed on "Z" Day which will be notified later.

2\. INTENTION. (a) The 172nd. Inf. Bde. will attack on the front of the 57th. Division, with the 173rd. Infantry Bde., 58th. Divn. on the right, and the 149th. Infantry Bde., 50th. Division on the left. Flank Assaulting Battalions are:-
Left .... Right ....

(b) The Battalion will be the reserve Battalion of the 172nd. Infantry Bde. The assaulting battalions will be disposed as follows:-

2/4th. Bn. S.Lan.R.	Left Assaulting Battalion.
2/10th. Bn. K.L.R.	Centre Assaulting Battalion.
2/5th. Bn. K.L.R.	Right Assaulting Battalion.

Boundaries are as follows:-
The Divisional Boundaries are indicated by Green Lines
The Left Boundary passes through 7c - 7b and 8c.
The Right Boundary passes through 13d, 14c, and 14b.
The Battalion Boundaries are:-

Left Battalion.	Left.	Divisional Boundary.
	Right.	Line cutting 7.d.10.30 8.c.00.80, 8.a.40.00, 8.b.00.35, to point on final objective 8.b.75.75.
Right Battalion.	Left.	Boundary Line from 13.b.60.15 to point on final objective at 8.d.95.60
	Right.	Right Divisional Boundary.

(c) The 172nd. Infantry Brigade will attack and capture the objectives shown on the attached map "A"
The first objective is the RED dotted line.
The Second and final objective is the RED solid line.
The jumping-off line is the GREEN dotted line.

3\. DISPOSITIONS PRIOR TO THE ATTACK. In accordance with relief orders issued separately, (imaginary) the Battalion will relieve the .... Battn. in VULTURE TRENCH on the Z - 2/Z - 1 night.
Upon completion of relief the Battalion will hold the defensive line taken over from the out-going Battalion.

4\. RECONNAISSANCE. Prior to the relief mentioned in para. 3, O.'s C. Coys. Specialist Officers, etc. will have made their reconnaissances of VULTURE TRENCH for the purpose of taking over. Also as far as possible for preparation of this attack. On Z - 1 day, the hours of daylight will be used to the full for reconnoitring.

(a) Routes to Support Areas.
(b) Routes to Assaulting Battalions and their Company Headquarters.
(c) The Area of Assembly, and (d) the positions of the Assaulting Battalions Reserve Companies after ZERO hour
and for pointing out objectives.

Special care will be taken in reconnoitring the stream running approximately East and West cutting the Divisional Boundary at 7.c.05.20.

(Continued)

5. ASSEMBLY. On the night prior to the attack, commencing at Zero minus 8 hours, the Battalion will move forward from VULTURE TRENCH to the Support position about BOAT FARM - HUN FARM AREA.
The Support Areas allotted to Companies are as follows:-
"A" Coy.AreaWest of TANK FARM - HUN FARM Road with
Coy. H.Q. at BOAT FARM.
"B" Coy.AreaEast of TANK FARM - HUN FARM Road with
Coy. H.Q. at LINK FARM.
"C" Coy.AreaWest of TANK FARM - HUN FARM Road with
Coy. H.Q. at COMFORT FARM.
"D" Coy.AreaWest of TANK FARM - HUN FARM Road with
Coy. H.Q. at MALIC HOUSES.
Battalion Headquarters will be at HUN FARM.

O.'s C. "A" and "B" Coy. will commence to move forward to their Support Areas by pre-reconnoitred routes at ZERO - 8 hours. O.'s C. "C" and "D" Coys. will commence to move forward at ZERO minus 7 hours.

Companies will move forward by platoons under their own arrangements.
O.'s C. Coys. will inform B.H.Q. when they are in position by use of the code-word "PARTRIDGE" which will be sent in duplicate. Messages by runners.
B.H.Q. will then move forward to HUN FARM.
One Battalion of the 171st. Infantry Brigade will occupy VULTURE TRENCH before ZERO.

6. BARRAGE. The attack will be made under cover of an artillery barrage, which will come down at ZERO hour, 200 yards in front of the GREEN dotted line shown on the attached map.
The first lift will be at ZERO plus 6 minutes, and the barrage will move at the rate of 100 yards in 8 minutes.
All lifts will be 50 yards.
The protective barrage in front of the 1st. Objectives will become intense at ZERO plus 1 hour and 48 minutes, and will begin to creep at ZERO plus 1 hour and 50 minutes.

7. ACTION. All Companies will be prepared to go forward to support any one or all of the assaulting battalions at a moment's notice. No Company will move without first having direct orders from B.H.Q.
O.'s C. Coys. will carefully guard against dissipating their forces by dribbling them up in small parties.
The role of the Battalion is not to reinforce but to counter-attack or fill up any gap which appears so great as to warrant such action.
O.'s C. Coys. will arrange special observation to keep an outlook on the progress of events, and to intelligentlyanticipate any orders to move.

8. ORDERS. No copies of Battalion or Company Orders, nor any orders of the Assaulting Battalions forwarded for information, will be taken into the line.

9. COLLECTION OF CAPTURED DOCUMENTS. In the event of Companies having to move forward, the Intelligence Officer will detail two men, specially to examine dug-outs in the captured area, and to collect all documents found therein. These documents will be forwardedto B.H.Q. immediately.

10. SITUATION REPORTS. In the event of Companies having to go forward, O.'s C. Coys. will make special efforts to keep Battn. Headquarters advised of the location of their troops. Reports will be sent in to B.H.Q. hourly until the

(Continued)

10. SITUATION REPORTS. – Contd.
situation is clear. As soon as the situation permits the Intelligence Officer with two runners will reconnoitre Company positions and report result as early as possible to B.H.Q.

11. COMMUNICATIONS.
The Battalion Signalling Officer will be responsible for establishing communication between Battn. H.Q. Coy. H.Q. and also to Assaulting Battn. Headquarters by means of:-
(a) Wire.
(b) Visual.
(c) Runners.
(d) Power Buzzer.

12. DRESS AND EQUIPMENT.
According to Special Instructions "A" issued to Coy. and Platoon Commanders on Oct. 28th. 1917.

13. ZERO HOUR.
ZERO hour will be notified to all concerned in duplicate messages by runners. O.'s C. Coys. will ensure that no reference to the day of assault or to Zero Hour will be made by telephone or wire, but only in writing, and then only to responsible officers.

14. CONSOLIDATION.
All ground gained must be held at all costs. The word "Retire" will never be used. Anyone using this word will be treated as an enemy and shot.

15. LIAISON.
The Intelligence Officer will arrange for forward liaison with the Reserve Companies of the attacking Battalions, and also with the H.Q., L.T.M.B.

16. CARE OF ARMS.
(a) All rifles will have breech cover, special long cover adjusted, and a piece of 4" x 2" in muzzle. Men will advance with rifles so covered. The bayonet will be fixed and the long cover pulled down over it.
(b) Breech covers will be attached to the small of the butt by means of a boot-lace.
(c) Before firing the long cover will be taken off and put in the pocket, 4" x 2" taken out, and breech cover unfastened, and left hanging from the small of the butt.

17. TRENCH BOARDS.
Trench Boards must not be removed from tracks or used for unauthorised purposes. Track "police" have orders to shoot at sight if this order is broken.

18. R.A.P.
Position of R.A.P. is at MALTO HOUSES 13.a.78.75.

19. ACKNOWLEDGE.

2/Lieutenant,
A/Adjutant,
2/5th. S.Lan.R.

Issued by runner at 12.30pm
on 28/10/17
Distribution
No. 1 Copy to O/C "A" Coy. No. 2 Copy to O/C "B" Coy.
3 " to O/C "C" " No. 4 " to O/C "D" "
5 " H.Q. 172nd.Inf.Bde. (for information.)
6 & 7 War diary
8 9 0

War Diary

Appendix XLII/12

SECRET.

Copy No.....

2/5th. S.LAN.R., OPERATION ORDERS NO. 58.

Ref. Map,
Sheet HAZEBROUCK 5A
1/100,000

***

6th. Dec. 17.

1. MOVE. The Battalion less portion of Transport will move to the HERZEELE AREA by train in accordance with attached Time-table on December 7th. 1917.

2. PARADE. The Battalion will parade outside B.H.Q. at 4 a.m. on 7th. instant. Order of march:-
   H.Q. Sigs. - Band - A - B - C - D.
   Greatcoats, lapelled up, will be worn.
   Transport will march in rear of the column. Officers chargers will be with their respective owners.

3. ROUTE. B.H.Q. (LANDRETHUN CHATEAU) - AUTINGUES - NIELLES - AUDRICQ.

4. ENTRAINING & DETRAINING OFFICER. Major A.H. SCHULTZ will be entraining and detraining Officer, and will arrive at the Station half an hour before the Battalion entrains.

5. BREAKFASTS. Breakfasts will be under Company arrangements. A large breakfast must be provided with two full courses. A full hour must be allowed from the time at which breakfasts are served.

6. LOADING PARTY. "D" Coy., less Nos. 1, 2, 3, 4 and 5 of Lewis Gun Sections will report to the Staff Captain at AUDRICQ STATION at 9 a.m. on December 7th. They will travel by the omnibus train to PROVEN and will unload the train and then join the Battalion in the new Area.
   "D" Coy. will proceed with the Battalion as far as AUDRICQ STATION.

7. BILLETS. All Billets will be left scrupulously clean and in a sanitary condition.

8. RATIONS. The unexpired portion of the day's rations will be carried on the man. Men must be warned that there will be no further issue of food for the day. Tea will be provided on arrival in Camp.

9. COMPLETION. O.'s C. Coys. will report to B.H.Q. by runner the completion of the move, on arrival in the new Area.

A.P. St.George
2/Lieutenant,
A/Adjutant,
2/5th. S.Lan.R.

Issued by runner at 11.30am
to:-
No. 1 Copy to O/C "A" Coy.
No. 2 " to O/C "B" "
No. 3 " to O/C "C" "
No. 4 " to O/C "D" "
No. 5 " to Q/M
No. 6 " to T.O.
No. 7 " to Major A.H. Schultz.
No. 8 " to S.O.
No. 9 " File.

SECRET. TRAIN MOVES 7th. DECR 1917.

Station of Departure.	Time to start entrain ing.	Depart.	Arrive PROVEN	Report to entrain ing Officer at AUDRUICQ STATION.
AUDRUICQ.	8-0 a.m	9-0 am	12.30pm	7.45 a.m.

SECRET.

T R A I N   M O V E S - 17th. DECEMBER, 1917.

STATION OF DEPARTURE.	TIME TO START ENTRAIN -ING.	DEPART	ARRIVE PROVEN	DEPART PROVEN	DESTINATION	ALL PERSONNEL LESS TRANSPORT PERSONNEL	REPORT TO EN- TRAINING OFFICER AT HERZEELE.
HERZEELE	8 a.m.	8.28 a.m.	9.24am.	10 a.m.	BOESINGHE.	2/5th. Bn.S.L.R.	7.50 a.m.

XL IV

SECRET.

Copy No. 8.

Reference Map HAZEBROUCK 5A 1/100000

2/5th. Bn. S.Lan.R., OPERATION ORDERS NO.53.

ADMINISTRATIVE INSTRUCTIONS.

No. 1.

1. The Battalion will move to the ELVERDINGHE AREA on December 17th. from HERZEELE by train. Times to be notified later. Transport will move by road in accordance with attached table.

2. The Battalion will be billeted in the new area in BOESINGHE Camp (Sheet 28/ 1/40,000 B.5.d.4.3.) and will take over from the 8th NORFOLK REGT.

3. ADVANCE PARTIES. Captain C.W.STEPHENSON and 10 other ranks will move to new area to-morrow, 16th. instant by bus, starting from Brigade Headquarters at 9 a.m.
The undermentioned will report to Captain C.W.STEPHENSON at 8 a.m. tomorrow morning, the 16th. instant, outside "D" Company Headquarters.

- 1 Other Rank from Q.M.Stores.
- 1 do. from Transport.
- 1 do. B.H.Q.
- 1 do. "A" Coy.
- 1 do. "B" "
- 1 do. "C" "
- 1 do. "D" "
- 1 Signaller. } B.H.Q.
- 1 Batman. }

The following will be taken over:-

- (1) Defence Scheme.
- (2) Aeroplane Photographs.
- (3) Maps of the Area.
- (4) Area Stores.
- (5) Work in progress round Camps and Horse Lines.

Certificates as to cleanliness of billets will be given and taken.
This party will be rationed up to and including 17th. December, 1917.

4. MECHANICAL TRANSPORT. Two lorries have been allotted to the Battalion and will report to Brigade Headquarters at 7.30 a.m. on the 17th. instant. Lieut. Timson will detail two guides to conduct these lorries from Brigade Headquarters to loading points.
Written instructions as to destination of lorries will be handed to drivers before proceeding to ELVERDINGHE AREA. 1 blanket per man will be taken by motor lorry These will be rolled in bundles of 10 and labelled. "A" and "D" Coys. H.Q. and Transport blankets will be sent to Q.M. Stores by 7.30 a.m. on the 17th. instant "B" and "C" Coys. blankets will be deposited on the main road near point D.11.d.6.3. under a guard of one man from each Company by 7.30 a.m. The Guard should be fully equipped and have their unconsumed portion of the day's ration.

5. BAGGAGE WAGONS. Baggage Wagons will report at 10 a.m. on the 16th. instant. All Officers' Valises surplus stores etc. will be at the Q.M.Stores by 9.30 a.m. 16th. instant.

6. BILLETS. All billets will be left scrupulously clean. Certificates must be obtained from Officer i/c Advance Party of incoming Battalion as to cleanliness, sanitation etc.

7. REFILLING POINT. On December 17th. Refilling Point will be at ZONNEBLOOM CABARET near ELVERDINGHE (point B.6.c.8.?.) The Q.M. will send a guide to refilling point to guide wagons to his headquarters.

8. COMMAND OF TRANSPORT. C.O. No.4 H.T.Coy. A.S.C. 57th. Divisional Train will be in charge of the Brigade Transport during the march.

9. WASHING BOWLS. All washing bowls will be returned to Q.M.Stores by 9.30 to-morrow the 1[illegible]th. instant.

10. ACKNOWLEDGE.

2/Lieutenant,
A/Adjutant,
2/5th. S.Lan.R.

No. 1 Copy to O/C "A" Coy.
2 Copy to O/C "B" Coy.
3 " to O/C "C" Coy.
4 " to O/C "D" Coy.
5 " to Q.M.
6 " to T.O.
7 " to Lieut. Timson.
8 " to C.O.
9 " to File.
10 " to War Diary.
11 " to " "

APPENDIX XLV

SECRET.

Copy No. 11

2/5th. BN. S. LAN. R., OPERATION ORDERS NO. 54.

Reference Maps,
BIXSCHOOTE, 20 S.W.4. 1/10,000.
ST.JULIEN, 20 N.W.2. 1/10,000.
BELGIUM. 28 N.W. 1/20,000.
HOUTHOULST FOREST,
(Special Sheet, 1/10,000.)

24/12/17.

1. On the night 25/26th. December, 1917, the 172nd. Infantry Brigade will relieve the 171st. Infantry Brigade in the line.

2. The Battalion will relieve the 2/8th. K.L.R. in the Front Line of the Right Subsector on the night 25/26th. December, 1917.

3. Relief will take place in accordance with the attached table.

4. On completion of relief Companies will be located as per proforma to be issued later.

5. Guides will be at BOESINGHE CAMP by 1 p.m. on the 25th. inst.

6. CLARGES STREET is for UP-TRAFFIC - HUNTER STREET is for DOWN TRAFFIC. RAILWAY STREET will be used by 2/5th. S.L.R. going in.

7. The Platoon Commanders of the odd platoons, and 2nd. i/c of the even platoons will proceed to the line on the night 24/25th. December, to learn the situations and exact dispositions of their respective platoons and sections, and will make all the necessary arrangements for meeting their platoons.

8. All blankets will be collected and rolled in bundles of 10 and dumped outside the Drying Room opposite B.O.R. by 10 a.m. 25th. instant. Officers' valises will also be collected. Blankets must be labelled.

9. DRESS. Packs will be carried, and leather jerkins will be worn. Greatcoats will be taken inside the pack. 2 Extra pairs of socks and 120 rounds of S.A.A. per man. Two days' rations will be carried, and two water-bottles per man will be taken. These will be issued later.

10. LEWIS GUNS. All L.G. equipment etc. will be taken into the line, and brought out on relief.

11. All defence schemes and other documents, concerning Company sectors will be taken over on relief. Copies of receipts will be sent to B.H.Q.

12. Relief of Companies will be reported to B.H.Q. by "B.A.B." Code.

A.P.S. Grant
2/Lieutenant,
A/Adjutant,
2/5th. S.Lan.R.

No.1 Copy to "A" Coy.
2 " to "B" "
3 " to "C" "
4 " to "D" "
5 " to Q.M.
10 " to C.O. (for H.Q.)
12 " to War Diary.

No. 6 Copy to T.O.
7 " to O/C 2/8 K.L.R. (for information)
8 " C.O.
9 " 2nd. i/c Battn.
11 " War Diary.
13 " Spare.

2/5th. S. Lan. R.

Date.	Unit.	From.	Relieving.	Time.	Destination.	Route.	Remarks.
Dec 25th.	2/5th. Bn. S. Lan. R.	BOESINGHE CAMP.	2/5th.K.L.R.	Not to pass CANAL BANK before 5pm.	FRONT LINE RIGHT Subsector.	RAILWAY STREET	100 yards between platoons.

SECRET. Copy No. 11

2/5th. Bn. S. Lan. R.

ADMINISTRATIVE INSTRUCTIONS
in connection with
O.O.54.

1. DUTIES. Major A.H.SCHULTZ will detail 1 N.C.O. and 4 men from those not going into the trenches to report at PASSERELE FARM U.21.c.6.8. at 2 p.m. 25th. instant, to act as Bomb Storemen as permanent duty until the Brigade is relieved. They will be rationed by 172nd. Bde. H.Q.

2. TRENCH & AREA STORES O.'s C. Companies will forward a list of all Trench and Area Stores to this Office.

3. HOT FOOD. Orders for this have been issued.

4. TRANSPORT ROUTES. Routes for Transport are as follows:-
BOESINGHE BRIDGE to U.21.a.10.5. - U.28.c.7.5. - Vee Bend U.11.c.95.65.
Wheeled transport can be used up to Vee Bend U.11.c.95.65.
Pack animals can be used to B.H.Q. at EGYPT HOUSE.

5. R.E. MATERIAL. R.E.Material ca be drawn direct from the R.E.Dump KOEKUIT (U.11.c.80.25) List of Stores drawn will be forwarded to B.H.Q.

6. S.A.A. & GRENADES. The Bombing Officer will submit all indents for supply of ammunition to B.H.Q.

7. CAMP. The Camp will be left scrupulously clean and in a sanitary condition, and a certificateto this effect obtained from O/C Advance Party of Incoming Unit, copy of which will be forwarded to this Office.

A. R. St George

2/Lieutenant,
A/Adjutant,
2/5th. S.Lan.R.

24/12/17.

SECRET. APPENDIX XLIII Copy No.9.....

ADMINISTRATIVE INSTRUCTIONS, No.2.

1. MOVE. The Battalion, less Transport personnel, will move to the ELVERDINGHE AREA to-morrow, 17th. instant, by train in accordance with attached time-table.

2. ENTRAINING OFFICER. Lieut. L.M.DEAN will be Entraining Officer and will report to the Staff Captain three quarters of an hour before the train is due to start. He will accompany the train to PROVEN and will act as Entraining and Detraining Officer there and at destination.

3. BREAKFASTS. Breakfast will be at 5.30 a.m.

4. PARADE. The Battalion will parade at 7.15 a.m. at point D.11.d.8.3. in order H.Q. - Band - A - B - C - D.

5. BLANKETS. Reference Administrative Orders No.1, para. 4. Blankets will be deposited at 6 a.m. and not as stated.

6. FIELD KITCHENS. (Ref.Map, HAZEBROUCK 5A 1/10,000). Cookers will be at Cross-roads N.W. of H in HOUTKERQUE at 7.50 a.m. C.Q.M.S.'s will be held responsible that these cookers are at this point punctually, and that they are carrying rations for a hot meal in the evening.

7. MESS CART. Officers' Mess-baskets will be collected to-night, and will call at "D" Coy.'s Headquarters at 9 p.m. and at "C" Coy.'s Headquarters at 9.30 p.m. to collect both "B" and "C" Coy.'s Mess Kit. These times will be strictly adhered to. The Mess-cart will call at B.H.Q. on its return from Companies. Officers will arrange with local people to provide mess utensils for to-morrow morning.

8. REFILLING POINT. The Q.M. will arrange for a guide to be sent to Refilling Point at Sheet 28, B.8.c.8.3. to meet Supply Wagons as soon as possible after arrival.

9. COMPLETION. O.'s C. Coys. will report to B.H.Q. by runner the completion of the move.

10. EMPLOYMENT. O.C. "C" Coy. will detail 2 O.R. to report to B.H.Q. at 8 a.m. on the 18th. instant for duty at PENSIONS FARM D.21.c.2.5.

11. COURT OF ENQUIRY. The undermentioned Officers, N.C.O.'s and men will remain behind to-morrow, and will report to Major Schultz at 9 a.m. at "A" Coy.'s H.Q.

Captain T.M. DONALD.
Lieut. H. WEST.
241238, C.S.M. BALL T.
240384, Sergt. ROBINSON.
240688, " BANKS J.
240341, " ROGERS A.V.
240942, L/Cpl. HOLLAND J.
241838, Rfn. ELLISON.
240349, " MARSH J.
and 3 Batmen.

The above will retain their day's rations.

12. ACKNOWLEDGE.

A.P. St.George.
2/Lieutenant,
A/Adjutant,
2/5th. S.Lan.R.

APPENDIX XLVI [illegible]

[illegible]

Secret 1/5th S. Lan. R.

[illegible] Orders 55

MAP REFERENCE

BIXSCHOOTE

20 S.W. 4 1/10,000

1. This evening Thursday the 27th inst 'B' and 'C' Coys. will be relieved in the FRONT line by two Companies of 1/4th S. Lan. R.

2. When relieved B and C Coys. will move back to BABOON CAMP where they will come under the orders of O.C. 1/4th Bn S. Lan. R.

3. Whilst at BABOON CAMP B and C Coys. will not be used for working parties

4. Companies moving to the line will use RAILWAY STREET, HUNTER STREET [illegible] [illegible] for down traffic

5. The relieving Companies of
7/4th Bn S. Lan. R. will leave
BABOON CAMP at 3 p.m.

6. 1 N.C.O. per platoon will
[illegible] remain in the line till
5 a.m. 28th inst in order to
assist the two Companies of
the 7/4th S. Lan. R. to learn the
line positions. These N.C.O.'s
will report at PASCAL FARM
at 4.45 p.m. 27th inst to
conduct the relieving platoons
to their positions.

7. On being relieved B and C
Coys. will be rationed by
O.C. 7/4th Bn S. Lan. R. and the
two companies of the 7/4th will
be rationed by this unit.

8. The B and C Coys. will [illegible]
all [illegible], and [illegible], in
use for [illegible] [illegible] [illegible] [illegible]
tea and water, and hand
[illegible] [illegible] [illegible] [illegible]
numbers with an [illegible]
as the system in force

for obtaining and distributing same.

9. The second Water Bottle per man will be taken down to BABOON CAMP and there handed over to Sgt. J.S. Woollett of Advanced Q.M. Stores at COLDSTREAM CAMP, with instructions to retain them in his custody.

10. O/C B and C Coy. will cause being collected in a central spot in rear infantry areas all wiring materials sent up them last night for special purposes. They will hand this material over carefully to our opposite numbers to enable the latter to start wiring the front tonight with a minimum of delay.

11. O/C B & C Coy. will also hand over carefully all reports etc. which are required daily.

12. Completion of relief will be reported to B.H.Q. by Code Word "XMAS".

13. Acknowledge.

A.R. McGregor 2/Lt
Adjt.
7/8th R. Ir. S.I.R. [illegible]

No 1 Copy to B Coy
" 2 do to C Coy
" 3 do to A Coy
" 4 do to D Coy
" 5 do to 7th/8th S.I.R.
" 6 do to Co.
7 do to War Diary
8 do to do
9 do to 172nd Inf. Bde.

(Nos 3–5: for information)

(No 9: for information)

27th December 1917.

APPENDIX XLVII

SECRET. Copy No. 12

2/5th SOUTH LANCASHIRE REGIMENT
ORDER No. 15

December 29th 1917.

Reference Maps:- HOUTHULST Pt 1/10,000
Special Map J1 1/10,000.

ATTACK. (1) B and C Coys will carry out an attack on the enemy's posts round TURENNE CROSSING on the night of 30/31 December 1917. ZERO HOUR will be 8-0 p.
B Coy will attack on the RIGHT; C Coy on the LEFT.

OBJECT. (2) To capture and consolidate the enemy's posts; to kill Germans and to secure prisoners for identification.

OBJECTIVES. (3) B Coy.
1. COLIBRI FARM
2. TURENNE CROSSING.

C Coy.
1. Post at V.1.c.75.60
2. Post at V.1.d.00.55 (one section will be posted at about V.1.c.55.60)

APPROXIMATE STRENGTH (4)
(a) Attacking Parties. 3½ platoons (2 platoons B Coy, 1½ platoons C Coy)
(b) Support Parties. 1½ platoons (1 platoon B Coy, ½ platoon C Coy)

ASSEMBLY. (5) The attacking parties will be formed up as follows:-
B Coy.
Leading platoon will be formed up on the West side of BERTHIER FARM - TURENNE CROSSING Road on a line from V.7.b.10.45 to the road facing North.
The second platoon immediately in rear.

C Coy.
Leading platoon will be formed up on the line V.1.c.35.50 to V.1.c.40.30 with half a platoon immediately in rear.

Assembly will be completed by ZERO - 30.

WITHDRAWAL OF POSTS (6)
(a) The following posts will be withdrawn to
V.1. No. 1 will be withdrawn at ZERO-60 and relieve V.1. No.5, when V.1 No. 5 will go to PASCAL FARM.

V.1 No. 2 will be withdrawn at ZERO-30 to the vicinity of V.1. No. 4

U.6. No. 1 will be withdrawn at ZERO-30, 100 yards to a disused series of fortified shell holes.

(b) V.1 No. 2 and U.6. No. 1 will reoccupy their posts at ZERO + 30 or as soon after as possible, reporting same to O.C. Operations.

(c) V.1 No. 1 will be occupied by the support ½ platoon of C Coy as soon as operations allow. This platoon will be accommodated at U.6.d.90.30 previous to attack.

SUPPORTS (7) B Coy.
One platoon at V.7.b.00.80. This post will be sent out from post V.7. No. 1 at first opportunity after the capture of objectives.

C Coy.
Half platoon at V.1.c.60.50 This post will be sent out from V.1 No. 1 post at first opportunity after capture of objectives. (see para 6 (c)).

Support parties will consolidate above positions as soon as they are taken up.

ADVANCE (8)

At ZERO HOUR attacking platoons will advance under a creeping barrage. Leading platoons will capture and consolidate first objectives mentioned in para 3. Second waves will leapfrog through leading waves and capture and consolidate second objectives mentioned in para 3.

CONSOLIDATION (9)

(a) As soon as the objectives have been gained all men except observers must consolidate, especially during the first half hour.

(b) One section of Supporting Parties will carry forward the following material:-
- 3 coils plain French concertina wire.
- 6 long screw pickets
- 2 shovels.

This material will be carried forward to attacking parties as soon as the situation permits.

(c) The remaining three sections will each carry forward a similar amount of material for their own use.

ARTILLERY ACTION (10)

(a) The attack will be supported by -
- 66 18 pounders
- 23 4.5" Hows

In addition XIX and II Corps Heavy Artillery will stand by for counter-battery work and engage selected points on flanks and rear of enemy's line including VAN DYCK and DAVOUST FARMS.
Artillery of Divisions on our right and left will also co-operate.

(b) Creeping and standing barrage from ZERO to ZERO+25
Protective barrage from ZERO to ZERO+60

(c) From ZERO to ZERO+12 one gun per 18 pounder Battery will fire smoke shell. These guns will be superimposed on the creeping barrage.
Two guns of left group will also fire smoke shell in enfilade.

(d) 4.5" Hows will fire on selected points and known enemy emplacements.

(e) The creeping barrage will allow B Coy to attack TURENNE CROSSING at ZERO+13 and C Coy to attack V.1.c.75.60 at same time.

ACTION OF TRENCH MORTARS (11)

(a) Light T.Ms will bombard following points from ZERO to ZERO+19 :-

(1) L.T.	1 mortar on M.G.	V.1.c.90.80	Bombard from ZERO to ZERO plus 19.
	1 mortar on TURENNE CROSSING		
	2 mortars on M.Gs at	V.1.c.35.95	
		V.1.a.5020	
		V.1.a.30.10	
		V.1.a.10.17	
	1 mortar on M.G.	U.6.b.15.70	
	and post	U.6.b.25.80	
	1 mortar on M.G.	U.6.a.80.60	
	and post	U.6.a.90.70	

(2) 4" Stokes Mortars will fire Thermite on the following positions :-

2 mortars on	COLIBRI FARM	ZERO to ZERO plus 2
2 mortars on	TURENNE CROSSING	ZERO to ZERO plus 5
2 mortars on	V.1.c.75.60	ZERO to ZERO plus 2

ACTION OF MACHINE GUNS (12) — 172nd Machine Gun Coy will put down a box barrage paying particular attention to V.1.b. and V.1.c. - ample clearance being allowed to attacking troops.

ACTION OF LEWIS GUNS (13) — Lewis Guns will be carried forward by attacking parties. Twenty four magazines to each Lewis Gun.

CO-OPERATION BY UNITS ON FLANKS (14) — (a) The 2/10th Bn. Lpool Regt will co-operate with fire from rifles and Lewis Guns on enemy's front line posts from ZERO to ZERO plus 19.

(b) The 1st and 175th Infantry Brigades have arranged to co-operate with rifle, Lewis Gun and machine gun fire on enemy's front line posts paying special attention to GRAVEL FARM.

MEDICAL ARRANGEMENTS (15) — (a) R.A.Ps will be at EGYPT HOUSE and PASCAL FARM.

(b) There will be advanced Medical Aid Posts at TAUBE FARM and U.6.d.70.30.

(c) The M.O. will arrange for evacuation of wounded as far as EGYPT HOUSE and PASCAL FARM. O.C. 2/2 Wessex Field Ambulance will be responsible for evacuation from R.A.Ps. An assistant M.O. will be at PASCAL FARM.

(d) No stretchers will be carried forward by attacking parties. Stretchers will be with supporting parties. Company stretcher bearers will be detailed by Os.C. Attacks to collect wounded. These stretcher bearers will be with supporting parties.

PRISONERS & DOCUMENTS (16) — (a) Prisoners must be taken and will be sent under escort via POLECAPELLE Railway Station to PASCAL FARM where they will be searched.

All documents found in pill boxes or on prisoners will be sent down to Brigade H.Q. in a sandbag with prisoners.

DRESS & EQUIPMENT (17) — (a) If snow remains on the ground white shirts, headgear and rifle covers will be worn.

(b) One Mills' bomb per man will be carried.

(c) Box Respirators will be carried at the alert. If white shirts are worn S.B.Rs will be worn underneath.

(d) All equipment will be carried under white shirts if worn.

(e) If there is no snow equipment will be normal. In either case skeleton equipment will be worn.

(f) No papers, letters, or identification of any kind will be carried by troops taking part in the attack.

COMMUNICATIONS. (18) (a) The Signalling Officer in conjunction with Brigade Signalling Officer will be responsible for running a line from pill box at U.6.d.70.30 to EGYPT HOUSE and from BERTHIER FARM or TAUBE FARM (as decdded later) to PASCAL FARM.
Four runners will also be at H.Q. of Os.C attacks.
(b) Communications from EGYPT HOUSE :-
Telephone to Brigade.
Power Buzzer to PASCAL FARM thence by telephone to Bde.
Visual to VEE BEND, thence to Bde.
Runners to VEE BEND and PASCAL FARM.
(c) Wireless from PASCAL FARM to Bde.

HEAD-QUARTERS (19)

O.C. Operations - Lt-Col W.L.OWEN M.C.	EGYPT HOUSE
O.C. Right attack - Capt J.A.CROWE	TAUBE FARM
O.C. Left attack - Capt A.W.MESSAM	Pill Box at U.6.d.70.30

Major A.H.SHULTZ will be at PASCAL FARM.

Light T.M.Bty	SIGNAL FARM
4" Stokes mortars	TAUBE FARM.

CODE (20) The following Code Words will be used in connection with this operation :-

Operations postpones 60 minutes	CABBAGE.
Operations cancelled	POTATO.
Have formed up	CRESS;
All objectives taken	MUSTARD.
All doing well	CELERY.
Much resistance	BEANS.
Weak resistance	PEAS.
Prisoners returning	SEEDS.
Many casualties	ONIONS.
Held up	LETTUCE.
One Company of 2/4th Bn. S.L.R. will relieve one Company of 2/5th Bn. S.L.R.	CARRY ON.

LIGHT SIGNALS. (21) The signal that all objectives have been taken will be a rocket bursting into three different colours RED, GREEN and YELLOW.

SYNCHRONIZATION OF WATCHES. (22) Watches will be synchronized at Brigade H.Q. at 9-0 a.m. and PASCAL FARM at 11-30 a.m.

REPORTS. (23) (a) Os.C. attacks will make such arrangements as will ensure that O.C. Operations is kept informed of the progress of events with the least possible delay.
(b) All ranks taking part in the attack will be assembled at BABOOB CAMP after they have been relieved so that a full account of the attack may be compiled.

RELIEF OF ATTACKING TROOPS. (24) Attacking troops will be relieved at the earliest possible moment under orders of O.C. Operations.

REFERENCE TO ATTACK. (25) No reference to this operation will be made on any wire previous to the attack taking place.

(26) Please acknowledge.

W.L. Owen
Lieut-Colonel.
Commanding
2/5th Bn. South Lancs Regt.

Issued 30/12/1917 at

DISTRIBUTION :-

Copy No. 1. O.C. OPERATIONS.
2. O.C. Right Attack.
3. O.C. Left Attack.
4. O.C. "A" Company.
5. O.C. "D" Company.
6. H.Q. 172nd Infantry Brigade.
7. O.C. 2/10th Bn. K.Lpool Regt.
8. O.C. 2/4th Bn. S. Lancs Regt.
9. O.C. Left Front Coy (2/4th Bn. S.L.R.)
10. O.C. Support Coy (2/4th Bn. S.L.R.)
11. O.C. Battn on Right.
12/13 War Diary.
14 File
15 Spare.
16 "
17 "
18 "
19 "
20 "

APPENDIX XLVIII

2/5th Battalion South Lancashire Regt.

NOMINAL ROLL OF OFFICERS. 31st DECr 1917

HEADQUARTERS

Lieut-Col	Owen	W.L. (M.C.)	C.O.
Major	Schultz	A.H.	Second in Command
Captain	Hayward	R.C.	Adjutant
2/Lieut	St George	A.K.	Asst. Adjt
Lieut	Hadfield	J.L.	Transport Office
Lieut	Gregory	H.	Quartermaster
Lieut	Vinson	H.H.	Signal Officer
Lieut	Dean	L.M.	Bombing Officer
Lieut	Nimmo	A.A.	Intelligence Officer
Lieut	Marsden	T.B.	Medical Officer (U.S.A)

'A' COMPANY

Capt	Wallis	A.C.	Coy Commander
Capt	Donald	T.M.	2nd in C. 'A' Coy.
Lieut	Hargreaves	R	Platoon Cdr.
Lieut	Leake	R.L.	" "
Lieut	Davis	H.P.W.	" "
2/Lt	Martin	A.J.	" "
2/Lt	Ragg	G.W.	" "
2/Lt	Jones	F	" "

'B' COMPANY

Capt	Crowe	J.A.	Coy. Commander
Lieut	Bullen	H.G.	2nd in C "B" Coy.
Lieut	Brazener	W.F.	Platoon Comdr
2/Lt	Clarke	J.	" "
2/Lt	Farmer	W.H	" "

'C' COMPANY

Capt.	Milton	S.J.	O.C. Company
Capt	Messum	A.W.	2nd in C "C" Coy
Lieut	Le Mare	E.B	Platoon Cdr.
2/Lieut	Woollett	J.S	" "
2/Lieut	Adams	B.C	" "
2/Lieut	Notley	A.C.	" "

D. COMPANY

Capt	Stephenson	C.W.	O.C. Company
Lieut	Frodsham	F.J.	2nd in C "D" Coy
Lieut	Holland	W.H.E.	Platoon Cdr.
Lieut	Agabeg	J.W.	" "
2/Lieut	Handley	W.C	" "
2/Lieut	Quinton	P.F.	" "
2/Lieut	Russell	C.A	

DETACHED ETC

Capt.	Hayward	R.C.	Hospital (Sick)
2/Lieut	Guest	E.L.	Hospital (Sick)
2/Lieut	Stone	A.R.	172nd L.T.M.B.
Lieut	West	H.	Bde L.G.O.
2/Lieut	Castle	A.C.	Hospital (S.I.W.)

APPENDIX XLIX

2/5th Bn South Lancashire Regiment

Statement Showing Strength. 31st Decr 1917

Battalion Strength 40. Officers. 930. O Ranks.

Other Ranks on Company Strength.

A. Company.	243.
B. Company.	234
C. Company	223
D. Company.	230
Total.	930

Detached

Bde & Division	14
Hospital	30
Leave	16
Courses	20
M. G. Coy.	10
Bde. L.T.M.B.	12
Trade Test	2
Army School	1
Base	1
	106

1/5th Bn S. Lancs Regt

Army Form C. 2118.

Vol 12

Instructions regarding War Diaries and Intelligence Summaries are contained in F. S. Regs., Part II. and the Staff Manual respectively. Title pages will be prepared in manuscript.

WAR DIARY
or
~~INTELLIGENCE SUMMARY.~~
(Erase heading not required.)

Place	Date 1918	Hour	Summary of Events and Information	Remarks and references to Appendices
BOESINGHE	Jan 1st		The Battalion was relieved in the right sub-sector HOULTHURST FOREST on the night 31st/1st by 2/4 South Lancs. Regt. The relief was complete by 12 midnight and was satisfactory. The battalion arrived at BABOON CAMP at 3 a.m. on the morning of the 1st and the remainder of the day was spent in rest and cleaning up.	
	2nd		The Battalion left BABOON CAMP at 12 noon and marched to BOESINGHE STATION where they entrained for ONDANK RAILHEAD at 1.30 p.m. On arrival at the railhead at 2 p.m. the Battalion proceeded to DE WIPPE CAMP. The billets and accommodation were found to be good. Details from HOUNSLOW CAMP joined the Battalion here. Orders were received that the Battalion would proceed to STEENWERCK AREA on the morning of the 4th and road transport on the morning of the 3rd	Appendix II
	3rd		Kit inspections were held during the morning and the remainder of the day was spent in cleaning up and preparing for the move to STEENWERCK.	

D. D. & L., London, E.C.
(A8003) Wt. W1771/M2031 750,000 5/17 Sch. 52 Forms C2118/14

Army Form C. 2118.

WAR DIARY
or
~~INTELLIGENCE SUMMARY.~~
(Erase heading not required.)

Instructions regarding War Diaries and Intelligence Summaries are contained in F. S. Regs., Part II. and the Staff Manual respectively. Title pages will be prepared in manuscript.

Place	Date	Hour	Summary of Events and Information	Remarks and references to Appendices
	Jan 4th		The Battalion left DE WIPPE CAMP (BOESINGHE III AREA) at 8 [illegible] a.m. and marched to INTERNATIONAL CORNER RAILHEAD where they entrained for BAILLEUL WEST. Arrived there at 1.5 p.m. and marched to PONT DE NIEPPE which was reached at 4.15 p.m. Men were here billeted in evacuated houses which, on arrival were not found to be very clean but which afterwards were made very comfortable. The road transport arrived at 5.30 p.m. but the train transport until 2 a.m. the following morning.	Appendix II
	5th		Platoon Commanders held inspections in the morning seeing that men's clothing and arms were [illegible] clean. Games were afterwards indulged in and the afternoon was spent playing football.	
	6th		Training carried out according to programme. At 11.15 a.m. Company Commanders, Intelligence Officer and Assistant Adjutant went forward to reconnoitre the Line ARMENTIERES DEFENCES. Guides were taken and left with the Commander	

D. D. & L., London, E.C. (A6001) Wt. W1771/M2031 750,000 5/17 Sch. 52 Forms C2118/14

Instructions regarding War Diaries and Intelligence Summaries are contained in F. S. Regs., Part II. and the Staff Manual respectively. Title pages will be prepared in manuscript.

WAR DIARY
or
~~INTELLIGENCE SUMMARY.~~
(Erase heading not required.)

Army Form C. 2118.

Place	Date	Hour	Summary of Events and Information	Remarks and references to Appendices
			Contd	
PONT-DE-NIEPPE	Jan 6		No1 Platoon was taken up and left as a nucleus garrison in the defence of the town.	
	7		Training under Platoon Commanders in the morning. The C.O. with Company Commanders reconnoitred the ARMENTIERES DEFENCES starting at 9.30 a.m and returning at 4.30 p.m.	
	8		The Commanding Officer held a conference with Company Commanders in the morning at 9.30. Seconds in Command of Companies went to reconnoitre strong point in SOUTHERN AREA ARMENTIERES DEFENCES.	
	9		Parades under Company arrangements. The Commanding Officer Adjutant and Company Commanders proceeded to the line to reconnoitre positions, starting at 9.30 a.m. and returning at 1.30 p.m. In the afternoon the Commanding Officer addressed B & C Companies on parade, complimenting them on their good work in the line.	

D. D. & L., London, E.C.
(A7001) Wt. W1771/M2031 750,000 5/17 Sch. 52 Forms C2118/14

Instructions regarding War Diaries and Intelligence Summaries are contained in F. S. Regs., Part II. and the Staff Manual respectively. Title pages will be prepared in manuscript.

WAR DIARY
or
~~INTELLIGENCE~~ SUMMARY.

(Erase heading not required.)

Army Form C. 2118.

Place	Date	Hour	Summary of Events and Information	Remarks and references to Appendices
PONT DE NIEPPE	Jan 10th		Parades under Company arrangements. Company and Platoon Commanders with Signalling Officer, Intelligence Officer and Assistant Adjutant visited the line in the morning, ~~and~~ interviewed their opposite numbers. Guides were taken from each Company and from Headquarters. In the afternoon the Commanding Officer addressed 'D' Company and Headquarters on their good work in the line.	
	11th		Parades under Company arrangement. The Commanding Officer held a conference with Company Commanders in the morning & addressed 'A' Company on their good work at HOULTHURST in the afternoon. Major Schultz left to take over the Bn. School at LA BECQUE.	
	12th		Training carried out, football games taking place in the afternoon.	

D. D. & L., London, E.C. (A8001) Wt. W1771/M2031 750,000 5/17 Sch. 52 Forms C2118/14

Army Form C. 2118.

WAR DIARY
or
~~INTELLIGENCE SUMMARY.~~
(Erase heading not required.)

Instructions regarding War Diaries and Intelligence Summaries are contained in F. S. Regs., Part II. and the Staff Manual respectively. Title pages will be prepared in manuscript.

Place	Date	Hour	Summary of Events and Information	Remarks and references to Appendices
HOUPLINES Left Sub. Sector	Jan 13th		The Battalion relieved the 2/7 Kings Liverpool Regt in the line, leaving PONT DE NIEPPE at 3 p.m. and proceeding via ARMENTIERES and HOUPLINES. Very quiet relief which was complete by 9.30 p.m. left flank company having two very difficult posts to relieve. At 7.15 p.m. the enemy dropped a few shells on the Subsidiary Line close to Battalion Head Quarters but otherwise the night was very quiet. Snow fell from 4 a.m. and was about 5 inches deep by daybreak.	Appendix LII
	14.		Working parties were busy throughout the day on C. T's ck During the night patrols went out from each front line Company At 8 20 p.m. a patrol of 1 Officer 1 sergeant + 5 O.R's went out from centre Company and bearing due East entered a gap in enemy wire. A Very light was immediately sent up from enemy forward post covering this gap and almost	

Army Form C. 2118.

Instructions regarding War Diaries and Intelligence Summaries are contained in F. S. Regs., Part II. and the Staff Manual respectively. Title pages will be prepared in manuscript.

WAR DIARY
or
~~INTELLIGENCE SUMMARY.~~
(Erase heading not required.)

Place	Date	Hour	Summary of Events and Information	Remarks and references to Appendices
HOUPLINES	Jan 14th (Contd)		almost immediately on the patrol. The Officer i/c deemed it advisable to withdraw the patrol as the presence of snow on the ground made movement very obvious to the enemy. The patrol returned at 10.35 p.m. There were no casualties. At 9.45 p.m. an enemy patrol estimated at a strength of 9 was seen and challenged by our No 2 Post. They were near the wire in front of the post. On receiving no reply to his challenge the sentry threw a bomb which had the effect of scattering the party and they were not seen again. The Company patrol coming in later found an enemy cap and rifle at the spot where these enemy were last seen and it is presumed that they were dropped by one of the enemy patrol who may have been wounded.	

D. D. & L., London, E.C. (A800.) Wt. W1771/M2031 750,000 5/17 Sch. 52 Forms C2118/14

Instructions regarding War Diaries and Intelligence Summaries are contained in F. S. Regs., Part II. and the Staff Manual respectively. Title pages will be prepared in manuscript.

WAR DIARY
or
~~INTELLIGENCE SUMMARY.~~
(Erase heading not required.)

Army Form C. 2118.

Place	Date	Hour	Summary of Events and Information	Remarks and references to Appendices
HOUPLINES	Jan 15th		Heavy rain set in about 4 a.m. and this combined with a very sharp thaw soon put the trenches into an awful state and much work was required on them and on the bivouacs which were in many cases flooded. The rain continued throughout the night and into the early hours of next morning. The night was pitch black and it was absolutely impossible for large working parties to carry on. By midnight the forward posts were giving concern as they were then flooded and the trenches leading up to same were in many places blocked.	
	16th		By daybreak the men in the front line posts were beginning to suffer from the effects of exposure and general conditions. Working parties were out throughout the day clearing C. Ts etc. and men who had been out all night were at work trying to get the water out of their bivouacs. The night was very fine with the moon up until 9 pm & much work was done	

Instructions regarding War Diaries and Intelligence Summaries are contained in F. S. Regs., Part II. and the Staff Manual respectively. Title pages will be prepared in manuscript.

WAR DIARY
or
~~INTELLIGENCE~~ SUMMARY.
(*Erase heading not required.*)

Army Form C. 2118.

Place	Date	Hour	Summary of Events and Information	Remarks and references to Appendices
HOUPLINES	Jan 16th (Contd)		A strong party of 100 O.R. were out wiring the whole of the front line posts and excellent work was done each post being made very strong with wire all round it. Support Line Posts were all wired by their own garrisons.	
			A patrol went out from the centre company about 11.30 pm. The going was found to be very bad and they could not get across being up to the thighs in water.	
			Both day and night were exceptionally quiet	
	17th		Rain set in again and the trenches got worse and worse some parts being waist deep in water. Most of the bivouacs were now full of water and the men consequently suffered through lack of sleep and shelter. Working parties were out on C.T's, cutting drains + generally improving. At night much wiring was done on Support Line Posts. These were considerably strengthened.	
			Our M.G's + L.T.M.B's were very active until about	

D. D. & L., London, E.C. (A8001) Wt. W1771/M2031 750,000 5/17 Sch. 52 Forms C2118/14

Instructions regarding War Diaries and Intelligence Summaries are contained in F. S. Regs., Part II. and the Staff Manual respectively. Title pages will be prepared in manuscript.

WAR DIARY
or
~~INTELLIGENCE SUMMARY.~~
(Erase heading not required.)

Army Form C. 2118.

Place	Date	Hour	Summary of Events and Information	Remarks and references to Appendices
HOUPLINES	Jan 17th		eleven o'clock but the enemy made no reply	
	18th		Slightly better day but trenches still bad. Line very quiet all day. At night the Battalion was relieved by the 2/10 Battn K. L. R. in Front Line Posts and took up position in SUBSID. LINE previously occupied by the 2/10 Bn. K.L.R. The relief, which started at 4.30 pm was not complete until 11.30 pm it being extremely difficult to relieve the posts on the left.	Appendix LIII
			During our tour in the Front Line the Battalion suffered terribly from the conditions, having a good number of trench feet & many cases of sickness. This was to be expected as the men in many cases had to stand about for hours with water nearly to their thighs & feet rubbing under the circumstances became extremely difficult	

D. D. & L., London, E.C. (A'00) Wt. W1 71/M2031 750,000 3/17 Sch. 52 Forms C2118/14

Instructions regarding War Diaries and Intelligence Summaries are contained in F. S. Regs., Part II. and the Staff Manual respectively. Title pages will be prepared in manuscript.

WAR DIARY
or
~~INTELLIGENCE SUMMARY.~~
(Erase heading not required.)

Army Form C. 2118.

Place	Date	Hour	Summary of Events and Information	Remarks and references to Appendices
HOUPLINES	Jan 19th		Four Companies of the Battalion now in the SUBSID. LINE with Battalion Headquarters behind, close to ARMENTIERES -ERQUINGHEM RAILWAY CROSSING. Companies under command of 2/10 K.L.R. Working parties were supplied and the situation was generally quiet.	
	20th		Conditions normal.	
PONT DE NIEPPE	21st		Conditions normal all day. Battalion was relieved in SUBSID. LINE by 2/8 Battalion KLR at 6 p.m. and went into former billets at PONT DE NIEPPE. Relief complete and all in billets at 9.30 p.m. The men returned in very good spirits notwithstanding the fact that during their tour in the line of 5 days in the Front Line and 3 days in SUBSID. LINE the conditions had been so bad. The trenches in many parts were flooded & in some parts thigh deep. In addition plenty of the "bivvies" were untenable and the men consequently	Appendix LIV

D. D. & L., London, E.C. (A7001) Wt. W1-71/M2031 750,000 5/17 Sch. 52 Forms C2118/14

Army Form C. 2118.

WAR DIARY
or
~~INTELLIGENCE SUMMARY.~~
(Erase heading not required.)

Instructions regarding War Diaries and Intelligence Summaries are contained in F. S. Regs., Part II. and the Staff Manual respectively. Title pages will be prepared in manuscript.

Place	Date	Hour	Summary of Events and Information	Remarks and references to Appendices
PONT DE NIEPPE	Jan 21st (Contd)		suffered from loss of sleep. During the whole of the period in the line the enemy was very quiet.	
	22nd		The day was spent in cleaning up and checking equipment.	
	23rd		The whole of the Battalion was out during the day on Working Parties under the R. Es.	
	24th		Working parties were out as per previous day.	
	25th		Working parties out all day.	
	26th		As on three previous days.	
	27th		Church Parades in the morning.	
HOUPLINES			At night the Battalion relieved the 2/7th K.L.R. in the line taking up their former dispositions in ARMENTIERES SECTOR, HOUPLINES SUB-SECTOR.	Appendix LV

D. D. & L., London, E.C. (A8001) Wt. W1771/M2031 750,000 5/17 Sch. 52 Forms C2118/14

Instructions regarding War Diaries and Intelligence Summaries are contained in F. S. Regs., Part II. and the Staff Manual respectively. Title pages will be prepared in manuscript.

WAR DIARY
or
~~INTELLIGENCE SUMMARY.~~
(Erase heading not required.)

Army Form C. 2118.

Place	Date	Hour	Summary of Events and Information	Remarks and references to Appendices
HOUPLINES	Jan 27th (Contd)		Word having been received that this Battalion was to be disbanded and this to be ~~done~~ completed by the 29th inst. the Battalion Headquarters did not proceed to the Line with the Companies but returned to their old position by the ARMENTIERES — ERQUINGHEM RAILWAY CROSSING. This change was made at the last minute as urgent returns involving considerable labour had to be rendered and these needed the concentration of the whole of the Orderly Room Staff and continual supervision by the C.O. and Adjutant. The Headquarters of the 2/10 K.L.R. were sent to the line and our Companies operated under their instructions.	
	~~28th~~		The line was very quiet all night.	
			The trenches had considerably improved since our last visit but forward there was still a lot of water lying in the C.T's.	
	28th		Work was carried on all day in improving	

D. D. & L., London, E.C. (A8004) Wt. W1771/M2031 750,000 5/17 Sch. 52 Forms C2118/14

Instructions regarding War Diaries and Intelligence Summaries are contained in F. S. Regs., Part II. and the Staff Manual respectively. Title pages will be prepared in manuscript.

WAR DIARY
or
~~INTELLIGENCE SUMMARY.~~
(Erase heading not required.)

Army Form C. 2118.

Place	Date	Hour	Summary of Events and Information	Remarks and references to Appendices
HOUPLINES.	Jan. 28th (contd)		the trenches and improving and building new "bivvies".	
			At night our Headquarters took over from Headquarters of the 2/10 K.L.R.	
	29th		The day was very quiet and was spent in general improvements to the trenches throughout the Sector.	
	30th		At night the Battalion was relieved in the front line by the 2/10 K.L.R. and went back into reserve at the CONVENT in ARMENTIERES (B. 30. d. 50. 55) B and C Companies were billetted ~~at~~ in the vicinity of the JUTE FACTORY and 'D' Company at the LAUNDRY. 'A' Company were left behind in the SUBSID. LINE as Counter Attack Company under the 2/10 K.L.R.	Appendix LVI
			During this last tour in the line the weather was beautifully fine.	
			The enemy were very quiet	

D. D. & L., London, E.C.
(A7001) Wt. W1371/M2031 750,000 5/17 Sch. 52 Forms C2118/14

Instructions regarding War Diaries and Intelligence Summaries are contained in F. S. Regs., Part II. and the Staff Manual respectively. Title pages will be prepared in manuscript.

WAR DIARY
or
~~INTELLIGENCE SUMMARY.~~
(Erase heading not required.)

Army Form C. 2118.

Place	Date	Hour	Summary of Events and Information	Remarks and references to Appendices
ARMENTIERES	Jan 31st		Most of the Battalion were up the line during the day as Working Parties. At night "C" Coy relieved "A" Company in the SUBSID. LINE in order that all arrangements could be made for withdrawing equipment etc from "A" Company now leaving the Battalion the next day to go to the 1/5 Batt. South Lancs.	

W L Owen
Lieu. Col.
Commanding
1/4 South Lancs Regt

D. D. & L., London, E.C.
(A8004) Wt. W1771/M2031 750,000 5/17 Sch. 52 Forms C2118/14

SECRET. War Diary Copy No. 10....

I

2/5th. S. LAN. R., OPERATION ORDERS NO. 1.

* * * * * * *

1. The Battalion will move fom BABOON CAMP to DE WIPPE CAMP BOESINGHE III AREA 3/1/18 in accordance with timetable attached.

2. MECHANICAL TRANSPORT. 1 Motor-lorry has been allotted to the Battalion. This lorry will be at the junction of ELVERDINGHE & BOESINGHE ROADS. Reference Sheet 28 N.W. B.5.d.77.05 at 9 a.m. All blankets will be collected, rolled in bundles of ten, and labelled, and will be deposited at the point mentioned above not later than 8.45 a.m.
O/C "D" Coy. will detail a loading and unloading party of 12 men to report at 8.45 a.m. at B.5.d.77.05 and will also detail guard over the blankets. This party will proceed with the lorry.
All Officers' Valises will be dumped at the above- mentioned point at 10 a.m. The R.S.M. will also detail one policeman to act as guard, and will detail three police-men for loading purposes. Surplus Coy. Stores will also be dumped.

3. BAGGAGE WAGONS. Officer i/c Details, HOUNSLOW CAMP will detail two guides to be at No.4 H.T.Coy., A.S.C. 57th. Divisional Train by 9 a.m. on the 2nd. instant. Baggage Wagons will be returned to Train Coy. on the night 2/1/18 loaded ready for the move to new Area. These wagons should be loaded with the surplus stores not immediately required as motor transport is being provided on 4/1/18. Officers" Valises will go by this M.T.

4. MOVEMENT BY TRAIN. 2/Lieut A.J. MARTIN will report to the Entraining Officer at BOESINGHE at 12.30 P.M. and will take with him the Entraining Statement of the Battalion.

5. STORES FOR THE PREV-ENTION OF TRENCH FEET. All water-bowls, brushes, etc. in the camp will be handed over to Advance Party of incoming unit and receipts obtained.
Copies will be forwarded to B.H.Q.

6. GUM-BOOT STORE. 2/Lieut. J.S. WOOLLETT will hand over the Gum-boot Store to incoming unit. A complete list of stores will be forwarded to reach this office by 11 a.m. 2/1/18.

7. CLEANLINESS OF BILLETS. The Camp will be left scrupulously clean and a certificate to that effect obtained from the Advance Party of Incoming unit or from Camp Warden.

A.R.B. Frost [signature]
2/Lieutenant,
A/Adjutant,
2/5th. S.Lan.R.

No.1 Copy to O/C "A" Coy.
2 " to O/C "B" "
3 " to O/C "C" "
4 " to O/C "D" "
5 " to Q.M.
6 " to T.O.
7 " to C.O.
8 " O. i/c Details (HOUNSLOW CAMP).
9 " to 2/Lt. J.S.WOOLLETT.
10 " War Diary.
11 " War Diary.
12 " Spare.

SECRET. *War Diary* Copy No. 2....

21

2/5th. BN. S. LAN. R., OPERATION ORDER NO. 2.

1. TRANSPORT MOVING BY RAIL. Transport detailed in Table "A" attached will entrain at PESELHOEK Railhead on 4th. January, 1918.

2. TRANSPORT MOVING BY ROAD. Surplus Transport will move by road on 3rd. January 1918 in accordance with attached Table "B". Transport moving by road will be billeted on night 3/4th. January 1918 in GODE AREA.

3. ADVANCE PARTY. Lieut. L.N.DEAN proceeded to GODE AREA to arrange billets and horse lines.

A.P. St George

2/Lieutenant,
A/Adjutant,
2/5th. S.Lan.R.

No. 1 Copy to T.O.
" 2 " to War Diary.
" 3 " to do.
" 4 " to File.

TABLE "B"

Unit.	From	To	Starting Point.	Time passing starting pt.	Route.
2/5th. Battn. Sth. Lancs. Regt.	DE WIPPE CAMP.	GODE AREA.	POPERHINGE-BUSCHEPE Rd. (HAZEBROUCK) (50.21.56.07)	12.11 p.m.	WOESTEN - POPERHINGHE Rd. - BOESCHEPE - BERTHEN.

TABLE "A"

Unit.	Entraining Point.	Time of Departure.	Detraining point.	Personnel		Horses.		4 Wheeled Wagons.	2 Wheeled Carts.	To reach entraing. Point.
				Off.	O.R.	H.D. or L.D.	Chargers & Pack Animals.			
2/5th. South Lancs. Regt.	PESELHOEK Sheet 28 NW A.21.a.	1 p.m.	BAILLEUL WEST.	1	33	14	18	4 L.G. Limbers. 2 Cookers.	1 Mess Cart. 1 Maltese Cart.	11 a.m.

War Diary

SECRET. Copy No. 11

2/4th. S. LAN. R., OPERATION ORDER NO. [illegible]

LI

Ref. Maps,
HAZEBROUCK 5A
1/100000
Sheet 28 N.W.
1/20,000.

3rd. Jan. 1918.

1. On the 4th. January, 1918, the Battalion will move from the [illegible] III AREA to STEENWERCK AREA. Movements will be by march route and train in accordance with the attached time-table.

2. The Battalion will travel by the train leaving INTERNATIONAL CORNER at 10 a.m. for [illegible]. 2/Lieut. A.J. [illegible] will report to Captain [illegible] at 9 a.m. at INTERNATIONAL CORNER, and will take with him the Entraining Statement of the Battalion. O.'s C. Coys. Lieut. [illegible] for Q.M. Personnel, and the R.S.M. for Headquarters, will send entraining statements to reach H.Q. by 8 p.m. to-night, 3/1/18.

3. MECHANICAL TRANSPORT. Two motor-lorries have been allotted to the Battalion. These lorries will make one journey to INTERNATIONAL CORNER, and will take all men who are unable to walk. The M.O. will make out a list in conjunction with O.'s C. Coys. 2/Lieut. F.W. [illegible] will be in charge of this party who will parade outside the Guard-room at 7.30 a.m. He will call a roll from the M.O.'s list, and will conduct them to the station. 2/Lieut. F.W. [illegible] will then bring back the lorry to be loaded. O/C "A" Coy. will detail a guide to meet these lorries at 8 a.m. at [illegible] CABARET, Sheet 28 N.W. A.11.b.[illegible], and from there conduct them to the vicinity of the Guard-room.

4. BLANKETS, BAGGAGE, ETC. One blanket per man will be carried. The remainder will be rolled in bundles of ten and labelled, and will be dumped together with Officers' Valises and all Baggage and Stores, outside the Guard-room not later than 7 a.m. O/C "A" Coy. will detail a loading and unloading party of 4 men [illegible]. This party will proceed with the lorry. On arrival in STEENWERCK AREA these lorries will rendezvous on [illegible]-ARMENTIERES Road at point HAZEBROUCK 5A 4.I.[illegible]. Lieut. [illegible] will detail a cyclist to meet these lorries and conduct them to billets. The Q.M. will give each lorry driver a chit showing name of unit and destination.

5. BREAKFAST & RATIONS. Breakfast will be at 6 a.m. An extra good breakfast must be provided. The unexpended portion of the days' rations will be carried and men must be warned not to expect a further meal during the day.

6. PARADE. The Battalion will parade in the order H.Q., A - B - C - D, and Q.M. personnel. The head of the column will be at the Starting Point at 7.45 a.m. prompt. A Parade Statement will be handed in to the Adjutant before starting.

7. TRENCH & AREA STORES. All Trench & Area Stores will be handed over to incoming Unit or Camp Warden, and a receipt obtained. Copies will be forwarded to this Office.

(Continued.)

8. CLEANLINESS OF CAMPS. The Camp and Horse Lines will be left scrupulously clean, and a certificate to this effect obtained, and forwarded to this Office.

9. MESS BASKETS & H.Q. Stores. The ~~Mess~~ Maltese Cart will be outside B.H.Q. at 7 a.m. All Mess Baskets must be loaded on the Mess Cart by 7.15 am The Mess Cart will report at H.Q.'s Hut at 7 a.m., and must be loaded with the H.Q.'s Stores by 7.15 a.m.

10. COMPLETION OF MOVE. On arrival in new Billets, O.'s C. Coys. will report "ALL IN" to B.H.Q. as soon as possible.

11. ACKNOWLEDGE.

A.B. St.Groot?
2/Lieutenant,
A/Adjutant,
2/Bn. S.Lan.R.

Copy No.1 to O/C "A" Coy.
" No.2 to O/C "B" "
" No.3 to O/C "C" "
" No.4 to O/C "D" "
" No.5 to C.O.
" No.6 to Bnd. i/c
" No.7 to Q.M.
" No.8 to T.O.
" No.9 File.
" No.10 War Diary.
" No.11 War Diary.

TIME TABLE.

Date.	Unit.	From	Route.	Time of Passing Starting Point. ([illegible])	Time of Departure of Train from [illegible].	Remarks.
4th. Jan. 19[illegible].	2/5th. South Lancs. Regt.	[illegible]	[illegible] [illegible], [illegible] Junction, [illegible]	[illegible] a.m.	[illegible] a.m.	Distance between Companies. [illegible] yds.

War Diary

SECRET. Copy No. 8

PRELIMINARY OPERATION ORDERS No.4.

LII

10/1/18.

1. The 172nd. Inf.Bde. will relieve the 171st. Inf.Bde. in the ARMENTIERES SECTOR on the night 13/14th. January, 1918.

2. The Battalion will relieve the 2/7th. K.L.R. in the Front Line on the left.

3. The 2/9th. K.L.R. will be on the right, with the 2/10th. K.L.R. in Subsidiary Line, and the 2/4th. S.L.R. in reserve.

4. O.'s C. Companies will be required to send into the line 24 hours in advance:-
   - (a) One Officer per Company.
   - (b) One representative per Platoon.
   - (c) One Specialist Officer from H.Q. will also proceed with this party.

5. Lewis Guns and Teams will probably go into the line in advance of the Battalion and take over their posts by daylight.

6. Relief Orders will be issued later.

[illegible signature]

2/Lieutenant,
Adjutant,
2/5th. S.Lan.R.

Copy No.1 to O/C "A" Coy.
" No.2 to O/C "B" Coy.
" No.3 to O/C "C" "
" No.4 to O/C "D" Coy.
" No.5 to 2nd. i/c
" No.6 to Q.M.
" No.7 to T.O.
" No.8 to War Diary.
" No.9 to War Diary.
" No.10 to S.O.
" No.11 to File.

SECRET. 11 Copy No. 9...

2/5th. S. LAN. R., OPERATION ORDERS No.5.

LIII

Ref.Map,
Sheet 36 N.W.
1/20000

11/1/18.

1. With reference to Preliminary Operation Orders No.4 dated 10/1/18.
The Battalion will relieve the 2/7th. K.L.R. (171st. Inf. Bde.) in the HOUPLINES LEFT SUBSECTOR on the night 13/14th. instant.

2. GUIDES. Guides at the rate of one per Company from the 2/7th. K.L.R. will meet the Battalion at the LEVEL CROSSING (C.27a.2.1.) at 4.30 p.m. on the 13th. instant.
Guides will also be provided at Company Headquarters for each post in the line.

3. LEWIS GUNS. O.'s C. Companies will detail two Lewis Gunners (Sec. Cdr.& No.5) per Company to proceed at 3 p.m. to the line on the night 12/13th. instant. They will be attached to the teams of the guns they are relieving, and they will carry one day's rations with them. All filled magazines in tinned boxes will be transported and dumped as close to the Subsidiary Line as possible on the night 12/13th. instant. One man per Coy. will be sent with these tin boxes and will have the same ready to hand over to their Companies the following night. The T.O. and L.G.O. will make mutual arrangements for transport. The Lewis Gun Officer and the remainder of Lewis Gun Teams will proceed to the line on the morning of the 13th. and will relieve by daylight.
1 Guide per Post from the 2/7th. K.L.R. will meet the L.G.O. and his party at B.H.Q. in the line at 10.30 a.m.
The Lewis Guns will be carried in the Vickers Canvas Bags.
A.Aircraft mountings must be taken.
At least 32 magazines must be with each gun at its post, a reserve dump being formed at Company H.Q.

4. ADVANCE PARTIES. The Second-in-Command of each Company and Second-in-Command of each Platoon together with the I.O. will proceed to the line on the afternoon of the 12th. instant, and will get particulars of all dispositions etc. Each Post must be visited by night. Guides must be demanded from the Companies in the Line concerned. The Bombing Officer will proceed to the line on the morning of the 13th. and will take over all S.A.A., Grenade Dumps, S.O.S. Rockets, etc. The Bn. Gas N.C.O. will also proceed up the line on the 13th. and take over.

5. DRESS. Battle Order. Each man will carry 120 Rounds S.A.A.
Leather jerkins will be worn and greatcoats will be carried round the haversack on the back
Lewis Gunners will carry 50 Rounds S.A.A. in addition to their panniers.

6. VALISES. All Officers' Valises will be collected and dumped at the Q.M. Stores by noon on the 13th. instant.

(Continued.)

7. BLANKETS. All Blankets will be collected, rolled in bundles of ten, labelled, and dumped at Q.M. Stores by 12 noon on the 13th. instant.

8. MESS BASKETS. The T.O. will make arrangements to collect Mess Baskets from Company H.Q. and B.H.Q. commencing at 8 p.m. on the 13th. instant. All Baskets must be ready by 8 p.m.

8. RATIONS. Unexpired portion of the day's rations will be carried, and men must be warned that no further rations will be issued on the 13th. instant.

9. DOCUMENTS. All defence schemes, aeroplane photographs, maps, and other documents, concerning the sector will be taken over on relief and copies of receipts sent to B.H.Q. by 9 a.m. on the 14th. instant.

10. RELIEF. Relief of Companies will be reported to B.H.Q. by use of the code-words as follows:-

"A" Coy.	BOWNIE.
"B" "	JIMMY.
"C" "	CHARLIE.
"D" "	FROG.

11. BILLETS. All billets must be left scrupulously clean and certificates to that effect obtained from O/C Advance parties 2/7th. K.L.R.

12. SOUP KITCHEN. The Soup Kitchen at TISSAGE CAMP will be taken over by the BAND. L/C. COULTER is responsible for this.

2/Lieutenant,
Adjutant,
"Y" Battalion.

No. 1 Copy to O/C "A" Coy.
2 " to O/C "B" "
3 " to O/C "C" "
4 " to O/C "D" "
5 " to [illegible]
6 " to [illegible]
7 " to T.O.
8 " War Diary.
9 " War Diary.
10 " O/C 2/7th. K.L.R. (for information.)

SECRET.

TABLE ATTACHED 2/5th. S. LAN.R O.O.5.

Coy. 2/5 SLR	Position.	Relieving	Guides	Rendezvous	Route to Trenches	Remarks
D	Left Sector.	"D" Coy. 2/7 KLR	One per Company	HOUPLINES Rly Crossing, C.27.a.2.1. 4.30 p.m.	DURHAM AV. - CAMBRIDGE AVENUE.	Guides Posts w be arr ed for Coy. H.
C	Centre Sector	"B" Coy. 2/7 KLR	do.	do. 4.35 p.m.	WESSEX AV.	do
A	Right.	"A" Coy. 2/7 KLR	do.	do. 4.40 p.m.	SPAIN AV.	do
B	Subsidiary Line	"C" Coy. 2/7 KLR	do.	do. 4.45 p.m.	GLOUCESTER AVENUE.	do
H.Q.	do.	H.Q. 2/7 KLR	do.	do. 4.50 p.m.	do.	d

SECRET. Copy No......

2/5TH BN.STH.LANCS.REGT. OPERATION ORDER NO.6.

Ref.Map,
Sheet 36 N.W.
1/20000

17th.Jan. 1918.

1. The Battalion will be relieved by the 2/10th. Bn. K.L.R. in the HOUPLINES SUBSECTOR on the night 18/19th. Jan. 1918.

2. On completion of relief the Battalion will go into Support in the Subsidiary Line and will be disposed as follows:-

"A" Coy.	Right Battn.	Right Subsid.
"C" "	Right Battn.	Left Subsid.
"B" "	Left Battn.	Left Subsid.
"D" "	Left Battn.	Right Subsid.

B.H.Q. at H.5.b.9.8.

3. GUIDES. (a) O/C "A" Coy. will send one guide to be at junction of SPAIN AVENUE and Subsid. Line at 5 p.m. to meet "D" Coy. 2/10th. K.L.R.
(b) O/C "B" Coy. will make mutual arrangements with O/C "A" Coy. 2/10th. K.L.R. as to relief.
(c) O/C "C" Coy. will send one guide to B.H.Q. at 5.10 p.m. to meet "C" Coy. 2/10th. K.L.R.
(d) O/C "D" Coy. will send one guide to B.H.Q. at 5 p.m. to meet "B" Coy. 2/10th. K.L.R.
(e) Guides will also be supplied at Coy. H.Q. or at such other convenient place, for each post in the line. O.'sC Coys. will send locations where guides will be by 9 a.m. 18th. instant.
(f) 2/Lt. A.J.MARTIN will proceed to Right Battn. H.Q. 2/9th. K.L.R., to arrange for guides to meet "A" and "C" Coys. Details will be issued later.

4. LEWIS GUNS. Lewis Guns and Teams will wherever possible, be relieved by day-light to-morrow. The L.G.O. will call at B.H.Q. at 8.30 a.m. 18th. instant to make arrangements for relief. All Lewis Gun Equipment including magazines and tin boxes will be made up to full strength for the purposes of this relief.

5. S.A.A. & MAGAZINES. The Bombing Officer will beat B.H.Q. at 6.30 a.m. and will hand over all S.A.A. etc. on the arrival of his opposite number.

6. INTELLIGENCE. The I.O. will also hand over on arrival of hisopposite number.

7. DOCUMENTS. All defence schemes, aeroplane photographs, maps, and other documents, will be handed over, and receipts, obtained. These receipts will be sent in duplicate to B.H.Q.by 12 noon 19th. instant.

8. TRENCH STORES. All Trench Stores will be handed over. Receipts on A.F. W.3405 will be sent in duplicate to B.H.Q. by 12 noon 19th. instant.

(Continued.)

9. VALISES. B.H.Q. Officers' Valises and Mess Basket will be dumped at TISSAGE DUMP by 6 p.m. The T.O. will convey these to B.H.Q. at H.9.b.9.8. O/C "C" Coy. will send valises to B.H.Q. in the line by 4.30 p.m. O/C "A" Coy. will send valises etc. to tram-way at bottom of SPAIN AVENUE. These must be sent for on completion of relief, in the Subsidiary Line. O.'s C. "B" and "D" Coys. will make their own arrangements.

10. BLANKETS. All Blankets will be collected, rolled in bundles of 10, and sent to TISSAGE DUMP by 4 p.m. These will be taken to the Q.M.Stores and clean blankets issued in exchange.
The Q.M. and T.O. will make necessary arrangements to bring one blanket per man with the rations.
Detailed orders will be issued to the QM. as regards the ration dumps for the right Battalion.
2/Lt. A.J.MARTIN will find out locations of ration dumps.

11. GUM BOOTS. All Gum Boots will be taken by the men with their ankle boots to the position they will occupy in the Subsidiary Line. These will be collected and returned to TISSAGE DUMP by 10 a.m. the following morning.

12. Relief complete will be sent to B.H.Q. by use of the following code-words.

"A" Coy.	DONNIE.
"B" "	JIMMY.
"C" "	CHARLIE.
"D" "	FROG.

O.'s C. "A" and "C" Coys. will also report relief complete by code-word to O/C 2/4th. S.L.R.

13. ACKNOWLEDGE.

2/Lieutenant,
Adjutant,
2/5th. S.Lan.R.

No.1 to O/C "A" Coy.
2 to O/C "B" "
3 to O/C "C" Coy.
4 " O/C "D" "
5 to O/C 2/10th. K.L.R. (for information.)
6 to O/C 2/9th. K.L.R. do.
7 to O/C 2/4th. S.L.R. do.
8 to Q.M. & T.O.
9 to C.O.
10 to War Diary.
11 to War Diary.

SECRET.

Copy No. 12

2/5th. S. LAN. R., OPERATION ORDERS NO. 7.

LIV

Ref. Map,
Sheet 36 N.W.,
1/20000

20th. Jan. 1918.

1. The 172nd. Infantry Brigade will be relieved by the 171st. Infantry Brigade on the 21st. January, 1918, and on the night 21/22nd. January, 1918.

2. The Battalion will be relieved by the 2/8th. Bn. K. L. R. in the Subsidiary Line on the night 21/22nd. Jan. 1918. After relief the Battalion will be in Billets at PONT NIEPPE.

3. GUIDES.
(a) O/C "B" and "D" Coys. will send one guide per Coy. to be at the Railway Crossing [illegible] at [illegible] p.m. The necessary guides for each Post in the line will be provided at Coy. H.Q.
(b) O/C "A" and "C" Coys. will send one guide per Coy. to be at SANDBAG CORNER [illegible] at [illegible] p.m. The necessary guides for each post in the line will be provided at Coy. H.Q.
(c) On completion of relief Companies will move to billets at PONT NIEPPE and will occupy the same billets as previously.

4. LEWIS GUNS.
All filled magazines in tin boxes will be dumped at TISSAGE DUMP by "B", "C" and "D" Companies, and at SQUARE FARM by "A" Coy. by 4.30 p.m. O.'s C. Coys. will detail two men as guards and loading party. These parties will proceed with limber. The T.O. will make the necessary arrangements for transport. The Lewis Guns in the Vickers Canvas Bags and A.A. Mountings will be carried out.

5. OFFICERS' VALISES AND MESS BASKETS.
Officers' Valises etc. will be dumped at TISSAGE DUMP and SQUARE FARM respectively by 4.30 p.m.

6. BLANKETS.
Blankets will be rolled in bundles of ten, labelled, and dumped at TISSAGE DUMP and SQUARE FARM by 4.30 p.m.

7. R.A.P. STORES ETC.
The Transport Officer will arrange for Transport to be at [illegible], at [illegible], at 12 noon, to convey blankets Officers' Valises and Mess Kit, and [illegible] Boxes to PONT NIEPPE.

8. ADVANCE PARTIES.
2/Lieut. A. [illegible] will proceed to PONT NIEPPE and take over B.H.Q. Billets.
O.'s C. Coys. will send their [illegible]'s to take over Billets.
The above parties will reach PONT NIEPPE by 12 noon.

9. GUM BOOTS.
All Gum-boots will be returned to Gum Boot Stores by 4.30 p.m.

(Continued.)

10. DOCUMENTS. All aeroplane photographs, documents, etc. will be handed over on relief, and receipts in duplicate obtained. These receipts will be sent to B.H.Q. by 9 a.m. the 22nd. instant.

11. TRENCH STORES. All Trench Stores will be handed over and receipts obtained. These receipts will be sent to B.H.Q. by 9 a.m. on the 22nd. instant.

12. COMPLETION OF RELIEF. Relief complete will be reported to in-coming Units by use of code-words.

"A" Coy.	[illegible].
"B" "	JENNY.
"C" "	CHARLEY.
"D" "	FROG.

O.'s C. Coys. will report in person to B.H.Q. as soon as they have xxxxxxxx arrived in Billets.

13. HOT TEA. The Q.M. will arrange for hot tea to be served to all ranks on arrival in Billets.

14. ACKNOWLEDGE.

2/Lieutenant,
a/ Adjutant,
2/5th. S.Lan.R.

Issued to:-

No.1 Copy to O/C "A" Coy.
2 " to O/C "B" "
3 " to O/C "C" "
4 " to O/C "D" "
5 " to C.O.
6 " to Q.M.
7 " to T.O.
8 " to O/C 2/5th. K.L.R. (for information.)
9 " to O/C 2/10th. K.L.R. do.
10 " to O/C 2/4th. S.L.R. do.
11 " to O/C 2/7th. K.L.R. do.
12 " to War Diary.
13 " to War Diary.

War Diary

SECRET. Copy No. 11......

2/5th. S. LAN. R., OPERATIONS ORDERS NO. 8.

LV

Ref. Map.
Sheet 36 N.W.
1/20000.

26/1/18.

1. The 172nd. Inf. Bde. will relieve the 171st. Inf. Bde. in the ARMENTIERES SECTION on the 27th. January, 1918, and on the night 27/28th. instant.

2. The Battalion will relieve the 2/7th. K.L.R. in the HOUPLINES Left Subsector on the night 27/28th. instant in accordance with the attached table.

3. On completion of reliefCompanies will be disposed as follows:-
"A" Coy. on the Right.
"C" " in the Centre.
"B" " on the Left.
"D" " in the Subsidiary Line.

4. GUIDES. Guides at the rate of one per Company will be at the Level Crossing C.27.a.2.1. at 4.30 p.m. Guides for each Post in the line will also be provided at the respective Company H.Q.

5. LEWIS GUNS.
(a) All filled magazines in tin-boxes will be transported and dumped as close to the Subsidiary Line as possible on the night 26/27th. instant. One man per Company will proceed with the transport, and they will act as guard over the ammunition.
(b) Lewis Guns and Teams, will wherever possible relieve by daylight on the 27th. instant. The L.G.O. and Lewis Gun Teams will proceed to the line on the morning of the 27th. instant. 1 Guide per Lewis Gun Post from the 2/7th. K.L.R. will meet the L.G.O. and his party at B.H.Q. in the line at 10.30 a.m. on the 27th. instant.
(c) Lewis Guns will be carried in the Vickers Canvas Bags A.A. Mountings will be taken. At least twenty magazines will be with each gun at its post, a reserve dump being formed at Coy. H.Q.
(d) 2 Lewis Guns from "D" Coy. will be handed over to "B" Coy. on the morning of the 27th. instant.
"D" Coy. will also send one gun and team to be attached to "A" Coy. on the morning of 27th. instant.

6. ADVANCE PARTIES.
(a) The 2nd.'s i/c Coys and 2nd.'s i/c Platoons together with the I.O. & S.O. will proceed to the line on the morning of the 27th. instant, and will obtain particulars of all dispositions, etc.
(b) The S.O. and Bn. Gas N.C.O. will proceed up the line on the morning of the 27th. instant, and take over their duties.

7. DRESS. Battle Order. Each man will carry 120 rounds of S.A.A. Leather jerkins will be worn and greatcoats will be carried round the haversack on back.
Lewis Gunners will carry 50 rounds of S.A.A. in addition to their panniers.

8. VALISES. All Officers' Valises will be dumped at the Q.M. Stores by 10am on the 27th. instant. Valises will be as light as possible.

(Continued.)

9\. BLANKETS. All blankets will be collected, rolled in bundles of ten, labelled, and dumped outside Q.M. Stores by 1 p.m. on the 27th. instant.
Each Coy. will take five rolls of blankets, and H.Q. [illegible] rolls blankets into the line.

10\. MESS BASKETS. The T.O. will make arrangements to collect Mess Baskets from B.H.Q. and Coy. H.Q. commencing at 2 p.m. 27th. instant. All baskets will be ready by 2 p.m.

11\. DOCUMENTS. All defence schemes, aeroplane photographs, maps and other documents, concerning the sector will be taken over on relief, and copies of receipts in duplicate, sent to B.H.Q. by 9 a.m. on the morning following relief.

12\. RELIEF. Relief of Companies will be reported to B.H.Q. by use of code-words as follows:-

"A" Coy. [illegible].
"B" " [illegible].
"C" " [illegible].
"D" " [illegible].

13\. BILLETS. All billets must be left scrupulously clean, and certificates to that effect obtained from Advance Party 2/7th. K.L.R.

14\. SOUP KITCHENS & GUM BOOTS. The soup kitchen, and gum-boot store at [illegible] will be taken over by L/C COULTER and 10 men from the Band.
This party will also provide the Gas Guard at the B.A.P.
They will also be responsible for socks.

15\. TRANSPORT. The Q.M. & T.O. will make the necessary arrangements for the necessary transport required on the 28th. instant and the night of relief.

16\. PLEASE ACKNOWLEDGE.

Captain,
Adjutant,
2/5th. S.Lan.R.

Distribution:-

No.1 Copy to O/C "A" Coy.
2 " to O/C "B" "
3 " to O/C "C" "
4 " to O/C "D" "
5 " to C.O.
6 " to O/C 2/7th. K.L.R. (for information.)
7 " to L.G.O.
8 " to T.O.
9 " to Q.M.
10 " to War Diary.
11 " to War Diary.
12 " Spare.

TIME - TABLE.

Coy.	Unit.	To.	Time of leaving Billets.	Time of arriving at Level Crossing C.27.a.2.1.	Route.	Rendez-vous for Guides. 1 per Coy.	Relieving	Remarks.
"B"	2/5 SLR.	FRONT LINE HOUPLINES SUBSECTOR LEFT.	3.15 p.m.	4.45 p.m.	ARMENTIERES - NOUVEL HOUPLINES.	Level Crossing C.27.a.2.1.	Left Company 2/4th. Y.L.R	100 yds. between Platoons.
"C"	do.	do.	3.30 p.m.	5 p.m.	do.	do.	Centre Coy. 2/4th. KLR.	do.
"A"	do.	do.	3.45 p.m.	5.15 p.m.	do.	do.	Right Coy. 2/4th. KLR	do.
"D"	do.	Subsid. Line.	3.50 p.m.	5.30 p.m.	do.	do.	Subsid.Coy. 2/4th. KLR	do.
BHQ.	do.	do.	4 p.m.	5.30 p.m.	do.	NIL.	B.H.Q.	do.

SECRET. Copy No. 12

2/5th. R. LAN. R., OPERATION ORDERS NO. 9.

Ref. Map,
Sheet 36 N.W.
1/20000 29/1/18.

1. The Battalion will be relieved by the 2/10th. Bn. (Scottish) K.L.R. on the night of the 30/31st. instant.

2. The Battalion after relief will go into Brigade Reserve in the vicinity of the CONVENT and JUTE Factory with B.H.Q. in the CONVENT at H.30.d.50.55.

3. "A" Company on completion of relief in the Front Line will go into Support in the Subsidiary Line, and take over dispositions etc. from "B" Coy. 2/10th. K.L.R. O/C "A" Coy. will make mutualarrangements with O/C "B" Coy. as to relief.

4. GUIDES. O/C "A" Coy. will send one guide to be at junction of C.T. and SPAIN AVENUE at 4.30 p.m.
O.'s C. "B", "C" and "D" Coys. will send one guide to be at B.H.Q. at 4.30 p.m.
Guides for each post in the line will be provided at Company Headquarters.

5. LEWIS GUNS. (a) Lewis Guns will be carried out in the Vickers Canvas Bags. A.A. Mountings will also be carried out.
(b) All filled magazines in tin boxes will be dumped at TISSAGE DUMP by 4.45 p.m.
Each Company will have two men to act as guard over the ammunition. This party will proceed with the limbers.
(c) Relief of Lewis Guns will wherever possible take place by daylight. The L.G.O. will make arrangements.
(d) "D" Coy. Gun and team attached to "A" Coy. will rejoin its Company on relief.
O/C "B" Coy. will return the 2 Lewis Guns from "D" Coy. on relief.

6. ADVANCE PARTIES. O.'s C. Coys. will detail two representatives per Company to take over billets. They will proceed in advance 2/Lieut. A.J.MARTIN will represent B.H.Q.

7. VALISES, BLANKETS, MESS BASKETS. All Officers' Valises, blankets rolled in bundles of ten and labelled, and Mess Stores will be dumped at TISSAGE DUMP by 5 p.m.

8. TRANSPORT. The T.O. and Q.M. will make the necessary arrangements for Transport. Rations for "A" Coy. will be brought to TISSAGE DUMP.

9. DOCUMENTS. All defence schemes, maps, aeroplane photographs, etc. will be handed over on relief. Copies of receipts in duplicate must be sent to B.H.Q. by 9 a.m. on the 31st.

10. RELIEF. Relief of Companies will be reported to B.H.Q. by use of code-words:-

"A" Coy.	SHERRY.
"B" "	PORT.
"C" "	CLARET.
"D" "	MADEIRA.

(Continued.)

11. GUM-BOOTS. Gum Boots will be worn as far as [illegible]. At "[illegible] DUMP" Gum Boots will be handed in to the Gum Boot Store, and ankle boots put on. "A" Coy. will retain their gum-boots, and usual procedure of exchange carried out.

12. SOCKS. Dry socks can be obtained at the CONVENT on relief except for "A" Coy. "A" Coy.'s socks will be sent up with their rations. Lieut. [illegible] will detail one man to remain at the Gum Boot Store to collect "A" Coy.'s socks. This man will be rationed by "A" Coy.

13. SURPLUS KITS. The Q.M. will arrange for all officers' surplus kits to be sent to the CONVENT with the exception of "A" Coy's

14. ACKNOWLEDGE.

[illegible]

Captain,
Adjutant,
2/4th. R.Lan.R.

Distribution:-

No. 1 Copy to O/C "A" Coy
2 " to O/C "B" "
3 " to O/C "C" "
4 " to O/C "D" "
5 " to Q.M.
6 " to O/C 2/10th. KLR (for information.)
7 " to O/C 2/4th. SLR (do.)
8 " to O/C 2/5th. KLR (do.)
9 " to I.O.
10 " to Lt. L.V.Dean.
11 " to War Diary.
12 " to War Diary.

Appendix XVII

2/5 Battalion South Lancashire Regt.

Nominal Roll of Officers 31st January 1918

HEADQUARTERS

Lieut. Col.	Owen	W. L. (M.C.)	C.O.
Major	Schultz	A. H.	Second in Command
Captain	St George	A. R.	Adjutant
2/Lieut.	Martin	A. J.	Asst. Adjutant
Lieut.	Hadfield	J. L.	Transport Officer
Lieut.	Gregory	H.	Quartermaster
Lieut.	Davis	H. P. W.	Signal Officer
Lieut.	Dean	L. M.	Bombing Officer
Lieut.	Nimmo	A. A.	Intelligence Officer
Lieut.	Holland	W. H. E.	Lewis Gun Officer
Lieut.	Marsden	T. B.	Medical Officer (U.S.A.)

"A" Company

Capt	Wallis	A. C.	
Capt	Donald	T. M.	Company Commander
Lieut.	Hargreaves	R.	2nd in C. "A" Coy.
Lieut.	Leake	R. L.	Platoon Commander
2/Lt.	Ragg	G. W.	" "
2/Lt.	Jones	H.	" "

"B" Company

Capt.	Crowe	J. A.	Company Commander
Lieut.	Bullen	H. G.	2nd in C. "B" Coy.
Lieut	Brazener	W. L.	Platoon Commander
2/Lt.	Clarke	J.	" "
2/Lt.	Farmer	W. H.	

"C" Company

Capt.	Milton	S. J.	Company Commander
Capt	Measum	A. W.	2nd in C. "C" Coy.
Lieut	Le Mare	E. B.	Platoon Commander
2/Lt	Woollett	J. S.	" "
2/Lt	Adams	B. C.	" "
2/Lt	Hotley	A. C.	" "

"D" Company

Capt.	Stephenson	G. W.	Company Commander
~~Capt.~~ Lieut.	~~Wallem~~ Rodsham	H. J.	2nd in C "D" Company
Lieut.	Agabeg	T. W.	~~Platoon Commander~~ Platoon Commander
2/Lt.	Handley	W. C.	" "
2/Lt	Quinton	P. L.	" "
2/Lt	Russell	C. A.	" "
2/Lt	Munn	W.	" "

Detached etc.

2/Lieut.	Guest	E. L.	Hospital (Sick)
Lieut	West	H.	Bde. L. G. O.

Appendix LVIII.

2/5 Battalion South Lancs. Regt.

STATEMENT
SHOWING STRENGTH
31st JANUARY 1918.

BATTALION STRENGTH 38 Officers 712 O. Ranks

OTHER RANKS ON COMPANY STRENGTH

A Company	196
B Company	183
C Company	172
D Company	161
TOTAL	712

DETACHED

Bde & Division	16
Hospital	42
Leave	9
Courses.	18
M. G. Coy	9
Bde L. T. M. B.	9
Trade Test	1
Army School	-
Base	1
Rein. Camp	2
505 Coy R.E.	34
Bde School	16
M. T. Depot	2
Aust. Tun. Coy	7
Area Comdt.	4
	180

Army Form C. 2118.

WAR DIARY
or
~~INTELLIGENCE SUMMARY.~~

(*Erase heading not required.*)

Instructions regarding War Diaries and Intelligence Summaries are contained in F. S. Regs., Part II. and the Staff Manual respectively. Title pages will be prepared in manuscript.

2/5 S Lancs Regt
Vol 13

Place	Date	Hour	Summary of Events and Information	Remarks and references to Appendices
ARMENTIERES	Feb 1st		A very busy morning was spent from the early hours, withdrawing equipment etc from the men of "A" Coy who were proceeding to the 1/5 South Lancs. The party, Lieuts. R Hargreaves & H. F. W. Davis & 100 O. Rs. left ERQUINGHEM at 10.45 am in busses, joining their new Battalion at LAIRES. News was afterwards received of the fine reception accorded this party on arrival at their new home.	
	2nd		The Battalion was relieved by 2/7 K L R in the CONVENT and "C" Company, which was in the SUBSID. LINE by 2/6 K.L.R. The Battalion less "C" Coy at HENIGATE CAMP, STEENWERCK at 6.30 p.m. by "C" Coy did not arrive until 11.30 p.m. having had a very poor relief & a long way to march.	Appendix LXVII
STEENWERCK	3rd		The day was spent in a thorough clean up & [illegible] handing in equipment.	

D. D. & L., London, E.C. (A7001) Wt. W1771/M2031 750,000 5/17 Sch. 52 Forms C2118/14

Army Form C. 2118.

WAR DIARY
or
~~INTELLIGENCE SUMMARY.~~
(Erase heading not required.)

Instructions regarding War Diaries and Intelligence Summaries are contained in F. S. Regs., Part II. and the Staff Manual respectively. Title pages will be prepared in manuscript.

Place	Date	Hour	Summary of Events and Information	Remarks and references to Appendices
STEENWERCK	Feb 4th		Working parties, consisting of every available man from the Battalion, were out the whole of the day, starting at 8.30 A.M. and returning at 5 p.m. In the afternoon we lost a further 150 O.Rs ~~left~~ who proceeded to join the 2/4 Battalion of the South Lancs. Captains A.R. St George and S.J. Melton & Lieuts. H.G. Buller & H. West were also transferred to this Battalion but were unable to join their new unit with this draft as they were not then available.	
	5th		Every available man of the Battalion was out on Working Party from 8.30 A.M. until 5 p.m.	
	6th		Working parties as the day previous.	
	7th		The same working parties were again found.	
	8th		Hardly a man left in camp as every one was out on Working Party as previously	

D. D. & L., London, E.C. (A7001) Wt. W1771/M2031 750,000 5/17 Sch. 52 Forms C2118/14

Army Form C. 2118.

WAR DIARY
or
~~INTELLIGENCE SUMMARY.~~

(Erase heading not required.)

Instructions regarding War Diaries and Intelligence Summaries are contained in F. S. Regs., Part II. and the Staff Manual respectively. Title pages will be prepared in manuscript.

Place	Date	Hour	Summary of Events and Information	Remarks and references to Appendices
STEENWERCK	Feb 9th		Usual working parties provided. In the afternoon Captain S. T. Miller & Lieut H. G. Bullen left the Battalion to join their new unit the 7/4 Battalion South Lancashire Regt. Captain J. M. Donald, back from leave, also left us to proceed to the 1/5 Battalion South Lancs Regiment.	
	10th		No working party today, the Brigadier-General inspecting a further draft of 100 O.Rs ready for the 7/4 South Lancashire Regiment & also the surplus personnel awaiting posting. The Brigadier-General afterwards spoke to the men saying that he regretted that he had to lose so many of the old battalion & that he was pleased to know that quite a number would still remain with him. Before he left he was given three hearty cheers.	

D. D. & L., London, E.C. (A8005) Wt. W1771/M2031 750,000 5/17 Sch. 52 Forms C2118/14

Instructions regarding War Diaries and Intelligence Summaries are contained in F. S. Regs., Part II. and the Staff Manual respectively. Title pages will be prepared in manuscript.

WAR DIARY
or
~~INTELLIGENCE SUMMARY.~~
(Erase heading not required.)

Army Form C. 2118.

Place	Date	Hour	Summary of Events and Information	Remarks and references to Appendices
STEENWERCK	Feb 11		Working party was out all day of every available man.	
	12th		Every available man left the Camp on Working Party.	
	13th		Working parties as previously	
	14th		Working parties went out as usual	
	15th		Every available man in working party.	
	16th		As per previous day.	
	17th		No working party today & men were allowed a rest after strenuous week. A further 120 O.R. left us to join the 7/ South Lancs.	
	18th		Every available man again out on Working Party	
	19th		Working parties as previous day. This party having done work at a place at least 10 kilometres from Camp was conveyed back in motor-busses.	

D. D. & L., London, E.C.
(A800) Wt. W1771/M2031 750,000 5/17 Sch. 52 Forms C2118/14

Army Form C. 2118.

WAR DIARY
or
~~INTELLIGENCE SUMMARY.~~
(Erase heading not required.)

Instructions regarding War Diaries and Intelligence Summaries are contained in F. S. Regs., Part II. and the Staff Manual respectively. Title pages will be prepared in manuscript.

Place	Date	Hour	Summary of Events and Information	Remarks and references to Appendices
STEENWERCK	Feb 20th		No working party sent out today but men employed on work in Camp.	
	21st		Not being required for work the men were employed on improvements to the Camp + later in the afternoon were all taken to the baths.	
	22nd		Considerable work was done on the Camp all day by the men, none being employed on Working Party.	
	23rd		Improvements to the Camp were carried out all day.	
	24"		As on previous day	
	25"		In early morning 29 O.R. left to join the new Machine Gun Battalion. In the afternoon the surplus personel 25 Officers and 182 O.R. left STEENWERCK and proceeded to DOULIEU where they became C Company of the new No 2 Entrenching Battalion.	

D. D. & L., London, E.C.
(A5001) Wt. W1771/M2031 750,000 5/17 Sch. 52 Forms C2118/14

Instructions regarding War Diaries and Intelligence Summaries are contained in F. S. Regs., Part II. and the Staff Manual respectively. Title pages will be prepared in manuscript.

Army Form C. 2118.

WAR DIARY
or
~~INTELLIGENCE SUMMARY.~~
(Erase heading not required.)

Place	Date	Hour	Summary of Events and Information	Remarks and references to Appendices
STEENWERCK	1918 Feb		The Battalion was formally disbanded on the 5th February	
	26th		4 Officers & 100 O.Rs. (from A Coy) were transferred to the 1/5 South Lancs	
			4 Officers & 270 O.Rs. (from B C & D Coy) were transferred to the 9th South Lancs.	
			31 O.Rs were sent to join new Divisional Machine Gun Batt	
			and on the 26 February the surplus personnel of	
			25 Officers & 182 O.Rs. proceeded to join the newly formed	
			No 2 Entrenching Battalion	
			The disbandment of such a fine Battalion was felt very keenly by both Officers & men who however realised that although very unfortunate it was very necessary and each left determined to keep up the good name of the old Battalion with the new Battalion he was posted to.	
			A.C. Wallis	

D. D. & L., London, E.C.
(A7853) Wt W809/M1672 50,000 4/17 Sch 52a Forms/C/2118/14

SECRET.

War Diary

Copy No. 9

2/5th. S. LAN. R., OPERATION ORDERS NO.11.

Ref.Map
Sheet 36 N.W.
1/20000

1st. Feb. 1918.

--o--

1. The 172nd. Infantry Brigade will be relieved by the 171st. Infantry Brigade in the ARMENTIERES SECTION on the 2nd. February, and on the night of 2/3rd. February.

2. The Battalion will be relieved by the 2/7th. K.L.R. in the vicinity of the CONVENT, and on completionof relief will proceed to MENEGATTE CAMP, B.19.a.4.3.

3. ADVANCE PARTIES. One Officer and one N.C.O. per Company, and Lieut. A.A.NIMMO and one N.C.O. for B.H.Q. will proceed to MENEGATTE CAMP to-morrow morning, the 2nd. instant to take over billets, and make the necessary arrangements.

4. LEWIS GUNS, VALISES, MESS STORES, BLANKETS, ETC. O/C "C" Coy. will dump all ammunition in tin boxes, Officers' Valises, Mess Kit, etc. at TISSAGE DUMP by 4.45 p.m. He will detail a loading party for this. This party will proceed to MENEGATTE CAMP with the limbers. Lewis Guns in Vickers Canvas Bags will be carried out, also A.A. Mountings.

5. BAGGAGE.

(a) O.'s C. "A", "B" & "D" Coys. will dump all blankets, rolled in bundles of ten and labelled, valises mess stores, etc, outside their Company Headquarters by 1 p.m. All Lewis Gun Equipment will be dumped by 1 p.m.

(b) Blankets etc. for personnel of B.H.Q. will be dumped at the CONVENT GATE by 1 p.m. HQ. Officers' Valises will also be dumped by 1 p.m.

6. TRANSPORT. Two baggage wagons will report at the CONVENT for blankets etc. The Q.M. and T.O. will make the necessary arrangements for transport.

7. BILLETS. Billets must be left scrupulously clean and in a sanitary condition, and a receipt to this effect obtained from O.C. Advance Party of incoming Unit.
One representative per Company and one from B.H.Q. will be left behind to hand over billets.

8. RELIEF. Arrival of Companies in the new area will be reported to B.H.Q. by runner.

Captain,
Adjutant,
2/5th. S.Lan.R.

Distribution:-
No. 1 Copy to O/C "B" Coy.
2 " to O/C "C" "
3 " to O/C "D" "
4 " to C.O.
5 " to Q.M.
6 " to T.O.
7 " to Lieut. A.A.NIMMO.
8 " War Diary.
9 " do.

2/5th. S.Lan.R.

Unit.	Coy.	From	To	Relieved by	Route	Replacing in STEENWERCK AREA.	Time of leaving Billets.	Remarks.
2/5 S.L.R.	"A" & "B"	JUTE FACTORY	[illegible] CAMP.	2/7th. K.L.R.	ERQUINGHEM.	2/5th. K.L.R.	3 p.m.	Companies at 100 yards intervals.
do.	"D"	LAUNDRY.	do.	do.	do.	do.	3.10 p.m.	do.
do.	H.Q.	CONVENT.	do.	do.	do.	do.	3.20 p.m.	do.
do.	"C"	SUBSIDIARY LINE.	do.	do.	do.	do.	On relief	